Makers of the City

LEWIS F. FRIED

Makers of the

CITY

The University of Massachusetts Press

Amherst

Library of Congress Cataloging-in-Publication Data

Fried, Lewis.

    Makers of the city / Lewis F. Fried.

      p. cm.

    Includes bibliographical references.

    ISBN 0–87023–693–8 (alk. paper)

    1. American literature—20th century—History and
criticism. 2. City and town life in literature. 3. Cities and
towns in literature. 4. Cities and towns—United States—
Historiography. 5. Farrell, James T. (James Thomas), 1904–
1979—Criticism and interpretation. 6. Goodman, Paul,
1911–1972—Criticism and interpretation. 7. Mumford,
Lewis, 1895–   . 8. Riis, Jacob A. (Jacob August), 1849–
1914—Criticism and interpretation. I. Title.

PS228.C53F7   1990

810.9′321732—dc20   89–5201

British Library Cataloguing in Publication data are available.

Acknowledgment is made to the following sources for
permission to quote from material under copyright:

James T. Farrell Papers, Van Pelt Library Manuscript
Division, University of Pennsylvania;

The Empire City, by Paul Goodman. Copyright © 1942,
1946, 1959 by Paul Goodman. Reprinted by permission of
Random House, Inc.;

Making Do, by Paul Goodman (New York: Macmillan, 1963).
Copyright © 1963 by Paul Goodman. Reprinted by permission
of the estate of Paul Goodman;

The City in History, by Lewis Mumford. Copyright © 1961
by Lewis Mumford. Reprinted by permission of Harcourt
Brace Jovanovich, Inc.;

Sketches from Life by Lewis Mumford. Copyright © 1982 by
Lewis Mumford. Reprinted by permission of Doubleday, a
division of Bantam, Doubleday, Dell Publishing Group, Inc.

Contents

Acknowledgments

PARTS OF this book were read by Edgar M. Branch, Gene Brown, Jules Chametzky, Kathe Davis, Steven Esposito, Sanford Marovitz, Peter Parisi, Jack Salzman, and Taylor Stoehr. I am grateful for their suggestions and encouragement. I owe a special debt of gratitude to Nenos Georgopoulos and Douglas Radcliff-Umstead whose critiques of the entire manuscript were invaluable.

I am indebted to J. Riis Owre who aided my work on Jacob A. Riis and gave me permission to quote from the Riis holdings in the Library of Congress and the New York Public Library; to Lewis Mumford who encouraged my reading of his archival holdings; to Edgar M. Branch and Cleo Paturis who helped me in my work on Farrell and allowed me to quote from material belonging to the Farrell estate in the Farrell Collection at the University of Pennsylvania's Van Pelt Library; and to Taylor Stoehr and Sally Goodman who answered my questions about Paul Goodman and generously made available a number of Goodman's early essays.

Thanks also to Alexander Alland, Sr., William Boelhower, Thomas M. Davis, James T. Farrell, John Fierst, Norman Fischer, Percival Goodman, and Leo Hershkowitz for their courteous help and advice.

My work was made much easier through assistance, early and late, given to me by Sally Arteseros of Doubleday; Esther Brumberg of the photography archive section of the Museum of the City of New York; Michael Cole of Kent State University's Interlibrary Loan; Ellen S. Dunlap, research librarian at the Humanities Research Center, University of Texas; Anne Gordon, librarian of the Long Island Historical Society; Kenneth A. Lohf, librarian for rare books and manuscripts at Columbia University; Kenneth McCormick of Doubleday; Neda Westlake of the Van Pelt Library of the University of Pennsylvania.

Thanks are in order to my friends whose encouragement and support were so helpful: Peter and Helen Benson, Normand and Barbara Berlin, Anne Carver, Adeline Esposito, Thomas and Margaret Magnani, Marylee and Dale Richards, Lawrence and Celeste Starzyk, and Igina Tattoni.

Acknowledgments

I owe a very special debt of gratitude to Ms. P. Wilkinson, the managing editor of the University of Massachusetts Press, for her reading of the manuscript. Thanks also to Rita Locke and Wilma Crawford for their kind assistance.

Parts of this book have been previously published and appear here in revised form. I am grateful to the editors of the journals and books in which they first appeared for permission to use some of the material here:

Jacob A. Riis: A Reference Guide, ed. and intro. Lewis Fried and John Fierst (Boston: G. K. Hall, 1977);

"Jacob A. Riis and the Jews: The Ambivalent Quest for Community," *American Studies* 20, no. 1 (Spring 1979);

"Jacob A. Riis and the Making of His Self," *In Their Own Words* 3 (Spring 1986);

"James T. Farrell: Shadow and Act," *Jahrbuch für Amerikastudien* 17 (1972);

"Bernard Carr and *His* Trials of the Mind," *Twentieth Century Literature* 22, no. 1 (February 1976);

"The Kingdom of *The Empire City:* Paul Goodman's Regional Labor," *Artist of the Actual: Essays on Paul Goodman,* ed. Peter Parisi (Metuchen, N.J.: Scarecrow Press, 1985).

Makers of the City

Introduction

THIS IS not a book about cities. This book deals with writing about cities. I am concerned with how individuals in fact portray the city and how they make use of the social and literary traditions they find pertinent. In other words, I want to discuss how writers domesticate the "otherness" of the metropolis and why they are impelled to do so. Specifically, I focus on Jacob A. Riis, Lewis Mumford, James T. Farrell, and Paul Goodman, four American thinkers whose works are almost wholly given over to discussion about the desirable city and its community. Reading their meditations, one is invariably struck by what urban historians neglect. Re-presenting the city in terms of their own personal and intellectual loyalties, these four writers remind us that writing mediates the urban environment, that rhetoric interprets the metropolis and comes to stand *for* it, if not *in* its place.

Riis, Mumford, Farrell, and Goodman are bound together in a number of ways. Bracketing the development of the twentieth-century American metropolis, they pose similar questions, share a common method of writing, and affirm the value of the authentic city for national life. They contend that the city transcends its material character; for them the city is, in part, the humanizing imagination it transmits. Modern America has produced few other writers who were as intent upon depicting the significance of the city in these ways. [1]

II

Riis, Mumford, Farrell, and Goodman span the history of modern urban development and its struggle for an adequate descriptive language, from the 1890s (the beginning of *the* epoch in which the city became an indisputable challenge for American life and letters) to the 1970s (a time in which the city was accepted as a commanding, if not *the* dominating aspect of American civilization). The writings of these men sweep across these decades, presenting a city and a literature unlike those composed by and

3

Introduction

found in professional urban planning, community studies, sociology, history, and politics. These writers offer us the city as a meaning in process. Moreover, they depict the city in terms of what they understood was the pattern of their lives and they did this in the literary and intellectual traditions that spoke to their expectations.

Their narrative strategy is to develop a rhetoric capturing the possibility for urban change, denying the city as an environment of seemingly fixed conduct and meanings. Embarked on this project, they knew themselves as writers insistent upon capturing the richness and complexity of experience so often categorized and deprived of novelty in empirical urban analysis. They sought to make a place in the rendition of human affairs for what is called the justice of the human situation—the subjective fullness of engagement.

Their writing centers on the engagement of man and the city. They are concerned with the possibilities of choice in everyday life. They are attentive to the intangible directives of social myth, religious fable, and national dreams. They rarely stray from what they take as specific examples of human nature and what it has become in its created environment. In these commitments, they make a moral use of their past and suggest the ethical criteria of future city planning, for they portray the unredemptive pathos of the metropolis as well as the humanizing community it *ought* to be. Riis's evocation of fraternity through images of the fallen metropolis, Mumford's opposition of the organic city and mechanized megalopolis, Farrell's portrait of a parochial community opposing the liberalizing urban heritage, and Goodman's use of the fabulous to indict the coercive metropolis—all form a progressively subsuming meditation, each challenging the next, each indicating gradually more spacious ways of knowing, depicting, and remediating the minatory city. The city can be recalled to its idea: human nature can be enlarged; a "true" self can be rescued.

In their affirmation of the city's virtues, these men are philosophically radical, raising questions about values of the city found in classical political thought. How do we *know* the city, and what kind of discourse is most able to depict it? Why do people choose to live in it? Does it enhance human nature? In what ways is the good life made possible by the city? What may we believe about its prospects? These writers argue that the city can be apprehended but only with all the classical connotations of that act. To gaze upon the city is to climb toward its idea and, finally, to be purified by it. For these thinkers, the city is *enacted*.

4

Introduction

Their work differs from and even challenges the adequacy of the modern urban sciences: professional social work, city planning, statistical sociology—those empirical inquiries that bring the city under physical control by conceiving of it as a series of causes and effects subject to quantification and abstraction. Mathematical data, for instance, becomes one way of summing up the movement and situation of a public. Systems such as public transit and categories of the city's population such as the technically skilled can be statistically rendered to represent part of the city. By understanding the relationship between these and other factors, a planning commission could arrive at conclusions regarding, for example, the future of urban manufacturing, and the work force. It was, and would continue to be, rare for urban agencies to ask: Manufacturing for what? or Are there moral criteria to judge urban growth? Value often became separated from fact; a charting of behavior supplanted a reading of the self-consciousness of a culture; a discussion of purpose was replaced by the discovery of cause. Reflection about the idea of the city, the whole city, was displaced by writing about the technically efficient, fragmented metropolis.

Thinking the city and analyzing urban affairs became separate activities. The post-Enlightenment questions about causality that urban sciences ask eroded the strength of questions such as What is the city? What does it *mean?* What is it transmitting? Similarly, the nature of writing about the city changed. On the one hand, thinking the city invokes the humanistic imagination the city transmits, if the writer is to be faithful to the city's role in preserving the continuity of human history. Tropes of decline and renewal sum up an understanding of a present situation within an informing cultural legacy. On the other hand, the prose of urban sciences has an assumed objectivity and is often designed to relate phenomena to lawful or lawlike statements. As historians have pointed out, much of this objectivity is due to the impact of nineteenth-century science and scientism upon social thought—the belief that the same methods used to ask questions of nature should be used to study society. The city came to be presented as a series of piecemeal abstractions; its affairs, mathematically describable; its language of analysis, often inaccessible to the common reader.[2] Of course, these are often dramatic claims, but they are ones that play an important role in the debates about the nature of the sociological imagination and the problematic objectivity of social sciences. They are also claims that Riis, Mumford, Farrell, and Goodman believed girded modern urban analysis, making a discussion of the authentic city and community seem less warranted but more imperative than ever before.

Not surprisingly, these men's writings represent what the urban sciences ignore: meditations connecting the humanistic and *humanizing* traditions of observers—*commitments to a way of seeing*—to their writing. These four thinkers felt that objective analysis lessens the chance to comprehend the city. The scientific method employed by the modern ensemble of urban planners does not see as legitimate experience that which is not objectively verifiable; it ignores the connection between the origin of meditation and its function; it insists on diminishing rather than affirming the relationship between writer and city; it ignores people in the completeness of their relationships, both with an informing past and with their symbolizing potential.

The work of these four is less "professional" or "academic" city history, less conventional urban historiography, than it is reflection emerging from the situation of the writer viewing the city as an icon. Therefore, the problems these thinkers face are fundamentally immediate ones about the bonds between writing and knowing. How is the city understood by an individual? Is there a rhetoric speaking to and of the human heritage? How can the particular be captured by the universal? What are the relationships between those myths that are fundamental to a culture's sense of self-explication—for example, the Judeo-Christian story of the first city—and its reliance upon an empirical, predictive social planning? What are the writer's commitments to depicting an open-willed future within the pattern of habitual conduct the city preserves? How does one portray the often contradictory epistemological claims of fable, religion, reason, and rationale that the city presents in architecture, in communal mores, in public institutions? The list is practically endless. As a result, *knowing* the metropolis demands an understanding, paradoxically, of the subjective nature of people as well as of the sum of their relations with what surrounds them, for the city is an "ecology of the human." This ecology is also conservative, preserving the fundamental questions of urban meditation.

Finally, at one time or another, Riis, Mumford, Farrell, and Goodman were all walkers in the same city: New York. They wrote about the chronologically diverse and various promises this city held, so that their work forms an almost continuous commentary on the difficulty of capturing the city in prose and on a shared city.

The modern American urban literature these writers helped create and the nature of their thought are the substance of my book.

6

Introduction

III

For Riis, Mumford, Farrell, and Goodman, meditation about the city is a pressing task. They invariably write about the crises of the metropolis and community. Cities, they argue, bind the promise of America to human conduct. The city objectifies the "givenness" of culture and its continuously reinterpreted legacy. As a result, theses about a desirable human character are translated into the civilization of cities. The city becomes a text to be deciphered. Making its meanings rational is the first step in realizing an authentic self and an authentic city. They can become developed and completed.

Never far from affirming the radical novelty of American life, these thinkers believe that the culture of European cities has exhausted its capacity for innovation. They see the American city and the American self as the means for breaking the thwarted history of the Western metropolis (or even a future conferred upon it by a speculative *Ur*-city). They depict the American city as insurrectionary, as having the chance to revolt against the seemingly inexorable formal destiny of the metropolis because of the experimental character of American conduct.

In a national literature given to depicting the pathos of life within the metropolis, these writers strikingly testify to the virtues of the city. The city can be a steward, if not an alma mater, shaping the good life. The city and its institutions generate and preserve opportunities to participate in the continuity of human existence: shared, rational experience and an equitable culture. In this sense, the city is the agent of humanization; it makes accessible a communalizing legacy of fraternity, creativity, and equality.

Yet the dissonance between irreducible needs and the modern city is the often tragic thesis of urban meditation. One must ask What are these human needs? In what way is the city as we know it modern? The four writers I study contend that the city must be comprehended, demystified, and *returned* to its humanizing idea. This triple labor becomes their task. As writers, they would bare the idea of the city, the spirit animating its essential democratic promises, yet they would also focus on man in his constraining situations. Acknowledging man as *the* artificer of the city, they discuss how humankind has become disempowered within and estranged from its major creation.

With these writers, it was a personal crisis or a visionary episode that linked the city to their idea of it. Their life was thrown into relief; they saw

7

their past either challenging the parochializing city of their youth or confirming its liberalizing heritage. Obsessed by the communitarian values of the Danish village, Riis stares aghast at the homeless and uncared for in the New York slums. A student of the regionalist movement, Mumford is ravished in a union with the transcendent on the Brooklyn Bridge, experiencing what the human situation in the city can be. Wanting to be a writer but finding no compelling subject, Farrell comes across Carl Sandburg's "Chicago" while working in a gas station and realizes that what he knows about his community's hostility to the liberal, progressive city would be his theme. Goodman, a writer who for much of his career was considered marginal because of his personal and political way of being, celebrates the free communities his characters struggle to maintain. These personal illuminations were put to public use; the writers I am studying drew upon these moments of transfiguration to renew the idea of civility.

The paradoxes of engaging literatures, namely multiple interpretations of experience (for example, the claims of the transcendent versus the empirical), nourish this tradition of writing. Riis, Mumford, Farrell, and Goodman are attracted to narration in gathering the epistemologies—if not the beliefs—the city preserves because they form a humanizing and humane collation of experience. They are, after all, what the city confers upon us and what we often live by and for. For these thinkers there is no urban history but the relation of the self to the urban heritage, and this animates their characteristic styles. For they are commitments to ways of depicting the city that break the spine of an often abstract and impersonal account. As a result, these writers transform the city into their text and into their language.

IV

I have tried not to make the four writers less variable than they actually are. Too often, we are inclined to look for the neatness and clarity that a topic or category bestows upon a situation, ignoring the significance of individuals as individuals, resisting terms like "movement" or "tradition." Moreover, we have come to tacitly accept the notion of a tradition as something akin to a cause, rather than a complex web of relations composed of, among other things, inspirations, influences, and expectations. In order to do justice to individual visions of the city it is necessary to subvert the dogmatic synopsis, to render it provisional by seeing the irony

Introduction

and paradox that these writers conferred upon their work. Our faith should be dispelled—and rightfully so—in abstractions deprived of people.

I discuss these men in terms of traditions they believed were relevant to their situation and in terms of the conventions that they announced they worked within. By presenting what they believed to be their pertinent subjects and literary strategies, I want to show Riis, Mumford, Farrell, and Goodman as writers who are engaged in a common enterprise and who affirm what they hoped would be the idea of a communalizing city. Although this book explores what conventions are blind to, the text does not offer to rewrite the work of these four as if it or they could be made better by an appeal to the most contemporary critical movement. Understanding the meanings of our cities, *as* and *in* prose is a step in comprehending how we express our own values. Moreover, our commitment to understanding writing is a commitment to originality. It is a dedication to prospects.

Chapter 1

Jacob A. Riis:
The City as
Christian Fraternity

O N THE evening of January 25, 1888, a middle-aged police reporter named Jacob A. Riis began a lecture that lasted for about two hours before the Society of Amateur Photographers at its headquarters on New York's West Thirty-sixth Street. By all accounts, "'The Other Half'—How It Lives and Dies in New York," illustrated with one hundred slides shown through a projector lantern, was a grim address. Later it would be copied and published by several New York papers. Scene after scene of urban misery stunned the audience. Glimpses of despair such as "Bandits' Roost," "A Baxter Street Alley," "Waked Up By Flashlight," and "A Black and Tan Dive," depicted a city in various stages of disintegration and dissolution. The plight of those disinherited from the basic needs of life—food, housing, work, a nurturing family and community—dramatically presented the failure of the city's public and private institutions to reverse the situation. After showing slide after slide of the homeless, of children given over to the streets, of the poor crowded into tenements, of those entombed within the slums, Riis ended his lecture with slides of Bellevue Hospital, the New York Morgue, the Blackwell's Island Penitentiary, the Lunatic Asylum on Ward's Island, and graves on Hart's Island.

So powerful were Riis's images of the city that the rarely squeamish New York press was anguished, if not morally revulsed. Riis's slides were "object lessons in squalor, vice and unclean and degraded humanity." A reporter observed that the "object of the exhibition was to picture to the audience the exact condition of the lowest phases of life as it at present exists in New York City." Another pointed out that "every place of misery, vice and crime that was not too horrible to show was presented." The lecturer, a journalist concluded, thought that "this treatment of the topic would call attention to the needs of the situation and suggest the direction in which much good might be done."[1]

Riis's chance to reach a wider audience was assured after he spoke at a benefit for the New York City Missions at the Broadway Tabernacle on February 28. A. F. Schauffler, vice-president of the New York City Missions, endorsed Riis's work by writing "I am glad to commend this lecture to the attention of any who want to awaken a new desire on the part of the Church to go out and save all who can in any way be reached. The lecture is an object lesson of the strongest kind." In short succession, Riis presented his now distinctive speech at various churches in Manhattan, Brooklyn, and Jamaica, Queens. Responding to his talk at the DeWitt Memorial Chapel on March 8, W. T. Elsing pointed out that "to the Christian Church, it reveals the urgent need of city evangelism." In May, Lyman Abbott asked Riis if he would contribute two articles on "The Other Half" to the *Christian Union*.[2]

As Riis began to lecture in upstate New York, New Jersey, and Massachusetts, he struck progressively deeper notes of concern. After listening to Riis in Jersey City, a reporter recalled how he sat "with others and watched the vivid portrayals upon the canvas until [his] soul cried out: 'Oh, my God; can't we help change these conditions?'" In a brief, touching letter from New Bedford, a woman wrote of how she was so moved by Riis's call to help the homeless children of New York that she and her friends enclosed twenty dollars to "send one little boy away, where he can have a chance to grow into Christian manhood."[3]

With the publication of *How the Other Half Lives* in 1890, Riis's portrait of the city reached a national audience. With his *The Children of the Poor* (1892), *The Battle with the Slum* (1902), and *The Peril and Preservation of the Home* (1903), Riis's interpretation of the metropolis fallen from Christian fraternity and stewardship had become a commanding plea for a new city of man.

Riis's efforts helped make the modern city we know. Due in part to him, laws were enacted making the tenement more habitable and safe; his labors increased urban responsibility for the homeless and the poor; public services were widened helping the child and the adolescent; the siting of small parks throughout the city became common; playgrounds were attached to public schools; civic organizations planning the neighborhood and the city grew with his encouragement. Even this list hardly does justice to the work of a man so involved in the urban planning and political reform movements of his day. Two of the most important figures of a younger generation of urban thinkers, Robert W. De Forest and Lawrence Veiller, put it best: Riis did "more to educate the general public about tenement-house reform than any other individual."[4]

The direct impact of Riis's written work and lectures is found in Ernest Poole's *Child Labor—The Street* (1903) and *The Harbor* (1915); in Stephen Crane's novels and stories of the New York Bowery; and in Lincoln Steffens's New York journalism. As a young man, Poole had "hungrily" devoured *How the Other Half Lives;* Riis's depiction of the tenements had struck him "as a tremendous new field, scarcely touched by American writers." Stephen Crane heard Riis lecture in New Jersey and that occasion must have confirmed the young reporter's confidence in his own decision to write about the tenements of New York. The young Lincoln Steffens found Riis a mentor and a guide to the city's police beat.[5]

Theodore Roosevelt left his calling card on Riis's desk. Riis soon began accompanying, and sometimes leading, the new head of the Police Commissioner's Board on nighttime tours of the unsavory parts of New York. Perhaps as a grateful tribute to Riis's loyalty (Riis had written a campaign biography of Roosevelt), President Theodore Roosevelt offered the governorship of the former Danish Virgin Islands to Riis. James Russell Lowell, surely no champion of the eastern European immigrant living in American cities, wrote to Riis, after reading *How the Other Half Lives:* "I felt as Dante must when he looked over the edge of the abyss at the bottom of which Geryon lay in ambush. I had but a vague idea of this horror before you brought them so feelingly home to me."[6]

Indirectly, Riis's presentation of the city helped augment the American literary imagination. Literary realists such as William Dean Howells and Hamlin Garland called for a modern American literature reflecting the spirit of a new age. The realists emphasized the need to depict the aspirations of the urban middle class and the moral climate of capitalist life— what for them was the essential nature of contemporary America. Yet they remained timorous and halting when confronting the city's polyglot, tenement zones. Riis's work pointed out the direction of yet another modern literature derived from the significance of the American city. The tenements and the problems they posed for an emerging national culture now warranted coverage. A successful portrait of the urban dispossessed did not depend on a mastery of sophisticated social theory. Rather, creating literature about the urban poor demanded a sense of civic mission, an impressionable nature, and a yearning to see for one's self what things were really like. In no small way, writers were encouraged to empathize

The City as Christian Fraternity

with the life of the city around them, especially with those in the tenements.

Clearly, the importance of Riis's writing went beyond affecting the sentiments of his audience. He had managed to portray the plight of urban America in a way that his readers could readily act upon because his interpretation spoke to and of their fears and hopes. Yet how could a Danish immigrant, essentially a villager, so successfully speak to an American audience about the need to reform the nation's cities? How could he adopt the rhetoric of an American elder preaching about the American future? What is the significance of his success? Part of the answer to these questions lies in Riis's sense of himself as an American in the making and in his notion of what America was. Another part lies in the nature of his writing.

His explication of his character molded his interpretation of and rhetoric about the minatory city. He knew firsthand the misery of the poor and unemployed. As a young man coming from Ribe, Denmark, to New York, Riis had been briefly part of the tramp migrations of the early 1870s. In New York, he had been homeless and starving. Looking for work, he had walked the city streets and slept in police lodging houses. In later life, as a police reporter and urban reformer, his bitter memories of his early years in New York inspired his writing. He saw his struggles to survive the city as tests of his sensibilities nourished by the rural community of his birth. Friendly, cohesive, and orderly, the town had given him his sense of the religious dimension of ordinary experience: of a nature immanent with the divine, of the values of fraternity, self-will, and human betterment.

America forced Riis to confront his identity. He began to see the city as a moral arena which defined *his* efforts, made at great cost, to integrate his European past and American future. His writings renewed paradoxes that were intensely personal yet that were acquiring a national durability. More than any writing of his generation, Riis's books spoke about the need to make America's past and present comport well. His work addressed the challenges the modern city posed to a nation attracted to the values and myths of its agrarian past. He invariably asked what the character of the American city was and what the future of an American society would be. His questions implicated almost every nativist fear about the transfiguration of the American city by the immigrant and the impoverished. The urban poor menacing those in a nation of seeming plenty; the assumed unassimilable emigrant masses from southern and eastern Europe slow to adopt the English language and Anglo-Saxon mores; the hordes of tramps

13

uninterested in work who seasonally flooded the city; the refugees contemptuous of the culture of capitalism; the yearning for revolution sup-
posedly cultivated by the tenements; the criminality that the lower class
was assumed to be attracted to; the sense of moral darkness that the slums
so physically conveyed—these are the motifs that Riis saw as inseparable
from the problems he posed about the divided city.

The nineteenth-century discovery of urban poverty and the dispossessed, conditions unamenable to the then-contemporary sermons about
hard work and temperance, took place within an epoch in which the
framework of explanations expanded. Contemporary studies such as Adna
Weber's *The Growth of Cities in the Nineteenth Century* (1899) described
the interdependent economies and politics of countryside, city, nation,
and world. Could the poor in great cities be explained only by reference to
a defective self or saloons? In this transformation of explanation from the
local environment to a larger theater of events, the newspaper reporter
occupied a favored position. His job depended upon dramatizing the
principle of compelling journalism: social change takes a human shape.
The individuals the reporter wrote about represented more than a particular misery or fortune; they represented the character of the city. Not
surprisingly, journalists-turned-novelists began to make the city itself a
protagonist, as if in its complexity it could explain the lives of its dwellers.
Abraham Cahan affixed to *Yekl* (1896) the subtitle *A Tale of the New York
Ghetto;* Frank Norris subtitled *McTeague* (1899) *A Story of San Francisco;*
Stephen Crane's *Maggie* (1893) is subtitled *A Girl of the Streets (A Story of
New York).*

The urban reporter had an audience that he could enlarge by finding an
interesting subject, by developing a strategy that gave moment to his
piece. The pressure of competition made for sensational journalism; it also
forced the reporter to open up the city. Above all, the police reporter had
to prove that the city in upheaval was *his* affair. As a reporter for the
Morning Journal put it, after listening to "The Other Half—How It Lives
and Dies in New York":

> Time was when little parties of explorers with fur-lined overcoats up to their
> chins and satin petticoats daintily lifted used to wend their ways for fun through
> these scenes of misery guided by a trusted detective. Time was when godly
> women passed like gentle spirits from the wretched garret of one tenement to
> the vault-like cellar of another, breathing hope and scattering the means of
> health and comfort. But "slumming" was voted bad form by the upper ten
> thousand and organized charities in the hands of agents hardened to pitiable
> scenes have to an extent replaced individual inspection with a subscription list
> and the Charity Ball.

The City as Christian Fraternity

Nobody comes into such close relation with every phase of life as the ordinary newspaper reporter. And no newspaper reporter becomes so familiar with the horrors of criminal New York as the police reporter.[7]

This familiarity informs Riis's writing. He depicted social neglect by preserving, ironically, an individual despair—be it a study of the sweatshop or a photograph of tenement dwellers. Riis rarely strayed from the human figure in front of him.

It is worth recalling the attraction of his writing in order to see not only how far apart Riis's work was from an emerging statistical sociology of the city but also how close he was to the sensibilities of his public. Riis had a gift for story. He projected moral and psychological states upon an occasion or character, conveying the immediacy of the situation as well as his concern. As Dr. Roger Tracy, the statistician for the city's Board of Health and for years a staunch friend of Riis's, put it:

He was the best story teller I ever knew, and had the greatest fund of stories to draw upon. Most of them were taken from his own experience and in everything that happened within his ken, if there was anything humorous he always saw it and could utilize it afterwards. This with his poetical imagination enabled him to write those reports of daily happenings that he contributed to the *Evening Sun* for about ten years. The way in which he would take an ordinary brief note from the file in Police Headquarters to which all the reporters had access and which the others sent in as mere items of news—the way I say in which he would take such a note and make an absorbing short story of it brimming with pathos, humor, and sympathetic insight was marvelous. . . . His imagination was so vivid that it sometimes brought on hallucinations, visions or waking dreams which seemed to him so real that he always insisted upon it that they were so and was rather impatient of criticism.[8]

Lincoln Steffens considered Riis's ability to tell a story as one of Riis's persistent strengths. He could simplify a situation so that the human figure and its emotional energy held the reader's attention. Speaking of the daily items of news that were accessible to all reporters, Steffens recalled that "only Riis wrote them as stories, with heart, humor, and understanding. And having 'seen' the human side of the crime or the disaster, he had taken note also of the house or the block or the street where it happened. He went back and described that, too; he called on the officers and landlords who permitted the conditions and 'blackmailed' them into reforms."[9]

Journalists such as Lincoln Steffens, Hutchins Hapgood, and Stephen Crane gave themselves up to the attractions of the city; Riis found himself *within* the metropolis. For all practical purposes, he was a man from a village caught by the lure and spirit of the New York streets. He believed that his journalism was a weapon in his struggle with a dehumanizing city.

15

Jacob A. Riis

He felt this claim so powerfully that he was uncomfortable with reporting that was more meditative and less engaged. A police reporter's work, he argued, "compels him always to take the short cut and . . . [keep] it clear of crankery of every kind. The 'isms' have no place in a newspaper office, certainly not in Mulberry Street. I confess I was rather glad of it. I had no stomach for abstract discussions of social wrongs; I wanted to right those of them that I could reach."[10]

Such goodwill had its price. Lincoln Steffens thought it important to mention how Riis's naïveté, his refusal to believe what he was told about the range of human nature, prevented him from broadening his journalism. As Steffens recollected with amusement:

> Riis was interested not at all in vice and crime, only in the stories of people and the conditions in which they lived. I remember one morning hearing Riis roaring, as he could roar, at Max [Riis's assistant], who was reporting a police raid on a resort of fairies.
> "Fairies!" Riis shouted, suspicious. "What are fairies?" And when Max began to define the word Riis rose up in a rage. "Not so," he cried. "There are no such creatures in this world." He threw down his pencil and rushed out of the office. He would not report this raid, and Max had to telephone enough to his paper to protect his chief.[11]

It is a testament to his faith in human nature that he was able to rescue the dignity of life from the tenement. He felt that once the "facts" were put before the reader, the solution to urban poverty would be obvious. Perhaps the best statement of this faith is found in *The Making of an American* (1901), in which he writes:

> I was once a deacon, but they did not often let me lead in prayer. My supplications ordinarily take the form of putting the case plainly to Him who is the source of all right and all justice, and leaving it so. If I were to find that I could not do that, I should decline to go into the fight, or, if I had to, should feel that I were to be justly beaten. In all the years of my reporting I have never omitted this when anything big was on foot . . . and I have never heard that my reports were any the worse for it. I know they were better. Perhaps the notion of a police reporter praying that he may write a good murder story may seem ludicrous, even irreverent, to some people. But that is only because they fail to make out in it the human element which dignifies anything and rescues it from reproach.[12]

To the sociologist and political economist of the 1890s, Riis's fascination with the figurative aspect of urban poverty did not lend itself to abstraction and generalization. As early as 1893, Marcus Reynolds, in *The Housing of the Poor in American Cities* (the prize monograph of the American Economic Association), argued that "too much attention has been paid to the personal and merely bodily discomforts of the occupants of our unsanitary tenements, while the far-reaching and more deadly evils, which have their origin here, are lost sight of in the lengthy descriptions of the want and suffering of the unfortunate poor." It is hard to imagine Riis talking about what kind of note cards to use and charts to make for gathered data—details that Lawrence Veiller saw as necessary in order to develop a uniform, modern professionalism. Adna Weber, subtitling *The Growth of Cities in the Nineteenth Century* with *A Study in Statistics*, appealed to a "method of measurement that can be used with some degree of refinement" to discover the difference between the structure of urban and rural populations. Not surprisingly, in the last decade of his life, Riis felt keenly the disparity between his own engaged reporting about the predicaments of individuals and an abstracting, quantifying sociology. In an uncharacteristic lapse of confidence, he wrote to Lincoln Steffens, who had known him when he was a police reporter, that "the day of scientific method has come, and I am neither able to grasp its ways, nor am I wholly in sympathy with them. Two or three times a week I am compelled to denounce the 'sociological' notions of the day and cry out for common sense."[13]

To read Riis anew is to ask how he mediated the claims of paradox and contradiction in the city he confronted. How did his sense of the past and his village inform his understanding and depiction of the modern American city? How did his proposals for a cohesive community address a city of diversity? What did he feel was the moral nature of self-development within a city of poverty? And how did he develop a characteristic style and rhetoric that made his concern so intensely shared, so nationally vital? We also ought to ask why such various figures as Theodore Roosevelt, Lincoln Steffens, and Jane Robbins agreed that Riis's life was culturally significant, worthy of emulation, that his urban thought and labors made him a representative American.[14]

II

Riis's quest for a desirable urban community cannot be understood apart from his interpretation of his own life. He could never free himself from the importance of the time and place of his youth: Ribe, Denmark, in the middle of the nineteenth century and America of the 1870s. His attempt to make his past accord with his present was never easy and was never satisfactorily achieved. His struggle augmented his notions of what the city should be and, above all, what it must not be.

How the Other Half Lives, The Children of the Poor, The Battle with the

Jacob A. Riis

Slum, *Theodore Roosevelt the Citizen* (1904), and *The Peril and Preservation of the Home* are not objective documents. They are the expressions of an immigrant trying to reconcile the opposing claims of the American city with the values of a pastoral Danish past. Organized upon the conflicts of his experience, his portrait of the city made sense to an American public because its notion of itself was also being articulated in terms of its agrarian past and industrial present.

Riis's valuation of daylight and darkness, wide vistas and narrowness, familial cohesiveness and fragmentation was formed in his rural childhood yet could easily be called upon to explain the American city. His hatred of the idle tramp, his disgust with police lodging houses, and his revulsion with the shaping powers embodied in the slum were transformed into images of the city that let him distance himself from his early hardships in New York. Writing about the city and its misery, he wrote about the importance of his past. His presentation of self celebrated fables of hard work and high individualism. Similarly, his fascination with New York's immigrants and their often ambivalent response to Americanization became a way of defining his own acculturation and lent itself to American nativism.

His autobiography, *The Making of an American*, and his homage to Ribe, *The Old Town* (1909), are revealing; they are close to a substantial body of American arts and letters that praised the strength and cohesion of village life but they seem far apart from the recollections and autobiographies of his contemporaries. Unlike many of the memoirs of European émigrés and American natives who took part in the various reform movements of the late nineteenth and early twentieth centuries, Riis's work presents a man comfortable with the values of his youth and at ease with the patriotic slogans of his time. An understanding of personally sustaining myths is absent from Riis's autobiographical work. He portrays himself as unaware of characteristic adult rites of passage, as someone underestimating or ignoring the meaning of events that would force him to reconsider his evaluation of himself. In short, he was confident that as long as he had faith in his ambitions and a supervening divine providence, he could master any crisis. This cast of mind set him far apart from the convictions of Lincoln Steffens, Hutchins Hapgood, and Abraham Cahan, reporters and writers who also wandered through the lower East Side and voiced their sense of life's often bitter and unresolved nature.

Riis's perception of his experience accounts for the popular appeal of his autobiography. *The Making of an American* confirmed the comforting fables of its time with its celebration of struggle and success. The book is part of the genre of American memoirs and fiction that interprets social and economic crises as proferred opportunities confirming resoluteness and confidence. Like Mary Antin's *The Promised Land* (1912) and Edward Bok's *The Americanization of Edward Bok* (1920), *The Making of an American* reads the hardness of immigrant life as a vindication of American idealism, equality, and upward mobility. These books were popular and remain popular because they reduce disenchantment with America to an unambiguous issue. They point to one's ability to seize (and wish for) the right opportunity.

In *The Making of an American*, Riis cast his life into mythic form, at one with the folk legends and values of an earlier Denmark, and presented it as a pattern repeated in minor and major forms of love, exile, hard work, and sanctified battle. The hardships of his adolescence and young manhood became the triumphs of his maturity. *The Making of an American* begins with his meeting his future wife, Elizabeth, then a young girl, as he was crossing a bridge. His reminiscence rarely strayed from their marriage (in fact, she contributes her own "story" to the book). "And is this going to be a love story, then?" Riis asks. "I don't see how it can be helped."[15] This is no happenstance beginning. It strikes a major chord. Through an indomitable will and trust in God's providence, the past and present could be bridged. The events of Riis's early years, marked by unfulfillment and despair, were to be repeated and resolved on American territory.

Unlike Abraham Cahan's eponymous protagonist David Levinsky, who in his fifties laments the loss of his identity and believes that he is closer to the Russian Talmud student of his youth than to his present American self, or Mike Gold's characters in *Jews Without Money* who identify their European past as the time of their most human, affective moments, Riis saw his present as the repetition and completion of his earlier years. In his youth, Elizabeth rejected him; this accounted, in part, for his wish to go to America. He made a childish attempt to reform a slum family, offering them money if they would clean their house. He had a chance meeting with the king; he did not know whom he was meeting. He felt he had disappointed his father, a schoolmaster, who had hoped Jacob would enter the learned professions. In America, Riis became, in succession, a roustabout, laborer, salesman, reporter, editor of a small Brooklyn newspaper, police reporter, and a major figure in the reform movement of the 1890s. Unfinished events in the past were completed. He married Elizabeth, waged a heroic battle against the tenements, was honored by the king, and

Jacob A. Riis

became a commanding individual in the struggle to make the city responsible for its inhabitants.

Whereas a psychoanalytic reading of his memoirs might suggest how and why he was unable to free himself from characteristic responses to figures of authority, his autobiography makes it clear that he was inclined to read the events of his life not only as a settling of past accounts but also as an allegory reflecting God's providence. Of school reform he writes, "Some of the schools our women made an end of a few years ago weren't much better [than those of my youth]. To help clean them out was like getting square with the ogre that plagued my childhood" (*MA*, 5). His crusade as a reporter against police lodging houses stemmed from a particularly cruel incident that occurred in one of them during his penniless days in America. His pet dog was clubbed to death and Riis was driven out of the station into the rain. With an immense satisfaction, he pointed out that "the outrage of that night became, in the providence of God, the means of putting an end to one of the foulest abuses that ever disgraced a Christian city, and a mainspring in the battle with the slum as far as my share in it is concerned. My dog did not die unavenged" (*MA*, 74). On Christmas Eve of 1874, he watched the lights of New York kindle. He had hit bottom. He writes that "not one was for me. It was all over. . . . Nobody cared." Seeing a meteor flash against the sky, he hoped—against his own knowledge of the situation—that Elizabeth might be his. When he returned to his apartment, he received a letter from his father. Elizabeth's fiancé had died; she was living with strangers. She soon became his wife. Clearly this is a fable of salvation: a passage from one world of despair and unfulfillment to a new land in which the hidden promise of the past is realized.

The childhood fights he took part in and the legends of his Viking ancestors shaped his sense of life as a moral battle. The chapter headings of *The Making of an American* ring with struggle: "I Go to War at Last and Sow the Seed of Future Campaigns"; "My Dog Is Avenged"; "The Bend Is Laid By the Heels"; and "I Try To Go To War for the Third and Last Time." Almost jubilantly, he recounted how he fought with anyone who blocked his will or affronted his patriotism: his German coworkers who unmercifully made him the victim of their pranks; the French consul who refused to help him go to France to fight the Prussians; a flunky barring his way to a meeting of Frenchmen. He declaims that "deep down in my heart there is the horror of my Viking forefathers of dying in bed, unable to strike back, as it were. I know it is wicked and foolish, but all my life I have so wished to get on a horse with a sword, and slam in just once, like another Sheridan" (*MA*, 378–79). Quickly ironic, he added, "I, who cannot sit on a horse!"

The strength of his message to America derived from what he believed to be the significance of his past. His autobiography makes it clear that the values of his youth suffered little abrasion in America; they provided him with a defensible notion of community and neighborhood. What is striking, at first, is how close Riis's description of village life is to Ferdinand Tonnies's *Gemeinschaft und Gesellschaft*, as if Tonnies's emphatic contrasts between the intimate community and the impersonal society defined Riis's childhood. What emerges from Riis's memoirs and letters are childhood scenes with wide, open horizons and a vast terrain that made for an aesthetic education. Ribe was characterized by face-to-face contact, the practice of Christian charity and forgiveness, a feel for economic autonomy, and an explanation for human motives and behavior bounded by local custom and village history. With its small scale and population, Ribe provided Riis with a measure to chart the capacities of American cities and neighborhoods to foster similar communal bonds and shared experiences.

The village's broad meadows and coastline suggested that nature was a necessary presence for an ethical community life. Riis came to echo Friedrich Froebel's argument that an aesthetic of order informs moral judgment. For Riis, vision was a moral sense: without seeing nature suggesting an infinite, omnipotent presence, how could one immediately perceive man's role in the world? As Riis observed in *The Making of an American*, Ribe's uncluttered horizon and landscape symbolized "human freedom and the struggle for it" (*MA*, 7). He contended in an address to kindergarten teachers that playgrounds would help slum children perceive "moral relations."[16] His explanation of tenement life drew upon the nature of Ribe's architecture and form, for Ribe was a village that could be grasped by the eye. It was not crisscrossed by narrow back alleys and rear courts where light, sky, and sun were blotted out.

For Riis, the metropolis could not express the immanence of God. As the city chewed its way into adjacent farmland and forest, it destroyed the possibility to sense the divine within nature that was, necessarily, sublime. Riis explained that "over against the tenement that we fight in our cities ever rises in my mind the fields, the woods, God's open sky, an accuser and witness that His temple is being so defiled, man so dwarfed in body and soul" (*MA*, 8).

Ribe's placid life indicated that the values of community could resist the avaricious spirit of the market. The town, as Riis recalled it, stood between

Jacob A. Riis

two epochs; one expressed common concern; the other marked the impersonal nature of a growing capitalism. In *The Old Town,* he traced the moral heritage of this transitory period:

> Varde was the next town, a little way up the coast. The symbol of that justice was an iron hand over the town gate which, tradition said, warned any who might be disposed to buy up grain and food-stuffs to their own gain, that for "cornering" the means of living, in Ribe a man had his right hand cut off. Good that the hand was never nailed on Trinity Church or on the Chicago Board of Trade, else what a one-handed lot of men we should have there and in Wall Street![17]

Ribe had little diversity. Its population—save for two Jewish families—was homogenous. Class antagonisms and extreme poverty may have been significant features of the town, but if they were Riis had little recollection of them. He observed that "there were no very rich people," and added that the poor "were not poor either in the sense in which one thinks of poverty in a great city. They had always enough to eat and were comfortably housed. There were no beggars. . . ."[18]

Ribe—the Ribe of Riis's memory and no doubt desire—served as the model for the fraternal, Christian community when Riis looked aghast at the filth and chaos of New York's tenement districts and suggested grafting rural values upon an urban mass wretchedly living in lower New York. He would come to support almost any activity that demystified the complexity of the city and made possible any form of agrarian life. He praised Woodbine, an entrepôt colony for training Russian-Jewish immigrants in agriculture (among other things), run under the auspices of the Baron de Hirsch Fund. He enthusiastically supported the National Farm School run by Dr. Krauskopf. He advocated transplanting the urban poor to abandoned farms and was impressed with the George Junior Republic's rural setting and military discipline, which made for a community of adolescents. Whether encouraging the work of the Small Parks Committee (he served as its secretary in 1897), playing an important role in the "play movement," fighting for schools to attach parks and playgrounds to their allotments, or starting a campaign to bring school gardens and flowers into the slums, he was engaged in sharing with the children of the tenements the values of his Danish past.[19] Toward the end of his career, he stated again the educational and economic values of his past: "Just now that mission [of the Danish nation] is to teach the world in *this city mad day* that husbandry, farming, is both patriotic and profitable, as indeed it must be since upon it rests all prosperity of man."[20] In fact, in his last years he bought a farm at Barre, Massachusetts, and tried to run it on a modern, efficient basis.

The City as Christian Fraternity

The Making of an American closes on a characteristic exuberance and confidence. "I dreamed a beautiful dream in my youth," he writes, "and I awoke and found it true" (*MA,* 441). Lying ill in a room in Elsinore and facing the Oersesund, he saw an American flag flying on the mast of a ship. He raised himself from bed, waved his handkerchief, and shouted. He knew then, he recollected, "that it was my flag; that my children's home was mine, indeed; that I also had become an American in truth. And I thanked God, and, like unto the man sick of the palsy, arose from my bed and went home, healed" (*MA,* 443). This scene is as utopian as its values are implicit: a set piece akin to visionary writing in which despair and sickness give way to a transforming dream of health and reason.

The success of Riis's interpretation of self can best be measured by what his contemporaries affirmed about his life and accomplishments. *The Making of an American* was compared to Lincoln's speeches and Emerson's essays. His life was the story of "hard won" and "highly honorable success."[21] Most of his colleagues saw him as he saw himself, and in his own time he became part of an American hagiography of the self-made man, battling for the welfare of others and inspiring those around him.[22] A spiritually robust man, Riis came to personify the humane social movements of the 1890s. It is fair to say that no one of his day can be more credited with exposing, dramatizing, and helping to correct the social shame of tenement life and the pathos of those forced to endure it. Such purposeful, humanizing work is always—and always should be—attractive: such success, even more so. In the year of his death (1914), he was mourned as "a man whom America could ill have spared in the story of her spiritual progress." A writer for *The Outlook* put it even better: "No man has ever more vitally and faithfully expressed and interpreted the American Spirit than Jacob A. Riis. . . ."[23]

However, his life had a darker side. It is a side his contemporaries chose to ignore and his autobiography slighted because, I suspect, it did not conform to the picture he wished to present. If faithfully and steadily confronted, it would have challenged Riis's thought and the popular evaluation of his work. Riis's unease with an increasingly explosive city and his temporizing portrayal of the urban poor suggest a complex relationship between his own life and his hope for community. The problem can best be approached by considering what kind of America he felt was in the making and what kind of self he felt he was becoming. For all his tales of determination and strenuousness, for all his attentiveness to his own struggle to preserve his individuality, *The Making of an American* remains a faceless

23

text. There is a bleaching of style as if Riis put into practice the thesis (which he often propounded in one way or another) that Americanization should whiten an informing, particularistic past when it contrasted too strongly with the color of what he believed to be the national culture.

His autobiography hints that the crises he faced were shattering and were resolved at the expense of less optimistic private reflection. Underneath his providential interpretation of success lay a restlessness, a discomfort with commitment to social and familial stability that he refused to accept in himself and others. He often came to reject self-doubts and responded to them as if they were trials of faith: trials to vindicate his belief in the benevolent God of Ribe and American promises of success conferred upon the self-driven and ambitious. As a result, his own life became paradoxical, suggestive of an American duality just as his fascination with the immigrant in quest of community was one way he had of judging his place and role within America.

He was uneasy with his worldly rise, yet could never rest upon his income. His parents' letters to him point out quite early the irreconcilable nature of his Danish past and his American present: "Everything is very big in America, my boy. You talk about dollars and we about pennies. Perhaps you would be able once to help your mother. . . . who knows, perhaps you will be able to help us 'on the green branch' once." Yet, his father counseled that to "be in America and not be influenced by the business life and the restless search for money would be impossible, I think, but . . . I am sure the Yankees will not be able to change you, my dear Jacob, so that you are so materialistic that you have no other interests than those things that rust and moths can destroy."[24]

The clash between a devout Christian piety and material rewards provided a frame for Riis's writing, particularly for *How the Other Half Lives*. Yet this discord corroded his sense of satisfaction. He once summed up his activities by rightly denying any financial motivation. "Really, I do not wish to be rich," he wrote to his adopted sister Emma, "and it would not help to wish it as it would fortunately never come true. I have no time to save money."[25] Nonetheless, it is difficult to believe that he fully appreciated his luck in rebounding from economic failure and his startling run of fortune as a reporter. Given his robust ambition, he was unsympathetic with those whose will was less resolute than his, with those whose lives were bad, and with those who could or would not work. His children's scrapes bruised his finances, or so he contended. One son, John, couldn't find an outlet for his wanderlust and restlessness and was insecure in the shadow of his dominating father. Riis admonished him not to submit to his impulses and warned him to stop asking for money. He came to write cautionary letters to a daughter who had made an unfortunate marriage, and he found himself enmeshed in an embittered correspondence with his son-in-law, Riis telling him not to expect any help from him. In his last years, he undertook a grueling lecture tour that hastened his death: he wanted to have money for his Barre farm.

In like fashion, his attitudes about ethnicity and acculturation were divided and rooted in the felt nature of his Danish years and American experiences. As a boy, he learned to speak English. As a middle-aged man, he analyzed American social conditions for a Danish newspaper in order to preserve his fluency in his native language. One of his most prized and satisfying decorations was the Order of Dannebrog, which he received in 1900. His private correspondence makes clear his delight at meeting groups of Danish-Americans. He was impatient, however, with immigrants whose passage into the competitive life of America was not as smooth as his had been. He would become angry at the thought of immigrants arriving without jobs or needed skills. He was unreceptive to the clannishness of the Italians, the Irish, and the eastern European Jews. His study of their presence in the tenements often focused on what he saw as a detrimental cohesiveness that made Americanization incomplete.

He was often perplexed and discomforted when he came across people who were indifferent to the consolidation of property, or nonchalant about pride of place, as if his own hard-won gains were somehow made inauthentic. His writing about the family is a good example. Often proscriptive and dogmatic, his study of family life was nourished by the family as *he* wanted it to be. This was based on the memory of his parents and on the love he had for his first wife. He saw the saloon, the streets, the sweatshop, and the tenement shred the American family. His defense of it celebrated property and the stability it conferred. Nonetheless, his praise of home ownership, of the moral nature of place, and of the loving home as a barrier against the cares of the world simply did not take into account the family's need to change if it was to endure the altering marketplace. He was unwilling to see that different families adapted to the demands of capitalism in different ways. He excoriated Jews for turning their homes into workplaces; for turning their children into little workers; for renting rooms to boarders. He did not see that this was the only way some families could survive.

Jacob A. Riis

In Waitsburg, Washington, the wife of a traveling actor caught his eye. In melancholy reflection, he compared her with his first wife who had died several years before:

> I have been contrasting in my mind that life of hers, with all its tawdry tinsel and cheapness with that to which mother [Elizabeth] and I went when we left her home. Poor we were, and with nothing in the prospect but a running fight . . . but wherever we went there was *home* because she was there. And with the light and the sweetness of it came strength to me to fight what seemed sometimes impossible battles and win. How utterly does the wife make the man and his career. Certainly it was so with me. . . . And now there sits that young wife and sings—she is whistling now, as if she didn't care a pin—and does not even know what she, what he is losing. I can't help it, I think a traveling theatrical life is awful. If I were a despot I would corral every troupe, marry them off properly, settle them in homes of their own and make them stay there, to do the *real* things of life, and not the empty make-believes. Am I awful? I suppose it is foolishness, but that is the way I feel about it. Do they ever cry out in secret for the home they lost, and feel like breaking their hearts over it? They must.[26]

Riis's description of the actors' lives, as with his sentiments about the home and domesticity, drew its individuality from his own struggles to make sense of his past and present. However, he could not hold at bay crises that revealed his difficulty in reconciling the community of Ribe with the society he identified as American. He was caught within this crisis of identity. In fact, there were *crises* of identity, periodic and often turbulent, suggesting how difficult it became for him to know himself. He went through some five conversions and came to see his writing as consecrated. Reporting the city and fighting for a Christian community were labors that he saw as part of a divine plan.

After becoming a reporter for the *South Brooklyn News* in 1874 and discovering that Elizabeth's fiancé had died, Riis waited, with little hope, to hear from her. During this turbulent period, he went to a Methodist revival at the Eighteenth Street Church. "I had fallen," he recalled,

> under the spell of the preacher's fiery eloquence. Brother Simmons was of the old circuit-riders' stock, albeit their day was long past in our staid community. . . . he brought me to the altar quickly, though in my own case conversion refused to work the prescribed amount of agony. Perhaps it was because I had heard Mr. Beecher question the correctness of the prescription. . . . In fact, with the heat of the convert, I decided on the spot to throw up my editorial work and take to preaching. But Brother Simmons would not hear of it.
> "No, no, Jacob," he said; "not that. We have preachers enough. What the world needs is consecrated pens." (*MA*, 134–35)

His conversion, occurring in a flash, rescued him from what he later saw as a life without purpose. In an age chilled by naturalism, Riis's confession gains in importance because it seems to have been shared by a host of figures participating in social reform. The progressive clergy preaching the social gospel empowered the laity to redeem society, thereby emphasizing the claims of the city upon Christianity. Riis, along with Vida Scudder and Jane Addams, believed in a redemptive order *within* the chaos of the city. Contesting the quantified description of urban poverty by professional social workers and sociologists, Riis saw nature and city enriched with the transcendent. Humanity is part of an immense theophany. The city is a study for the moral and religious imagination. "I had the feeling," he wrote,

> and have it still, that if you are trying to do the things which are right, and which you were put here to do, you can and ought to leave ways and means to Him who drew the plans, after you have done your own level best to provide. Always that, of course. If then things don't come out right, it is the best proof in the world, to my mind, that you have got it wrong, and you have only to hammer away waiting for things to shape themselves. . . . For nothing in this world is without a purpose . . . though we may not be able to make it out. I got that faith from my mother, and it never put her to shame. . . . (*MA*, 285–86)

Riis's theology suffuses his city writing. Success is the fundamental adjustment to an immanent, purposive order. Maladjustment is a socially visible phenomenon. For Riis, however, it is not the poor who have "fallen"; rather, it is the well-to-do who have ignored the claims of faith. The slums were an irrefutable sign of a divine task that had to be undertaken.

Yet Riis's belief in his consecrated task was hard pressed in America and it is revealing that during specific crises he would be unable to recall his name, the immediate sense of what he was doing, or where he was. Flash amnesia is not, in these instances, an applicable term for his plight. For example, during the editing of *How the Other Half Lives*, he traveled to Boston to lecture and decided to visit a friend. When a servant asked who was calling, Riis observed that he

> stood there and looked at her like a fool: I had forgotten my name. I was not asleep; I was rummaging in an agony of dread and excitement through every corner and crevice of my brain for my own name, but I did not find it. As slowly as I could, to gain time, I reached for my card-case and fumbled for a card, hoping to remember. But no ray came. Until I actually read my name on my card it was as utterly gone as if I had never heard it. (*MA*, 306)

He describes becoming haunted "by a feeling that I would lose myself altogether, and got into the habit of leaving private directions in the office where I would probably be found, should question arise" (*MA*, 306). While lecturing in a Brooklyn church, Riis recalls that a feeling kept growing upon me that I ought to be down in the audience looking at the pictures. It all seemed a long way off and in no way related to me. Before I knew it, or any one had time to notice, I had gone down and taken a front seat. I sat there for as much as five minutes perhaps, while the man with the lantern fidgeted and the audience wondered, I suppose, what was coming next. Then it was the pictures that did not change which fretted me; with a cold chill I knew I had been lost, and went back and finished the speech. (*MA*, 307)

That such a dissociation of self occurred again and again while he was discussing the need for Christian responsibility in an America challenged by the polyethnic city is evidence of the dislocation he felt. Forgetting his name, his place, and his self betrayed his hopes for a thoroughly Americanized identity: for himself and for others. These crises suggest the difficulties he would have in accepting those who were indifferent to his notion of a Christian, American community: those who were faceless, those who were without "place," those who had or wanted no anchor of property in the whirlpool of America.

III

Riis dated the start of his career in journalism from 1873. Twenty-four years old, trying desperately but unsuccessfully to peddle copies of *Hard Times,* and literally starving, he thought of his life as "wasted, utterly wasted." Hearing of an opening at the New York News Association, Riis applied for the job and got it. By May 1874, he was working for the *South Brooklyn News,* a four-page affair run by local politicians. In June, he became its editor and in quick succession bought it, sold it at a healthy profit, married Elizabeth, and briefly resumed his former editorial chores at the *News.* He later tried to support his wife by selling ads projected through a magic lantern at open-air fairs. This was a meager, taxing life, and by 1877, through the influence of a friend, Riis was taken on at the *Tribune* as a reporter on probation. He was soon assigned to police headquarters on Mulberry Street and also began working for the Associated Press. By the late 1880s he was a police reporter of some importance and in 1890 he accepted a job with the *Evening Sun.* During his rise, he had also written feuilletons entitled "Gotham Doings" for the Green Bay (Wisconsin) *Advance* and had reported on national affairs for a Danish paper.

The shape and substance of his journalism mirrors that of the city Riis inherited and came to write about. The pattern of the city's events and the form of its history attracted Riis, and he made use of their suggestive possibilities. As a police reporter, he was caught in the swell of almost every current making the city treacherous.

When he disembarked from the ship *Iowa* in 1870, Manhattan's population was given at 942,252. Discussing the resources of the city for 1870 and 1871, James Macgregor, Superintendent of Buildings, pointed out that the metropolis's "narrow streets, frightful tenements and filthy markets" vividly contrasted with Broadway, Fifth Avenue, and Central Park.[27] By 1880, the contrast would be even more vivid, with the island's population reported at 1,164,673. In 1890, the year Riis's major work about poverty in New York was published, Manhattan's population had grown to 1,515,301. The Tenth Ward, often the scene of Riis's wanderings, achieved its infamous distinction of being one of the most densely populated areas on earth, with 57,596 people, or, in more graspable terms, 543 people per acre. William Dean Howells could hardly believe its inhabitants to be human. Henry James described it as if it were the bottom of a fish bowl.[28]

The southern part of Manhattan once bore witness to patrician dreams and pastoral geography with such streets as Cherry, Pine, Mulberry, Delancey, and that happy invocation of the garden, the Bowery. As population increased and chewed its way into the northern meadows and pastureland, prosperous and prospering families moved along the vertical axis of the island. The former neighborhoods became the site of warehouses, small stores, commercial enterprises, and tenements. The well-known areas of the years of settlement were well known only in memory. As James S. Redfield put it in 1871: "A man need not be more than sixty years old to remember when the Battery was, to the fashionable world, what Fifth avenue and 50th street are to-day." Or, as R. G. White described it twelve years later: "A lad of fourteen or fifteen years of age who, born and bred in New York, had gone to Europe or to China in 1850, and had been detained there until now, would on his return be absolutely unable to recognize the place of his birth and his early education, except by the course of its principal streets, and by a very few public gardens and churches." By Riis's day, a fashionable Washington Square supplanted memories of the Potter's Field underneath it. The Bowery had become a tough area; Mulberry Bend, a slum; the Five Points, near Collect Pond, was remembered as an area controlled by crime and poverty.[29] Abandoned cemeteries, signs of a community's upward mobility or dissolution, marked the attenuated claims of human memory and devotion within the city.

Jacob A. Riis

A tenement was defined as a "house, building or portion thereof which is . . . occupied as the home or residence of more than three families living independently of one another, and doing their own cooking on the premises, or by more than two families on a floor, so living and cooking, but have common right in the halls, stairways, water closets or privies, or some of them." These structures began to dominate the lower quadrant of the island as it was abandoned in the move uptown. The "double-decker" tenement was an assault on human life. It covered 90 percent of its 25-by-100-feet lot, with four families on each floor. The absence of social engineering in such housing created huge problems. In an apt comparison, the Tenement House Committee of 1894 wrote that the

> only thing that bears the slightest similarity to this in Europe is to be found in the old houses surrounding the closes in High street in Edinburgh, which were constructed several centuries ago. . . . There, however, no cases can be found of such narrow rooms and dark and narrow halls as exist in the double-decker on the 25-foot lot in New York to-day. These permit an agglomeration of humanity which exists nowhere else, and which under a less rigorous code of health, a less keen watchfulness on the part of the authorities as to contagion, and firemen of less courage and efficiency, would create a state of affairs absolutely fatal to the public welfare.[30]

The same committee described New York's abominable rear tenements as prisons: they stand "almost in contact, at the rear, with the rear houses of the adjoining lots on three sides, so that the unfortunate tenants live virtually in a cage, open only toward the front."[31] The "dumb bell" tenement, designed by James Ware and submitted in 1879 to a competition sponsored by Henry Meyer, editor of the *Sanitary Engineer*, was of dubious value in enhancing the quality of its tenants' lives. Its air shaft produced unbearable odors and was little more than an opening for light and air.

The steadily growing stream of immigrants who often wanted to live in ethnic neighborhoods of their own, and the boundaries of the island itself made tenement building a timely job for greedy contractors and speculators. The Tenement House Committees of 1867, 1884, and 1894 could well recommend limitations on the proportion of the standard lot to be occupied, on fire-proofing materials, on sanitary amenities, and so on, but they could not deal with the nature of Manhattan as a container and the promise of America that hurried the immigrant to the port of New York. The price of land could only go up; the number of tenants on a piece of land could easily be increased; rooms would be built that would conform to the most minimal sanitary codes and dimensions.

The City as Christian Fraternity

It was relatively easy to view New York's slum population as an uneasy mob given to violence and anarchy. American letters, often drawing upon biblical images of the fallen city or upon the hope of a New Jerusalem, made it possible and popular to see the city as divided. One half was dark, resistant to Christian virtue and unamenable to social control and order. The other half dwelt in light; it was propertied, stable, virtuous, and domestic. Witness such titles signifying the divided city as G. G. Foster's *New York by Gas-Light: With Here and There a Streak of Sunshine* (1850); Matthew Hale Smith's *Sunshine and Shadow in New York* (1868); Edward Crapsey's *The Nether Side of New York: or, The Vice, Crime, and Poverty of the Great Metropolis* (1872); and J. W. Buel's *Metropolitan Life Unveiled: Or the Mysteries and Miseries of America's Great Cities* (1882). While these were historically convenient images rooted in shared theological assumptions, they also expressed apprehensions about social and economic realities. The darkened half of the city represented its population's moral degradation, a consequence of a defective will.

One of the most prominent examples of this urban iconography, if only because of its argument that the urban poor and the pagan remain so because of their resistance to the message of salvation, is found in the Reverend Peter Stryker's address to the congregation of an "uptown" church, the Dutch Reformed at Thirty-fourth Street. Speaking on April 29, 1866, about "The Lower Depths of the Great American Metropolis," Stryker declaimed that we

> may learn from the accounts given by modern missionaries, as well as the writings of the Apostle Paul, that the abominations of heathenism are fearfully great. . . . In the mind of the heathen there exists scarcely any obligation to restrain passion and lust. The only hindrance of any account is that which society may impose for its protection, and in many cases this is very slight. Of the obscenities practiced in many parts of the heathen world it would be improper to speak. . . . But alas! what is true of heathendom is equally true of certain localities in the most enlightened and Christianized parts of the world. In London, Paris and New York, the lower depths of vice and destitution may be found as fully exhibited and illustrated as they were in ancient Ephesus and Rome, as they are in modern Constantinople, Pekin or Calcutta . . . we may learn to avoid the first step which leads to moral degradation, and pity those who have fallen a prey to crime and poverty. [32]

This was not a new thesis but it is a telling example of the popular fear that the poor and unchurched of New York would remake the city. Charles Loring Brace (founder of the Children's Aid Society) argued in *The Dangerous Classes of New York* (1872), that the city should be compared to the Paris of the Commune: "there are just the same explosive social elements

31

beneath the surface of New York as of Paris." In one of the most feverish books viewing New York as a city whose surface blankets with difficulty a furious unrest, "A Volunteer Special" described the Draft riots of 1863 in his *The Volcano Under the City* (1887) and warned that "all men know that there is and always will be a volcano under the city, but they are justly sure that there is no need of an eruption."³³ By 1889, subterranean New York provided the drama of insurrection for Ignatius Donnelly's utopian novel *Caesar's Column*.

Fear of the immigrant is often found in the polemics directed against the ward boss, or Tammany Hall, or socialists and anarchists. This prejudice achieved its height by playing upon the memory of the sacked city. This was not an overdramatic possibility. It was fed by recollections of the 1863 Draft riots in which approximately twelve hundred people were killed; by the Orange troubles of 1870 in which a parade of Orangemen was attacked and three killed; by the Orange riot of 1871 in which fifty-two people were killed. Popular journals found anarchism and revolution attractive topics. The themes of the fall of a city or an insurrection were periodically heated up, and Americans came to think of their cities as hostages to be taken. Witness the spate of articles with such titles as "How to Quell Mobs," "My Dream of Anarchy and Dynamite," "Reminiscences of the Siege and Commune of Paris," "Mobs and Revolution," "The Physiognomy of Anarchists," and "Anarchists and Destructive Mania." Josiah Strong, who had gradually turned his pastoral concerns from the care of his Midwestern congregation to the evils of city life, invoked in one quick paragraph the spectre of the French Revolution, modern military weapons, the fragile structure of society, and human needs that had not been answered by contemporary civilization. In his words, it

> must not be forgotten that, side by side, with this deep discontent of intelligent and unsatisfied wants, has been developed in modern times, a tremendous enginery of destruction, which offers itself to every man. Since the French Revolution, nitro-glycerine, illuminating gas, petroleum, dynamite, the revolver, the repeating rifle and the Gatling gun have all come into use. . . . Society . . . is become more highly organized, much more complex, and is therefore much more susceptible of injury. There never was a time in the history of the world when an enemy of society could work such mighty mischief as today.³⁴

Religious and charitable societies were disturbed by what appeared to be an unmanageable urban population. The potential for losing touch with the foreign-born poor in the city increasingly preoccupied the Home Missionary Society, the American Sunday School Union, and the Association for Improving the Condition of the Poor. The urgency felt by these organizations can be gathered from the speeches given at the Christian Conference that met at Chickering Hall in early December 1888, a gathering Riis attended. Speakers covered a host of themes that had in common the topic of the unredeemed in the city. Lecturers discussed how the foreign "element" was responsible for vice and crime, how the non–Anglo-Saxon was resistant to assimilation, how a rising Catholic populace severely contested the hegemony of American Protestant mores. Protestant churches and their members, it was pointed out, had moved away from the most problem-ridden sections of the city. As a result, the poor in the tenements either simply did not know where a church could be found or were hostile to missionaries and home visitors they did not know.[35]

The city had its shepherdless multitudes; it also had its homeless children. Called newspaper boys, street arabs, and gamins, they were variously seen as tough, gritty kids, as ragged entrepreneurs with their own customs and honor, or as the unfortunate product of drunken immigrant families sloughing off their children onto city streets.

There is a literature that praises these children's shrewdness. They practiced, in small, the pattern of large commercial undertakings, if only in buying cheap and selling dear. Enchanted with their youthful exuberance and business acumen, G. G. Foster described how they operated when the presses had stopped and newspapers were ready to be sold:

> In a few minutes Nassau street swarms with the rough and ready little philosophers . . . determined to be served first or die. . . . The spirit of mercantile exploitation and multiplied profit-makers pervades in full force the business of selling newspapers. The principal speculators sell to about twenty sub-speculators, who pay two dollars a hundred and sell them again to the street boys for two shillings a dozen . . . thus making four per cent on their capital.[36]

Like the wholesalers Mark Maguire and Mike Madden, the newsboy could himself become a speculator and possibly "King of the Newsboys." Foster highly praised such a career. Maguire's ward had "strong thoughts of running him for alderman; and we sincerely trust they will. . . . Not half nor a quarter of those sent to City Hall are half so deserving of the confidence of their fellow-citizens, nor half so able to legislate for the benefit of the city. . . ."[37]

The young reflected the spirited enterprise of urban affairs: "If you impress him as a merchant, he informs you of a sudden movement in dry goods, an advance in gold, a decline in imports, of which you have never heard." For better or worse, the newsboys were seen as products of the city who knew little about rural life. In 1871 the *New York Times* sponsored a newsboys' and bootblacks' picnic. "They came to Oriental Grove," the editor of *Harper's* "Easy Chair" dramatically observed, "like the Spanish sailors of Columbus came to San Salvador. The country was a new world to them. One of the little pilgrims had never seen a tree but twice or thrice, and then upon the Battery!"[38]

In 1873, Charles Loring Brace had a more compelling, though no less interesting response to these children. He estimated that one hundred thousand children were at work in New York factories, and that between fifteen and twenty thousand were "floaters," drifting from one factory to another. Although he admitted that it was desirable to have a citizenry who worked hard and exhibited intelligence and pluck, he felt that homeless children (he estimated that lodging houses sheltered some twelve thousand of them), "the little slaves of capitalism," should be made available to the Western farmer. His essay "The Little Laborers of New York City" presents a montage of a city waif in various states of employment: standing on a corner illuminated by gaslight; being sent to the country; happily waving his hat while handling a crude plough; and content in the midst of a country family. City misery could be turned to rural advantages. The Children's Aid Society, he argued, "early saw the immense benefit in taking advantage of the peculiar economical condition of this country in treating questions of pauperism. They at once recognized the fact and resolved to make use in their plans, of the endless demand for children's labor in the Western country."[39]

IV

While Riis placed the "immiserated" and un-Americanized in city slums at the core of his journalism, he did not arrive at these subjects early in his career. What does emerge early is his attempt to analyze the city in terms of his rural background. Riis wanted to foster what best can be called a historically relevant Christian culture, one that could embrace and appreciate the industrial values and achievements of his time. The elements of the Social Gospel (cooperation, an individualism based upon and held in check by shared religious theses, a devotion to Christ through a robust service to people) were paradoxically wedded to the prominent features of an American secularism (rugged individualism, a bold entrepreneurial spirit, a pronounced chauvinism). His espousal of this self-devouring ideology that exalted notions of both universalism and particularism, one that committed itself to two contending interpretations of human nature and rational endeavor, invariably reflected the paradox and contradiction of his past and present. The notion of a Christian, capitalist society could be deployed to maintain the competitive market while ameliorating only its excesses. Witness the slogan—one that Riis liked—"philanthropy and five per cent"—an exhortation to build decent tenements and make decent profits.

For Riis, this ideology emphasized only one of the many versions of democratic civil life and identified it as the acceptable norm of a national culture. Pluralism was an intransigent refusal to participate in the life of a nation, an unwillingness to adopt its cohesive myths and values. In fact, Riis spoke increasingly of Americanization as the triumph of mores and aspirations that neutralized undesirable folkways, competing allegiances, and radical politics. He thought acculturation could be measured by its success in eradicating the unique, enriching past of a group that seemed reluctant to fully adopt the American language; to acquire property (which not only made for stable families but also for a shareholding in society); and to be Christian. Riis's understanding of what made a desirable community shaped his writing to the extent that it became *his* teaching about the fraternal Christian, capitalist city.

Little can be stated with accuracy about Riis's work with the *South Brooklyn News* because the complete run of the paper does not exist. What can be gathered from his own account and from the fugitive pieces that are extant is that he hoped to make the paper a presence in community affairs. At the beginning of his career he had to temporize his sense of justice in order to accommodate the politics of the paper's backers. When he achieved a measure of control, he took up the cause of political reform by blocking the removal of a precinct police captain. He even published a list of those who hadn't paid their bills with a local grocer.

Yet his work at this stage also addressed the major concern of his career: the nature of a desirable community that was stable and composed of people who felt that they had a share in a society that was not exploitive. Domesticity and property, the community's need to share assumptions about the nature of civic life, and an inclination toward a uniform community theology start to mark his work. Heady with his newfound domestic life, he praised the virtue of property. In his weekly editorials he declaimed the social value of the home. Our country, he wrote, "to fulfil its destiny, must be a nation of homes. Down with the boarding-house!" (*MA*, 178).

Jacob A. Riis

He shrank from what he took to be the agent and symbol of capitalism. In an essay remarkable for its undisguised sentiments, Riis described his journey back to Ribe. Dated January 18, 1876, and printed on March 4 of that year, "Across the Ocean: Leaves from the Journal of a Traveler" described a visit that took him through Hamburg. The city

> much as we had longed for it, did not hold us for long, nor interest us much. It is an old city and has never had any other importance than which its commerce gave it. . . . On the whole everything in Hamburg appeared to us to bear a stamp of Jewish avarice that was extremely repulsive—from the brokers at the Boerse, of whom the majority were unquestionably Jews, to the servant girls who with their badges of servitude, a sort of white pad on their head, paraded the streets. We were glad to leave, and when we paid our bowing and smiling Jew waiter at the hotel his "Trinkgeld," it was with the mental resolution that the city should not be honored by our presence oftener and longer than unavoidably necessary.[40]

The presence of the Jews, the Irish, the Italians, and the Chinese within New York came to represent something more dispiriting than Hamburg's affront. These immigrant groups challenged the aspiration Riis had for the city itself. He would portray them as factions unamenable to a shared, Christian culture, as if they were barbarians who chose to live outside the salvific city. Their desire to live within their own communities and culture signaled the city's need to transmit a common faith.

As Riis matured as a journalist, his reporting measured the shape of the modern city. His early pieces are marked by the realization that there was an interdependency between individuals and urban institutions and that this relationship was a clue to the kind of public in the making. Riis was clearly fascinated with the customs of ethnic groups and their adjustment, successful or not, to American life. Taken as a whole, his columns describe both the surface *and* the structure of metropolitan lives.

The city's withering anonymity struck him: the intimacy of the village was lost. Monuments suggestive of the loving community and its continuity were often abandoned if not forgotten. This neglect pointed to some inherent weakness of those living in the city or testified to the disintegrative power of the city itself. In one of his most poignant columns—one that appeared in the *World*—he told of how he came upon a deserted lot in the midst of "swarming east-side tenements." Writing in the third person, he described how he was

> confronted suddenly and rather awkwardly by an opening in the rear fence, through which he fell prone on his face while endeavoring to gain an idea of the locality. . . . It was a wide inclosure [*sic*] many times larger than an ordinary

yard and rather like a school play-ground, devoid apparently of all traces of vegetation. . . . Inquiry developed the fact that the graveyard had belonged to Methodists who built a church two generations ago where the school now stands. . . . His interest having been strongly excited, the reporter found a number of like spots scattered through the city—old burial grounds—the names and original owners of which have been forgotten by the busy world that lives and moves around them.[41]

A sense of the past, a cultivated, social act of memory, however, could rescue the community from the desolating effects of the city. He noted that sometimes there were "survivors" who resisted the amnesia of the metropolis. "Notably," he told his readers, "this is the case with Hebrews with whom it amounts to an article of faith. However sharply a Jew may trade with living men, he will not bargain about his father's dust or his grave. Hence there are many Jewish graveyards in odd places in New York."[42]

These graveyards marked the modern, anonymous city that erased the memory not only of individuals but also of entire communities. In fact, to live in the city was to chance the maelstrom. Images of turbulence, of being swept away and out of sight, of being swallowed, haunted Riis. He would speak of the dead hauled out of rivers and of the hundreds of men and women who yearly disappeared as a submerged population, "sucked under in the mad whirlpool of feverish metropolitan life in which only the sum, not the individual counts. . . ." These people, he lamented, were "lost, unmourned, and unsought."[43]

Riis dealt with the spectacle of this faceless misery by giving it a definable personality. He refused to see the crowd and the dwellers of the slums as a quantifiable mass existing in isolation from the city: people could not be abstracted from the conditions of their lives. Writing of the poor on Delancey Street who used to sleep on fire escapes and roof tops during the summer, Riis observed:

> The sultriness of those human beehives, with their sweltering, restless mass of feverish humanity; the sleep without rest; the silent suffering and the loud; the heat that scorches and withers, radiating from pavements and stone walls; the thousand stenches from the street, yard and sink; the dying babies whose helpless wails meet with no comforting response; the weary morning walks in the street, praying for a breath of fresh air for the sick child; the comfortless bed on the flags or on the fire-escape—these are the sights to be encountered there.[44]

In his eyes, the unredemptive city represented a fallen, menacing nature. Suicide, often traceable to poverty and business failure "has come to be regarded . . . as a disease, almost as much as cholera. . . ." Riis transformed the pastoral background of the shepherd's calendar into metropolitan occasions: each season proclaims its own physical and moral misfortune. Spring heralds the thawing of rivers and the rise of the drowned to the surface; it is complemented by a "boom" in abandoned babies. Summer announces itself by a "sort of human shower" that "regularly falls in the tenement districts of sleepers who roll off the roofs. . . ." Fall and winter watch the migrations of tramps to the city and their search for shelter.[45]

The sorrows of the city captured his writing, but Riis was also held by the larger perspective the city offered him. Like many of his contemporaries and a younger generation of novelists, Riis found the city compelling. He discovered it to be an entity that evoked his talent and identity. Against the background of the city, Riis described the growth of institutions pointing to a new, larger community in the making. Such a community conferred at least some social identity and order upon its members, placing them in a basic framework of responsibility and obligation. He began to write about police stations linked by telegraphs, the building of new hospitals and fire engine houses, the Board of Health, the work of city missions and foundling homes. For Riis, the question was less whether these institutions and projects were agents of social control than whether they were agents of a structured, moral community. In the absence of larger, private efforts integrating the poor and the immigrant into a national culture, these urban enterprises were making the new community and city habitable.

It is not surprising that cautionary observations reflecting the nativist fears of the time crept into his journalism. After all, he was a police reporter and concerned about the readiness of this force. Speaking of one of the oldest policemen on the beat, Riis mentions that "the department has to-day no more vigorous member and none with apparently better prospects of seeing the dawn of another century that is to test the soundness of Karl Marx's doctrines in conflict with locust clubs and official muscle." Describing the importance of the police telegraph system, he observes that in "times of riot and mob rule the first blows of the rioters have heretofore been aimed at the telegraph poles and wires of the Police Department." Emphasizing his admonition, he sketches the history of the 1863 Draft riots. Warning the public about the tricks used by beggars— "The race is numerous"—Riis praises the Charity Organization Society which winnows the fraudulent from the needy. The migrations of tramps, who swarm into the city during the late fall and winter and beg or steal, are held in check by periodic police raids: the tramps, often congregating in the "Bend" (Mulberry "Bend") are sent to Blackwell's Island. With the fall they come back to "prey on the city," a police captain tells Riis and blames the Board of Health for not closing the dens.[46]

Individuals asserting the values Riis himself champions—familial love, concern for one's neighbor, respect for religious institutions—become the subjects for his most sentimental and touching pieces. Such writings are evocations of the village customs and family life that he knew, and in them he defends the dignity of man. Riis is caught up in the unremitting anguish of the Brodsky family whose two-and-a-half-year-old daughter had simply vanished, disappearing from the neighborhood when she set "out of the house bound for her father's stand up the street to get a penny for candy." Riis writes about the Mahon family whose breadwinner, Mike, was killed working for the railroad. No company official bothered to tell Mahon's wife and children; the task fell to Riis. The trainmaster, Riis states, said it was a matter of no consequence. He praises Henry Gibbud and Smith Allen of the Florence Night Mission for rescuing young women from prostitution and for empathizing with human frailty rather than condemning it.[47]

The neglect Riis wrote about proclaimed how morally and politically one half of the city had been abused and exploited by the other. Riis did not take a divided city as a hypothesis. For him, it was fact: each half held the pertinent act of redemption for the other. The city had to embrace its marginalized. On the one hand, the rescue of the poor was an opportunity for Christian community. On the other hand, having respect for a uniform, Christian culture and its property would morally elevate the outcast. Yet the institutions and people Riis praised and the organizations that were successful, seemed to him to be too limited in themselves to develop a common, shared vision of community.

Riis's sense of the city's fragmentation was sharpened as he discussed the urban poor and the immigrant because he was also writing about the city's upper class. He helped publicize it. For a short time, he was something of a social feuilletonist, whose column "Gotham Doings" (dating from 1884) appeared in the unlikely Green Bay, Wisconsin, *Advance*. He writes about the famed gathering of people composing the "Patriarchs"—one of New York's patrician circles that included the Goulds, the Vanderbilts, and the Belmonts. His pieces are light, airy, and mocking. He had never written like this before; he would never write like this again. This episode can be seen as a rhetorical experiment, an attempt to develop a style conveying the froth of Fifth Avenue life to the provinces. Riis could change his persona and discover the distance betwen himself and the thoroughly self-appointed exemplars of American ways. The column gave him a chance to look closely at those Americans whose identity was socially confirmed but morally incomplete in relation to the poor. These sketches also suggest that for Riis the experience of America could be captured through its language. He could be Americanized by adopting the attitudes of an ironic American observer.

In "Gotham Doings," Riis poses as a worldly though frivolous narrator recounting, among other topics, the activities of Mr. de Bille, the Danish minister at Washington; the romantic life of Marion Langdon, "esteemed," as Riis contended, "the most beautiful girl in America"; the career of Lewis Leland, former proprietor of the Sturtevant House and now locked in an insane asylum; an anecdote about Matthew Arnold's visit to the Normal College.[48] Riis as narrator conveys his moral discomfort, suggesting his detachment from such affairs. He easily praises a charitable act by Jay Gould but reminds his audience that Gould "poses as a shrewd and reckless operator, whose success means the ruin of thousands, and . . . [in the eyes of many, he is] a sort of malicious ogre or moral vampire." Riis chats about the fifteen hundred thousand dollar house a banker was building on Fifth Avenue but observes that it is "a quite pertinent reflection [to notice] how many rich men in New York move into splendid new houses to die."[49]

As a whole, Riis's journalism became ethically spacious, measuring the city's moral health through oppositions: the rich contrasting with the poor, and the sensibilities of Riis the narrator counterpointing the judgments of Riis the moralist. Yet he had no adequate way of writing about the city as a whole, no method that could vigorously present the city's failure to develop a unifying Christian stewardship. Moreover, his work seemed inconsequential. "I wrote," he remembered, "but it seemed to make no impression" (*MA*, 267).

His discovery of photography was timely; it was also therapeutic. It helped satisfy his need for a redemptive task. In 1887, he began to experiment with photojournalism; pictures taken by others accompanied his writing. Shortly after, he read about flash photography. He had a technological advantage to deploy and he used it well, invading the East Side, "bent on letting in the light where it was so much needed" (*MA*, 268). This wasn't easy; the people who accompanied him on midnight excursions became less enthusiastic. He hired a professional photographer who, without Riis's permission, tried to sell Riis's photographs to someone.

The City as Christian Fraternity

Finally, Riis bought a camera. On a day in January he went to Potter's Field and took a picture of an open trench, soon to be filled with the dead.

He believed that his photography was an instrument for reform; he began by using his pictures to illustrate his writing and lectures, but after a decade, he simply abandoned making these portraits of the city. Yet his pictures are so wedded to his sense of self and the city he described that they provide us with his perspective on being of and in the city. His subject was not the conventional iconography of Manhattan—photographs of monuments, streets, businesses, and parks that advertised the city as a collection of objects and are invariably found in the New York guide books of the time. Rather, his slides (I shall refer to them as photographs) were of a city fallen from Christian community into neglect and fratricide. His photographs are a catalog of individuals crushed by narrow alleys, of people clustered tightly while working in dilapidated rooms, of individuals thrust into the darkness of tenements. What slowly emerges is a sense of the person, the family, the gang asserting whatever frail individuality could survive these gruesome conditions. The human subject does not bespeak its background; it becomes it.

The photographs are realistic because they are bound to the common objects of the slum: a plank serving as a bed; the rags and junk of a crowded flat; the worn, bleak, sad faces of the poor and the immigrant. The faces that are turned toward us seem to plead with us to redeem this moment of their lives or to remind us how distant their lives are from our own. Yet Riis's photographs also make visible the clash between the values of his village past and the immediacy of his urban present, for the pictures deal with the disappearance of nature as a standard of normalcy, the chaos that darkness represents, and the fear of social disorder. The low frame, the rubble that invariably fills the background, and the loss of a wide horizon, the absence of trees, of countryside, and the figures often posed against crumbling walls and shacks become facts revealing an order of meaning— the absence of communal responsibility. As a result, the photographs ought to be seen as a series of glimpses into a culture that is alien but that is profoundly related to our daily lives, for it is formed by a public withdrawal from human dependency. It is shocking because the daily aspects of earning a living or worshiping or having leisure time mock our own existence. Turgenev told Henry James that he began to write when he imagined a group of figures beckon him or an imagined character turn to him. So, I think, with Riis and the subjects of his photographs; it is easy to believe that the individuals framed by walls or fences or alleys seized the imagination of a man who had managed to escape the urban barriers and mazes of the poor's fate.[50]

By 1888 Riis had become a public figure. He no longer had doubts about the direction his journalism would take when he copyrighted the title page of his most famous book, *How the Other Half Lives*. It would be written by 1890 and published on November 15 of that year by Charles Scribner's Sons. During that two-year interval, Riis not only launched himself upon the first of a series of exhausting lecture tours but also began to publish his own essays about the poor and foreign born. "Homeless Waifs of the City" (*Harper's Young People*, January 22, 1889); "The Tenement-House Question" (*Christian Union*, May 1889); "Model Lodgings for the Poor" (*Christian Union*, April 3, 1890); and his major statement, a nineteen-page essay "How the Other Half Lives" (appearing in *Scribner's Magazine*, December 1889), have a common focus that would be widened when *How the Other Half Lives* appeared. These essays speak about the relationship between the cohesive family and the fraternal community; the bond between the disintegrative family and a rapacious society. The pieces resound with the characteristic moral slogans of the time: social reconstruction could only begin with a Christian dedication of the self. "Put yourself," Riis commanded, "if you would do the Master's work, *en rapport* with his cause. Get into personal contact and sympathy with those you would help." There is nothing unusual about this; it is advice that is also found, for example, throughout the history of the Association for Improving the Condition of the Poor. Riis was not slow to raise the ghosts of revolution, either: "That Other Half," he pronounced, "uneasy, suffering, threatening anarchy and revolt. . . . The thieves and murderers of our land are raised there [in the tenements]."[51]

His reading of family and society relies upon a triple order of urban interpretation: personal, communal, and theological. In fact, each of these is a different conceptual aspect of the other. Commitment to tenement reform binds the individual to a just society; commitment is a nostrum for the self, as well as the practice of stewardship, and also a social effort to contain upheaval. Just as self, society, and church were the makers of the Christian city, so were they also barriers against revolution. They could drain away whatever insurrectionary energies the poor had left to them.

The tenement challenged this triple concord. It was a monster that could enslave its creator: "the Frankenstein of our city civilization," Riis labeled it. It symptomized the disease of collective pride: "In the haste to become great, our city has lost opportunities for healthy growth that have passed not to return," he wrote. It consecrated rapacity: "The tenement that was born in the old homes of wealth and luxury, nurtured in greed and avarice in Jewtown and The Bend reaches uptown its third and last stage of development, a new baptism, under the tardy restraint of laws designed for the protection of the community as well as the helpless tenant."[52]

These are careful phrases. They present the felt, experienced values of a deeply pious man from the country, someone who would try to reconstitute the city by ridding urban analysis of assumptions hostile to the idea of the metropolis as a little community. What Riis did not and could not know were notions of the metropolis that would demand other terms of reform. Within a decade, the city would be seen as an expression of regional and extraregional resources; a historically shaped container; a preserver of diversity making experience shared and rational; a qualitatively and physically different habitation from the village that must create a large public rather than a small community; an inventory of human symbolizing and technical activity.

In substance, Riis's early essays are slender additions to previous literature about urban poverty and humane obligation. Yet *How the Other Half Lives* eclipsed in influence and popularity every American work written on poverty up to that time and had a wide audience in England as well. A reviewer for the (London) *Saturday Review* pointed out that "we know of no single book, in the enormous official and independent literature on the subject of overcrowding in English cities, that is at all comparable with the vivid and thorough chronicle of Mr. Riis." The *Chicago Times* called the work one "of immense, shuddering interest." "No book of the year," a writer for the *Dial* claimed, "has aroused a deeper interest or wider discussion than Mr. Riis's earnest study of the poor and outcast."[53] The book's concerns and Riis's now developed talent for dramatizing his subject far overshadowed works of that year addressing themselves to some of the same problems: who can remember (or who has read) Richard Mayo's *Emigration and Immigration*, or Charles Reeve's *The Prison Question*, or Havelock Ellis's *The Criminal*, or Austin Bierbower's *Socialism of Christ, or Attitudes of Early Christians Toward Modern Problems?* Or, for that matter, Ward McAllister's portrayal of the Four Hundred in *Society As I Have Found It?*

As a police reporter, Riis worked hard and long at chronicling the city's despair. The text of *How the Other Half Lives* was written quickly. The recollections and data of his earlier journalism apparently flooded his thoughts; the holograph manuscript shows little major revision. The book was written at night after Riis had put in a full day at his beat. He would pace the floors of the lower story of his house while planning the text. He told his readers, "I do most of my writing on my feet" (*MA*, 303). This outburst of energy was controlled as the book presented an emotionally demanding journey to the New York poor. In a letter, Riis pointed out that "I admitted my presentation of the case limped. I had purposely only seen the sick with which I was concerned. My aim was to arouse conscience and excite sympathy. In a crowd of a hundred the one who limps excites attention & sympathy—those who go on sound legs go unnoticed. Therefore I 'limped' purposely, was presenting wrongs to be addressed."[54]

So powerful was Riis's portrait of life in the tenements that few readers, it is fair to say, remembered the book's real plea: decent housing for the poor.[55] Riis had been influenced by the work of Alfred White whose flats, based upon his *Improved Dwellings for the Laboring Classes* (1879), were pioneering efforts to stem high-profit tenement construction; by Sir Sydney Waterlow's plans for improved London housing; by the experiments of Octavia Hill in England and Ellen Collins in America to tie housing and moral improvement together; and by such enterprises as the Improved Dwellings Association whose Riverside tenements, with flats renting from $1.50 to $2.50 a week, emphasized the need for family privacy. "How the Case Stands" in *How the Other Half Lives* is Riis's presentation of these achievements.

How the Other Half Lives brims with then-prevalent philanthropic attitudes as well as with fears about increased immigration, criminality, and revolution. It also concerns itself with a bust and boom economy which could easily smash the charitable institutions that dealt with the poor in cities, for example, the Charity Organization Society. Riis remains in the company of those social thinkers who saw the conundrums of American life as the subject of their attention: poverty in the midst of abundance; neglect in the midst of an intentional democratic nation. Riis drew upon the contemporary thought that spoke to these troubling paradoxes. Josiah Strong in his editions of the fulminating *Our Country* (1885)—the book had been edited twice before as part of the publications of the American Home Missionary Society—questioned the future strength of Anglo-Saxon America if it remained hospitable to other religions and immigrant groups indifferent to national values. Helen Campbell in *Prisoners of Poverty* (1887) pondered the fate of the workingwoman in large cities. How could this unique labor force maintain its dignity in the face of competition? Henry George in *Progress and Poverty* (1879) suggested that the system of taxation failed to generate capital and improvement by ignoring the taxable basis of land.

How the Other Half Lives held its audience not only because the book raised these well-known subjects, but also for other reasons. Riis avoided the attractions of both science and scientism common to thinkers of his day. He was not given to speculate on how human affairs could be expressed in terms of one or several overarching laws of evolution or on how social life might be discussed in terms of biology or chemistry or physics, or on how a picture of the quality of human life could be ignored in favor of a statistical reading of urban demography. Several months before Riis's book appeared, Franklin Giddings, in a landmark essay entitled "The Province of Sociology" that was published in the first volume of the *Annals of the American Academy of Political and Social Science,* urged his colleagues to remember that sociology "is an interpretation of psychical activity, organic adjustment, natural selection, and conservation of energy. . . ."[56] Riis would find this charge to the academy lacking in moral imagination.

How the Other Half Lives is the last great nineteenth-century sermon taking as its principle of organization the fall of the harmonious community: from brotherhood to fratricide. The book's central figures are debased people as Riis quickly sketched the history of the city declining from intimacy and order to exploitation and barbarism. The triumph of literary realism, the description of people and environment as bare, discrete data that do not necessarily implicate or reveal a transcendent principle, was an unusable victory for Riis, for to him the contemporary city embodied man's estrangement from God. To grasp a fundamental principle of human life is to accept the community as a revelation of the divine. Advising his son John, Riis explained that "you will realize what Jesus meant when he constantly put love of neighbor beside love of God. They are essentially the same thing. You can not love God whom you can not grasp, by Himself alone; but you can love Him through his children who bear his image in them. So, all theology becomes simple to me . . . love one another."[57] God's will is the immanent principle of fraternity in the city. His spirit is indwelling when the city makes actual a humanizing state of affairs.

The book's rhetoric is stunning, transforming the empirical data of urban development into moral values. *How the Other Half Lives* defends Christian capitalism by often depicting the modern city in biblical and pastoral images—tropes easily understood by a nation used to affirming its own divinely ordained destiny and virtuous agrarian past. In the book, metaphors of the ordered garden and a nature open for self-sustaining human labor violently contrast with a present decay and rot. The graceful mansions of the past had been turned into the slums of the present. History was *Abbau*, an unbuilding, and with it came an age of turmoil and rapacity. The "decorous homes of the old Knickerbockers" now harbored "promiscuous crowds." The "old garden where the stolid Dutch burgher grew his tulips" became the site for the infamous rear tenement. God's presence in nature was blackened by the shadow of the speculator. "It was rent," Riis argued, "the owner was after. . . . The garden gate no longer swung on its rusty hinges. The shell-paved walk had become an alley; what the rear house had left of the garden, a 'court.' "[58]

History is the cycle of fratricide: Riis stating that "the first tenement New York knew bore the mark of Cain from its birth, though a generation passed before the writing was deciphered" (*HOHL*, 5). From Genesis to Daniel, from the moral failure to recognize a human community, to the amazement that this violence is a text of its own, crying out for explication—this odyssey of the ethical becomes the historical "story" of *How the Other Half Lives*.

Riis's interpretation of the city is apocalyptic. He was quick to argue that the tenements were both a hidden city and the avenging consequences of a collapsed moral order. The tenements, he pointed out, "had bred their Nemesis, a proletariat ready and able to avenge the wrongs of their crowds" (*HOHL*, 11). In the strongest of his cautionary readings of everyday life, he warned:

> Crowding all the lower wards, wherever business leaves a foot of ground unclaimed; strung along both rivers, like ball and chain tied to the foot of every street, and filling up Harlem with their restless, pent-up multitudes, they hold within their clutch the wealth and business of New York, hold them at their mercy in the day of mob-rule and wrath. The bullet-proof shutters, the stacks of hand-grenades, and the Gatling guns of the Sub-Treasury are tacit admissions of the fact and of the quality of the mercy expected. The tenements of to-day are New York, harboring three-fourths of its population. When another generation shall have doubled the census of our city, and to that vast army of workers, held captive by poverty, the very name of home shall be as a bitter mockery, what will the harvest be? (*HOHL*, 14–15)

Because each member of the community—and city—was primevally bound to the other, each shared in and was shaped by the other's history. Whether called fratricide, or wandering without rest, or bearing the mark of Cain, these were but different ways of signifying the persistent, everwidening theme of the unregulated community. This theme would be dealt with as metaphor, myth, urban history, and social analysis. The empirical facts of tenement life, for example, make their appearance as an allegory of disordered nature. Tenements were "nurseries of pauperism" and touched "family life with deadly moral contagion." They made for the feral city in which the "wolf knocks loudly at the gate in the troubled dreams that come to this alley." The darkness of alleys and rooms reveals, even jestingly, a universe torn between sunlight and shadow, between the powers that make for order and those that make for chaos, for "the sun never shone into the alley from the day the devil planned and man built it." The slum is finally apotheosized as a natural force that breaches an invariable law of hierarchy. At the end of the book, Riis wrote that he "was told that during the fierce storms of winter it happened that this sea [where he was vacationing], now so calm, rose in rage and beat down, broke over the bluff, sweeping all before it. No barrier built by human hands had power to stay it then. The sea of a mighty population, held in galling fetters, heaves uneasily in the tenements. . . . If it rise once more, no human power may avail to check it" (*HOHL*, 226).

In one of the book's striking passages, he equates transiency with the loss of historical memory binding people to their place, community, and nation. Manhattan no longer had common traditions or shared, public experience. "The one thing you shall vainly ask for," Riis wrote, "in the chief city of America is a distinctively American community. There is none; certainly not among the tenements. Where have they gone to, the old inhabitants? . . . They are not here. In their place has come this queer conglomerate mass of heterogenous elements, ever striving and working like whiskey and water in one glass, and with the like result: final union and a prevailing taint of whiskey" (*HOHL*, 15–16).

The prose conveys Riis's discomfort. Starting with the word "vainly" and evoking the poignant theme of an irrecoverable past with "Where have they gone to" and moving to the jangling, discordant "conglomerate mass of heterogenous elements," Riis presents the babel of the contemporary city. Even more remarkable is Riis's pose: that of a city elder. Yet if this city history was a never-ending drama who else ought to pose as a mentor but a man from the village, praising its stability and conservancy?

The metropolis was really a series of neighborhoods. If a city map could be colored to represent its various nationalities, the map would show "more stripes than the skin of a zebra, more colors than any rainbow." This patchwork cartography illustrated how insular and competitive ethnic groups were, making a shared, common culture almost impossible. Riis's most compelling sketches, therefore, remain studies of various, impoverished nationalities within the city whose progress toward acculturation he tried to measure.

These groups were victims first and, later, representatives of the socially disruptive character of the tenements. They imitated what the city offered them. The Irish landlord, for example, became a rent gouger and profited from the saloon; he followed the custom of the country. The Italian, invariably exploited by the padrone, would exploit others if he ran a stale beer dive in the Bend.

There were groups that were simply unassimilable to the promised fraternity of Christian life; they would always remain aliens in Riis's thought. He was revulsed by the Chinese presence in New York. He argued that at "the risk of distressing some well-meaning but, I fear, too trustful people, I state it in advance as my opinion, based on the steady observation of years, that all attempts to make an effective Christian of John Chinaman will remain abortive in this generation; of the next I have, if anything, less hope" (*HOHL,* 67).

During these early days of fame, he declaimed that the Chinese "must go." His passion on this issue never abated and years later he wrote, seemingly without a qualm, "For . . . years now we have been discussing the immigrants. . . . Only as regards the Asiatic we have made a flat verdict of exclusion."[59]

His portrayal of the Russian and Polish Jews he came upon owed a great deal to his earlier sketch of Hamburg for the *South Brooklyn News* and shows how little his sentiments had altered. Taking the reader on a tour of Bayard Street, which he called "the high road to Jewtown," he described Jewish women "young and old alike with the odd head-covering, pad or turban, that is their badge of servitude—her's [*sic*] to bear the burden as long as she lives . . ." (*HOHL,* 43).

Jewish existence in *How the Other Half Lives* was an example of willful resistance to Christian American life. How could the city be redeemed if Jews opposed salvation itself? Jews, for Riis, were imprisoned within a conception of history that had become unnecessary. Their lives were, in reality, destined to repeat the patterns of their ancestors because their history was closed to the possibilities of salvation and hence the authentic community. Excluding whatever amiable traits they had or customs they practiced, they were creatures of the Bourse and a decayed civilization. In Europe, Jews could buy freedom only with gold. In "Jewtown" the pursuit of capital "has enslaved them in bondage worse than that from which they fled. Money is their God" (*HOHL,* 78–79). They stand, he pronounced,

The City as Christian Fraternity

"where the new day that dawned on Calvary left them standing, stubbornly refusing to see the light" (*HOHL*, 83).

In a quick study, he proved Hegel right: the family transmits capitalism. The Jewish family, as Riis described it, domesticated the spirit and method of capitalism while ironically trying to maintain its own integrity. As competition in the garment industry grew, the family transformed itself into an economic system. The home is now the site of piecemeal work: the child, a worker; the father, a boss. Psychological and mercantile relations cut across one another so that the members of the family were unable to exist in relation to each other as kin but rather as units of production. The sweatshop was a monument to "constitutional greed" and every fresh wave of immigration intensified the competition and the atomization of the family. The transition of home into factory or home-as-factory effaced the line between public and private experience: this was a line for Riis that could not be crossed without reversion to primitive life. When discussing the phenomena of the lodger, without whom many families could not survive economically, Riis judged that "it is idle to speak of privacy in these 'homes.' The term carries no more meaning with it than would a lecture on social ethics to an audience of Hottentots" (*HOHL*, 98).

Yet there was a solution that would pacify and acculturate the immigrant, the street arab, the workingwoman, and the poor: tenement-house reform. Riis wanted to halt land speculation which made the tenement an attractive profit-making venture. Echoing however softly Henry George's sentiments about socially unproductive wealth, Riis argued that the "danger to society comes not from the poverty of the tenements, but from the ill-spent wealth that reared them, that it might earn a usurious interest from a class from which 'nothing else was expected'" (*HOHL*, 202). Absentee landlords, inefficient management, and a tepid public climate could not be immune to moral sentiment, or so Riis believed. The housing question could, in fact, be approached as a business problem. When it was confused with charity, a system of relief was ineffective; the tenant could not be helped and the incentives for better management and investment became unattractive. Renting to the needy, he contended, on philanthropic terms, as "charity, pastime, or fad . . . will miserably fail, always and everywhere. . . . Upon any other plan than the assumption that the workman has a just claim to a decent home, and the right to demand it, any scheme for his relief fails. It must be a fair exchange of the man's money for what he can afford to buy at a reasonable price" (*HOHL*, 205–6).

On the face of it this is hardly a helpful solution. After all, what could the sweatshop worker or the Italian laborer afford? However, model tenement construction demonstrated the poor could be housed adequately and at a profit. If the landlord demanded it, the tenant would be responsible for his family's behavior. In "How the Case Stands," Riis outlined a number of tenement-house experiments that he saw as practical and as models for future construction. In fact, the tenement, he believed, had come to stay and "must itself be the solution of the problem with which it confronts us" (*HOHL*, 215). Taking into account the major factors of Manhattan's growth—its natural boundaries that prevented horizontal expansion, immigration to the city, increasing numbers of workers who wanted to live near their place of employment—an attractive investment program such as building seemed an adequate first step.

This is a practical proposal. In part, it reminds us of Riis's attraction to Henry George's argument that a tax on the full valuation of land benefits the larger community as well as those who aid the city by serving its social and industrial needs through construction. It also looks forward to progressive notions of the city responsible for its inhabitants.

Yet what was most appealingly simple was Riis's ease in presenting social and economic questions as essentially ethical ones to which answers could readily be given. His attack on the tenement (one that must not be underestimated for its grasp of the human problem) ignored the complex and tight web of city growth, regional economies, and national problems. Could the city be so easily analyzed that the problem of housing when solved would, in turn, remedy acculturation, sweatshop labor, and dissenting politics?

Riis's program could neither envision the *nature* of an interdependent urban economy nor come to grips with the plasticity of capitalism itself: its ability, as the Frankfurt school argued, to absorb contradictions rather than expose them. Certainly, Riis cannot be faulted for what seemed to be a progressive solution to the misery of his age. Rather, the terms that he seized upon complemented and made emphatic what he believed to be the controlling values of his Danish boyhood.

It is not surprising that his immediate target was Tammany Hall politics. The significance of Tammany was its ease of corruption and its immigrant constituency. Its open argument was that government was a system of favors, patronage, and protection. The city was for sale. These were lessons that reformers such as Jane Addams and Frederic C. Howe discovered had grateful pupils. Often an impoverished, immigrant electorate insisted that the city ought to do something for them, that politicians should fill the vacuum between a helpless individual and an indifferent government.[60]

How the Other Half Lives argued, and argued well, Riis's case against ward politics. He had despised graft and corruption in government from his start as a journalist. He detested the machinations of Boss Tweed. Watching the New York City Police Department act upon the caprice and greed of politically interested ward bosses and officers, Riis was revulsed by indifference to people and to law. His book vividly sketched the relationship between the poor and the network of power that made impossible a disinterested politics. "The rumshop," Riis stated, "turns the political crank in New York" (*HOHL,* 159). The saloon propelled its owners into politics and prominence; look at, he urged, the composition of successive Boards of Aldermen and the problem of graft. The barroom is the "gorgeous centre of political activity" for the Irishman whose "genius" is "public affairs" (*HOHL,* 21). The padrone and his ally the contractor managed to get city contracts for trimming garbage scows. This monopoly crushed independent contractors and increased the dependency of Italian laborers upon their employers' goodwill and politics. The cheap lodging houses of New York were the recruiting grounds for vote selling on election days; when a proprietor was caught, his pull with the boss earned a reprieve.

Riis's indignation was partly justifiable, although he was unable—or perhaps unwilling—to see the saloon, the ward boss, and the padrone as expressions of immigrant power within a city unresponsive to the needs of the poor and disempowered. Obviously, for Riis, there were favored immigrants and there were those who had to prove their worthiness as Americans. (It is interesting that Riis would often follow Theodore Roosevelt's bidding; and on at least one occasion he asked Roosevelt to help John Riis get a job.)

Riis's hope for a Christian city meant agreement had to be reached on those virtues that made for unity (thrift, temperance, language, theology), and on those that subverted the city by breaching any or all of these values. The aggressive competition of the "sweaters" from "Jewtown," while expressing "constitutional greed," furthered an insurrectionary politics. How easily, Riis mused, the poor, "won over by the promise of a general 'divide'" could join the ranks of the anarchists (*HOHL,* 95). Years later, he stated the problem less cautiously by arguing that the poor "in their ignorant groping for relief . . . are wont at times to wander off on wild theories, such as Socialism and even anarchy." Even the newsboys whom Riis admired for being self-reliant could fall victim to a menacing ideology. A boy "robbed of his chance to play," Riis believed, "will not be an honest and effective man—you can't depend on him at the polls."[61]

The culture of poverty, a term much debated years ago but one I think Riis would have no trouble affirming in its literal sense, could be broken by the will of the urban poor. Riis did not deny that the environment imprisoned those in the tenements. He did argue, though, that rehabilitation was effective only when the individual wanted and was given the opportunity to change the conditions of his life. He did not accept older assumptions about poverty; he did not believe it was caused by a moral flaw or that it was a sign of vice. He believed, however, that few could survive a childhood devoid of economic and moral choice. For Riis the qualities of a rugged individualism and of willful self-help were those of a valuable adulthood. For example, his disgust with the tramp was certainly shaped by the memory of his early days starving in New York. He believed that tramps refused to redeem themselves by work; they saw no sense in undertaking providential labor. They would not become part of the labor force. Moreover, tramps were confirmed in their idleness by charities that pauperized the spirit. In short, tramps would not change their ways. "Whence these tramps," Riis asked, "and why the tramping? are questions oftener asked than answered. Ill-applied charity and idleness answer the first query. . . . Once started on the career of a tramp, the man keeps to it because it is the laziest. . . . The devil has various ways of taking care of his own" (*HOHL*, 58).

More suggestively, tramps challenged the stability of the home and the sustaining value of place that Riis felt so deeply about. Tramps were free to wander, breaking the conventional ties of life. They were not bound to the tempo of the factory and if they were often compared in popular literature to the locust or grasshopper, they clearly challenged any moralizing about the rewards of postponing immediate pleasures.[62] In a self-revealing moment, Riis warned his son John about this distraction: "Your peril, my peril, the peril that yawns for us all, is to be idle."[63]

Older immigrants were bound to their customs and to what Riis saw as contentious political theories. Their children were not. Riis believed that the child could become a factor in Americanizing the community and city. *The Children of the Poor* examined the difficulty urban agencies had in meeting the needs of children, a unique clientele without legal recourse to assert rights to a life of dignity. Bringing children into the realm of law would, Riis believed, make them into citizens affirming the law. *The Children of the Poor* supplemented *How the Other Half Lives* and, like it, argued for an environment adequate to the child's growth. The education of children reflects the resources of the city; their future character could be created by the orderly city.

The city, as it was, could hardly respond to demands made upon it. In 1891, Riis argued, fifty thousand children between the ages of five and fourteen received no schooling. In fact, had they applied, the public schools could not accept them: there was no room. The easy evasion of factory laws and the grinding struggle for the necessities of life forced children into the workplace or onto the streets. As a result, children uneducated and deprived of genuine citizenship, imperiled themselves and the city. "The problem of the children," he wrote, "is the problem of the State. . . . Clearly, there is reason for the sharp attention given at last to the life and doings of the other half. . . . Philanthropy we call it sometimes with patronizing airs. Better call it self-defence."[64]

How could one rise from the slums? It was a "dumping ground" from which only the strong could escape, while the "sediment," that "contingent that always lives from hand to mouth with no provision and no means of providing for the morrow," remained (*CP*, 65). Their children were indifferent to learning, to self-help, to the promise of democracy. In fact, they were also indifferent to life outside the slums. Riis told the story of a girl who stayed with his own family in then-rural Richmond Hill, but who "went back to her old tenement life, because 'all the green hurt her eyes so.'" He noted that the slum "had its fatal grip upon her" (*CP*, 65). In short, there were simply not enough opportunities in the city to guarantee growing up well.

Rescuing the entire family was unlikely. The working day enslaved it. Familial love became parental greed. Riis had no shortage of examples. In one instance, parents refused to send their sick infant for medical treatment because without that child, the landlord would be pitiless and evict them. In another case, a father wasted his time playing checkers while his daughter was forced to work. In yet another example, parents broke the factory laws by simply lying about the ages of their children who were working in the sweatshops.

Riis did not concern himself with the "professionalization" of the family—its invasion by educators and "visitors"—though he did make it clear that an alternative had to be found for the family incapable of caring for its children *as* children. He championed kindergartens, boys' clubs, industrial schools, and the Children's Aid Society because they functioned as surrogate families. They fed, washed, sheltered, and trained the poor and homeless young. The Fresh Air Fund, which took children on Hudson River excursions, and placed youths during the summer on farms, restored to city children what Riis believed to be the proscriptive value of normal life: the moral imperatives of Nature. "Down in the worst little ruffian's soul," he wrote, "there is, after all, a tender spot not yet pre-empted by the slum. And Mother Nature touches it once" (*CP*, 173). The kindergarten led young children out of the tenement and into the classroom; it "delivers them," as he said ". . . to the public school" (*CP*, 181). Industrial schools and the Children's Aid Society's farm resettlement program trained children for useful, socially productive work. Advocacy of these programs was pragmatic; they made good common sense—especially when there were no other choices. Children are, properly, both wards *and* creations of the State; they would come to possess it.

Riis knew the lure of city streets and argued that the gang could be turned into a club by providing it with a different environment appealing to the spirit of the adolescent. The *creation* of a childhood for ruffians—as Riis fondly called them—was an orderly and ordering process. If anything, Riis was uncongenial to what he felt were city temptations: competing and irreconcilable values that pitted the customs of the family against those of the street. In this sense, the city was invasive, though Riis would not come to see the conflict of city ways and family behavior as a desirable process making a democratic public.

He was not inclined to be tolerant of childhood and adolescence as periods for testing authority, as periods for discovering that the city itself could teach more than the limited family. Perhaps his dislike of teenage rebellion and wanderlust came from what he saw as his wasted years: the arduous time he spent tramping around America. His view of this period in his own life might account for his liking a disciplined education. He spoke, with some reservation, about the helpful nature of military drill for boys; its value was proven in reform schools where it was found to be "a most useful ally in dealing with the worst and wildest class of boy" (*CP*, 240). He was taken with the Battalion Club at St. George's and looked approvingly upon the spartan quasi-military life of the George Junior Republic. The success of these educational ventures could be measured in what they produced: an enterprising, propertied class of youth having common causes. He recounted with satisfaction the odyssey of a tenement youth who was sent to Schoharie County, New York. He became "an active Christian, married, and worth property, and expects in a few years to have his farm all paid for" (*CP*, 165).

The challenges Riis threw down for saving the city's children had their consequences and revealed at best a short-sightedness and at worst a careless ambivalence. For whatever reasons, he did not separate his hope for a furiously expanding economy—with its bust and boom cycle—from the need for cheap labor. He argued that "letting foreign workmen in in shoals to crowd our market" was responsible for the difficulties youth had getting jobs. The stocking of farms with tenement children might be initially attractive, but Riis was blind to the obvious reasons older tenement youth had for quitting their assigned families—too much work and no excitement.

Ironically, his notions of a healthy childhood unavoidably widened the distance between immigrant parents and their children by splintering the family. For parents, America was a hard reality; for children, it was a promise. Helping to break down children's sense of the worth of their families' pasts made inevitable Americans estranged from their European background. Certainly, this order of alienation was unavoidable but Riis did not see it as a major problem. He did not forcefully address this issue that bedevilled Jane Addams: the contempt on the part of reformers and immigrant children themselves for an older way of life that was a kingdom of ends in itself.

For example, Riis was pleased by the great drive for knowledge he witnessed in the Jewish community, a community that is "set apart, set sharply against the rest in every clashing interest, social and industrial; foreign in language, in faith, and in tradition; repaying dislike with distrust; expanding under the new relief from oppression in the unpopular qualities of greed and contentiousness, fostered by ages of tyranny unresistingly borne" (*CP*, 45).

Nonetheless, he saw the tradition of Jewish education as unnecessary and regressive in America. Ironically, the physical conditions of Hebrew school, Jewish particularity, and the lower East Side might all speed up the transition from an antique faith to an enlightened society. In *How the Other Half Lives* Riis had spoken of the Jews stranded on the road to

Jacob A. Riis

Calvary. How could they be brought into the modern world? In *The Children of the Poor* Riis would propose half-humorously that there might be a higher purpose within their isolation. He happily perceived that the

> daily transition, they [the rabbis] say from the bright and, by comparison, aesthetically beautiful public schoolroom to these dark and inhospitable dens [tenement Hebrew schools], with which the faith that has brought so many miseries upon their race comes to be inseparably associated in the child's mind as he grows up . . . to reflections that breed indifference, if not infidelity in the young. It would not be strange if this were so. If the schools, through this process, also helped pave the way for the acceptance of the Messiah, heretofore rejected, which I greatly doubt, it may be said to be the only instance in which the East Side tenement has done its tenants a good Christian turn. (*CP*, 49)

How the Other Half Lives and *The Children of the Poor* presented Riis's broad theses about urban community and character, and his ideas underwent no fundamental change in his later works. Disorder in social life, the chaos bred by the tenements, and the inability (or refusal) of their dwellers to be at one with a Christian America pointed to political and moral loss. An uncaring, uninformed city made the slum. In turn, the slum demands a new city in which love, stewardship, and responsibility are principles of community. Tenement reform, therefore, from financing to construction, is morally and socially necessary. Such reform would stay what Riis called "The Man with the Knife" in *How the Other Half Lives*. By breaking the web of tenement life, the family could be reconstructed. A decent place to live would prevent the workplace from contaminating the family. In large measure, the city would be a watchful family. Americanized by the school, politically neutralized by housing that encouraged family life and thrift, and consecrated by Christianity, the city would transcend the great society; it would be a city in which parks, schools, factories, and houses offered a moral teaching.

Riis's early work suggests the extent to which his writing would be of one piece. Just as his first two books did, his later ones exhorted to action a generation of Americans who believed that they shared a common heritage and, therefore, a fundamentally common response to urban problems. They were sympathetic to the realities and also to the myths of an agrarian America that made the heterodox city appear to be a challenge to the American past and its promise. Yet it would be foolish to reduce Riis's achievements to congruence with this pastoral fable. He helped make the resources of the city deal with what he believed to be the authentic needs of the self and family. His later writings and work helped strengthen the growing alternatives to tenement life if only by bringing them to public attention. No less important, these works spoke on behalf of the disempowered.

The Battle with the Slum, essentially a variant of *A Ten Years' War* (1900), enumerated the accomplishments of the tenement-house reform movement of the 1890s: the destruction of the Bend, better and more vigorously enforced housing codes, the creation of small parks, the work of settlement houses, and improved school construction laws. Yet the book is most important because it registers Riis's growing uneasiness with an impersonal sociology and a social work devoid of common sense. The quality of human affairs had been lost sight of by an emerging, professionalizing social science. He contended that this

> is what it comes down to in the end: common sense and common honesty. Common sense to steer us clear of the "sociology" reef that would make our cause ridiculous, on Fifth Avenue and in East Broadway. I have no quarrel with the man who would do things by system and in order; but the man who would reduce men and women and children to mere items in his infallible system and classify and sub-classify them until they are as dried up as his theories, that man I will fight till I die. One throb of a human heart is worth a whole book of his stuff.[65]

The city has a "great and terrible longing for neighborliness where the home feeling is gone with the home. . . ."[66] Riis began to translate his *descriptions* of human behavior, so compelling in *How the Other Half Lives*, into a reading of behavior. The cry of the slum is a plea for fraternity. The boy throwing rocks is assaulting a city that denies him a decent childhood; the fury of a mob dramatizes a plea for decent housing; the gang's life on the streets is a reaction against an indifferent family.

Human concern and a desire for community must be the motives of social reconstruction. Emphasis must be placed on "neighborliness" so that we resist seeing the city and its inhabitants as abstractions. The disinherited were not the problem; indifference to their dehumanization is.

The Peril and Preservation of the Home, the William Bull Lectures of 1903, accentuated the nature of Christian obligation as *the* struggle for reform. Reminding his audience that it was its brother's keeper, Riis observed that this obligation sounded the "key-note of the whole modern reform movement, the new charity, the new school, the social settlement and all; and thank God for it!"[67]

The Peril and Preservation of the Home made much of the contrast between the effects of tenement life and those of nature on the individual. The tenement masses were attracted to the tumult of the city; they had turned "their backs upon the country, upon the woods and the fields, when we offer them a refuge there." The poor were deprived of their "resources" and "individuality." No doubt, Riis was thinking of the Long Island community of Homewood when he claimed that "it is only a man who can think that is at home in the fields. The slum never thinks; it is all the time trying to forget. There is nothing good to think of, nothing worth remembering." Homewood had been a practical disappointment. A way out of the slums, it was a community built by the City and Suburban Homes Company consisting of about one hundred homes. After four years, only ten homes had been completely paid for; three were under contract, and fifty-six were on twenty-year mortgages. As Riis saw it, without an investment in land which was a commitment to place, the family became destabilized. The home would perish. In his words, the best home "always in my mind, is that of a man with his feet upon the soil and his children growing up there."[68] This could not happen in the city.

It is easy to read *The Peril and Preservation of the Home* as Riis's catalog of the healthy family. The book is a plea for patriarchy; an assault upon the restiveness of modern women; an offensive waged against the city that made the home little more than a shell for eating and sleeping. The complexity of city life, given its wide range of opportunities and chances for geographic mobility, could hardly be undone by Riis's proposals. The book should be seen as an attempt to simplify contemporary urban problems by asserting that Riis's historical picture of the family is *the* family. The book became Riis's effort to prevail against professional social science and social work by arguing for a proscriptive, moral norm governing family and nation: this in the face of a challenging pluralism that he so well described in his earlier works.

Nonetheless, Riis tried to accommodate the brittleness of his theory to a changing order of facts. Christian principles would control this rapprochement. "You will fight," he exhorted his Philadelphia listeners, "in vain for the people's homes till you know what afflicts them. The glory of our present-day Christianity is that at last it plants itself squarely on the facts— seeks them out first and then applies the remedy. Never fear them. If they clash in any way with scholastic theory or even theology, make sure they *are* the facts, then seek the fault in your theory."[69]

The facts as Riis saw them were defensive and sentimental. The framework within which he had experienced his village and its Christian fraternity was too small to apply to the city. In *The Battle with the Slum* he had written that "character implies depth, a soil, and growth. The street is all surface. Nothing grows there; it hides only a sewer."[70] He had come to believe that the trend of rural migration to cities would reverse itself. While this optimism about the attraction of rural life ran against the grain of fact—witness the gloomy readings of the American countryside ranging from N. H. Egleston's *Villages and Village Life* (1878), to Hamlin Garland's stories of the misery of farming in *Main Travelled Roads* (1891), to *The Report of the Commission on Country Life* (1911)—Riis shored up the values of his early years. He invoked Jeffersonian notions of the city as a canker, keeping alive the tradition of American arcadian letters that had never realistically depicted life on the farmlands. Ignoring the crises that brought about Populist politics and the decay of New England farms, Riis strongly clung to the guiding memories of his childhood and the little successes of organizations such as the Children's Aid Society in settling children on farms.

Early in his newspaper career, he had moved to Richmond Hill (in Queens), a semirural village that was far away from the slums of the lower East Side. Such a move was hardly a strategy for those in the tenements. Yet there was a way out. The city itself might be "pastoralized." If the city could be carved around parks, meadows, and shoreland, Nature as a morally organizing presence would regulate social existence. The biblical images of Adam in the garden of his dominion and of a redeemed people nourished by the traditions of a place and practicing a stewardship that made fraternity possible were never far from Riis's notions of a just city and social order. He did not feel that the city had become uninhabitable; rather, its citizens had forgotten what a city must become. Urban life was devastated by a moral amnesia; the tenements made an urban Fall and fratricide visible. Hence, Riis's fascination, almost gnostic, with the ethical portent of urban darkness and daylight, his fight for school playgrounds and small parks, his dedication to bringing flowers into the slums and their schools.

There was yet a more effective way of breaking the grip of the tenements and that was by encouraging agricultural and agriculturalizing programs, such as the Woodbine Colony and the National Farm School. Recalling a visit to the National Farm School, Riis described a walk along a country road at sunset, and seeing, alongside a horsedrawn cart,

> a sunburned, bearded man, with an axe on his shoulder, talking earnestly with his boy, a strapping young fellow in overalls. The man walked as one who is tired after a hard day's work, but his back was straight, and he held his head high. He greeted us with a frank nod, as one who meets an equal. . . . This was the Jew of

59

Jacob A. Riis

my dream, no longer despised, driven as a beast under impossible burdens, in the Ghetto of men's contempt, but free and his own Master. . . . The Jew redeemed to the soil, to his ancient heritage, a prince among his fellows, a man among men.[71]

Riis contended that agricultural work opened a window for the soul to "discern the day of freedom." The path to it is one, he proposed, that "we have long known, [it] must be by way of the soil. *There* is the real freedom. There man's soul can expand. That way lies not only economic independence, but the ethical rehabilitation of man."[72]

In his declining years, Riis spoke emphatically about restocking the soil and about the redemptive possibilities of farming. The garden, the city, and man became the terms of his postlapsarian drama. At a Chautauqua lecture delivered in 1908, he invoked the saw that "God made the country, man made the city." Insisting that the city could be remade, he spoke about how this hope could be traced "to the beginning. *Man's Eden was a garden.* The traditional 'instinct survives.'" He continued by pointing out that "the man in the garden is yet the ideal. . . . *He is the ideal citizen.*" Reform addresses human nature within the theology of history. The "*real slum . . .* is *unregenerate human nature,* and in fact it is so."[73]

In the last years of his life, Riis returned to the soil and to a village. He bought a farm in Barre, Massachusetts, partially to satisfy his second wife, Mary Phillips. He noted in a letter to his son John that running the farm on a modern basis and sharing their expertise with neighbors was somewhat analogous to settlement work. He and his wife "would . . . hate to prosper while our neighbors failed."[74] His relocation suggests the closeness of his thought and life. He would practice, he would live urban reform in its most fundamental and preparatory way. He would be a farmer speaking to the city.

He hoped that Mary Riis could run the farm; he wanted, as he put it, to be as lazy as Rip Van Winkle. The realities of farm life were otherwise as his account books and letters of his last year show. It was hard going, but he talked of his efforts as those within the broad movement of national rehabilitation. It is worthwhile to look again at Riis's commencement address at Barre High School. Riis proclaimed that "Just now that mission [of the Danish nation] is to teach the world in this *city-mad day* that husbandry, farming, is both patriotic and profitable as indeed it must be since upon it rests all prosperity of man."[75] His finances couldn't equal the demands made on them, and Riis decided to embark on another lecture tour—characteristic of his youthful exuberance. He must have been desperate;

he had cardiac problems. On April 23, 1914, he collapsed in New Orleans and died on May 26.

V

It is impossible to isolate Riis's achievements. Sharing the values of those who can be called urban thinkers of good will, typified by such individuals as Josephine Shaw Lowell, Colonel George Waring, Ellen Collins, and Charles Loring Brace, Riis changed our expectations of urban life, of what we could fundamentally ask of and from it. In great measure, he brought to the public's attention and into existence decent housing, adequate schooling, small parks and school playgrounds, city services for the indigent, and a child's right to grow up free from brutality and the sweatshop.[76]

He labored to make the city express the ideals he knew as Christian, fraternal, and democratic. Try as he might, he could not divorce himself from a city that was so unlike his own hopes for it. He sought to humanize it and in so doing demystified it, reminding those of his generation and succeeding ones that the raison d'être of urban planning is to make a decent, humane life possible.

As he found himself swept by fascination for the city, so he came to define himself: the terms of urban analysis that he chose were often the problems that shaped his own life. He felt that the city could remedy an incomplete human nature and a fragmented society by appealing to those conditions that reconciled his present with his past. Ironically, for all his praise of those who might be redeemed by the soil, he discovered that farmers, too, were entrepreneurs and tied just as meanly to the currents of the market and the greed of the speculator as were the urban poor. In public, he rarely permitted his audience to share in his own occasional doubt about the need to make the American city a transfiguration of the Danish village. What would prevent the city from supporting a principle of moral order derived from the sublimity of nature, a cooperative, fraternal agenda, an integrity of the self, a life of Christian concern?

Privately and infrequently he spoke about the cost of these struggles and his memories of them. In the year before he died, he meditated upon the self-sacrifice that appealed so much to him, and he felt that he had essentially compromised his character. He called the altruism that he valued "the thing which I never had a chance to practice and wouldn't have, had I had it. I have been too brutally prosperous, and a selfish beast ever."[77] At the height of his fame, he recalled that Ribe, the village of his youth and

61

model to rehabilitate the city of slums, "was especially favorable to the development of the tubercular contagion, if abroad. The country is low and marshy and fogs come in from the North Sea almost every night."[78] He urged his sister, a year before his death, to let Ribe be a trope of the past. "For our ideal's sake, it is better that the old city remain only a childhood memory."[79] Such recollections are both bemused and bitter; perhaps they were written in momentary weakness when he was hard pressed to affirm the virtues of the agrarian life to the polyglot city.

His career remains his victory over doubt. More than any other reformer or writer of his age, he opened the city for inspection and attempted, albeit dogmatically, to find what kind of fraternity transcended the economic and social barriers preventing a common understanding. He championed the shared moral destiny of city dwellers.

It would be a mistake, though an interesting one, to see Riis intuitively beginning his own urban meditations as Aristotle instructs, establishing the role of *oikos* for the family, and then attending to the desirable city and its constitution. It would be intriguing to see Riis as an epigone of Thoreau insisting upon an inquiry into the self beginning with the house and ending with a universe of renewal. But this is not Riis, and it is not his argument. He was not interested in refreshing the tradition of classical political thought. He did not know it.

Riis's practical, humanly centered work looked forward to those writers who would insist that people were at the center of the city and would focus on the moral and humanizing relationships that are finally realized. Riis demonstrated that this urban meditation could be done. His work came from the agony of what he saw and from the conflicts he tried to mediate. Riis's refusal to turn the city into anything other than a fraternal dwelling is part of his bequest to others.

More so than any American city writer before him, Riis reminded the public that the city was not its wholly physical nature, but the manifestation of the transcendent in human affairs. By doing so, he made judgments of the city depend upon criteria apart from the city's material arrangements: the city should not be evaluated as a network of roads and harbors, or in terms of its capital production. It must be seen as a grand ethical human creation. As a result, Riis prepared the way for those who would talk of the metropolis in terms of its nonmaterial nature—as the expressions of man's character that made the shape of the modern city dependent upon symbolic and symbolizing capacities, upon its commitments to a

The City as Christian Fraternity

morally humanizing past, and upon its conservancy of socially valuable myths.

Ironically, Riis's focus on what he took to be the most immediate terms of inquiry—the slums he had tramped and the Christian, industrialist culture he championed—soon turned to be too limiting and too parochial for urban thinkers. The most immediate successors of Riis, notably Robert De Forest and Lawrence Veiller, in *The Tenement House Problem* (1903) argued that the secular city itself is the case in and for planning about the slums. After Riis, the next commanding American urban thinker, Lewis Mumford, would argue that the basic unit of inquiry was the region; its city, an immense historicalizing agent; its individuals, enacting a fundamental conflict embodied in art and technics. Mumford's inquiry is capacious, asking how the city transmits the continuity and continuum of thought and how it makes accessible to all its inhabitants these opportunities that liberate them from the contingency of isolation.

Chapter 2

Lewis Mumford:
The City as Man

I N *Sketches from Life* (1982), his most sustained reminiscence, Lewis Mumford writes about how the city brought him to maturity, giving him a sense of its educative powers. His self-understanding, as he presents it, became inseparable from his gradual knowledge of what the city and its communities were, and what they could be. Like Riis, Mumford found that urban thought became impoverished if the terms "city" and "community" did not involve morally transfiguring opportunities: specifically, the democracy of participating in and sharing humanity's cultural and natural heritage. And again like Riis, Mumford's reflections trace his refusal to think about the city apart from humans as they do exist and might live. People are depicted amidst their creations. For Mumford, as for Riis before him, writing about urban form, city design, and regional affairs is, ultimately, a discussion of the city's ability to provide not only a decent life, but also the good life.

"I was a child of the city," Mumford recalls, adding that "for the first thirty years of my life I knew the country only as a visitor, though the occasional summers I spent on a Vermont farm before 1910 had first and last an influence on me that offset my long incarceration in what Melville called 'the Babylonish brick-kiln' of New York."[1] This is a pronouncement, emphasizing the perennial, major concerns of Mumford's work. On the one hand, Mumford speaks of the historical separation of city from countryside: a symptom of divided man expressed by the urban bricks of captivity and the natural life of the farm. On the other hand, the controlling theme of eutopian writing is begun: the city as parent. Ancient and modern, how many men of letters—or the protagonists of their work— have started out with parochial ambitions in city streets only to become transfigured by the idea of the authentic city? An urban education, so this tradition suggests, begins with a curious wandering across an inchoate metropolis and ends with the revelation that a city re-presents man's generative powers. The city becomes a teacher to those who live within it. It is the incarnation of reason.

Sketches from Life begins with Mumford as a child experiencing the welter of the metropolis—its schedules, its holidays, its promises of adventure and education—and gradually and self-consciously enacting its promises. The metropolis takes form; it becomes a city to be interpreted, and *Sketches from Life* portrays Mumford's life from a childhood composed of urban scenes to an adulthood of self-discovery reading the possibilities of human nature within the city and its region. In *Sketches from Life,* Mumford speaks of how he turned his pleasant but limiting upbringing into the universalizing promises of New York. His intensely personal yet urban rite of passage from accepting the city as a banal composition of sentiments and places to seeing the city and himself as a part of a transcendent pattern happened because of a sweeping illumination. I should add this was because he, like the Melville and Whitman of Manhattan, was a wanderer in the city, seeking its meaning.

Mumford was born in 1895. He did not know who his father was. His mother was a domestic and later ran a boarding house. Stories about his mother's employer's nephew were, in reality, hints about paternity and suggested a comfortable if not exotic birthright to Mumford. They must have also strengthened the boy's sense of a vast city concealing other lives and fortunes. It seems thin but plausible to suggest that the issues of fecundity and imperiousness, motifs of Mumford's urban studies, might have been rooted in this premonition of family.

Mumford's early life was an education in the affective geography of the city. The boy's grandfather rambled into "every part of the city" and broke down the barriers of other families' lives, making the child feel "at home everywhere." This education in and of the city became his patrimony. "I made my own way," Mumford recalled, "without patronage or favor, indeed without any external advantages except those which my native city offered me. This is a far more munificent gift than any family could bestow. . . . Walt Whitman's Mannahatta was my Mannahatta, too: 'City of orgies, walks, and joys.' That is why my city, not my family, properly set the stage for this narrative" (*SL*, 35).

Manhattan came of age, he believed, when he did, and its vitality reflected his own exuberance. He watched Manhattan change so dramatically that it had to be seen as a literal container of competing architectural styles and human purposes. He describes his city walks by identifying himself with the spirit of place: he invokes Melville and Whitman and places himself near the city's now characteristic monuments, testaments to physical and cultural energies. In an urban, epic catalog, Mumford reflects upon the technical and intellectually renewing powers of this new age:

> I was there as a boy; I saw it all. The city grew along with the visible proofs of my own growth. The disappearance of "Little Coney Island," an amusement park at 110th Street and Broadway; the rise of Columbia University on the site of the old Bloomingdale Insane Asylum; the slow, tortuous building of St. John's Cathedral, never again to be such a satisfactory monument as in the brute stone of its original Romanesque form; the main building of the New York Public Library on the site of the old reservoir at Forty-second Street, which I used to follow as a high-school student on occasional walks home in the afternoon. All this went on before my eyes, like the later covering over of the gaping railroad yards between Vanderbilt and Lexington Avenues. Not least, the new green double-decker motor buses, careening along Riverside Drive, gave one a fresh sense of the city in movement. (*SL*, 21)

Central Park, the pastoral uptown, the imposing municipal buildings from Park Row to Broadway, the grimy, tumultuous lower East Side, the decaying Bowery, the financial enclave of Wall Street—these were vividly contrasting parts of one city. They served unique functions yet they could easily present themselves as models of cities in their own right if not as a sign of a fractionated city. The kinds of satisfactions they offered to people, their physical scales, and their uses of nature were not lost on Mumford. He began to consider what urban neighborhoods offered and what they did not; what human satisfactions they answered and what needs they ignored. The problem of the desirable community and city attracted him. *Sketches from Life* tells of his excitement discovering experiments in urban planning such as the garden city and regionalism aspiring to make the city a satisfying home for man.

Mumford's rambles encouraged him to demystify the city. His own grasp of what he saw became the foundation of his characteristically independent judgments about urban life. Like Riis, Mumford appropriated New York. His speculations, no matter how vastly different, also came from the ground up. Writing of his "solitary walks" across the city, Mumford spoke of their larger merit: they were odysseys. He had gone on these walks "as a man who sought to take in visually and make the fullest possible use of the life about him. To quote Ulysses: 'Much have I seen and known: cities of men and manners, climates, councils, and governments.' For in my ideal scheme of education, this mode of seeing and knowing must both precede and supplement the knowledge we receive from books, statistics, or computers.[2]

The City as Man

Mumford's discovery that he lived within an immense city happened in his childhood. That the city was sublime was a revelation that came fortuitously and mystically. In a passage from *Sketches* that must be quoted in its entirety, if only to convey its significance as the book's organizing illumination, Mumford recalls the moment in which he became one with the city, transfigured by its idea. Walking along the Brooklyn Bridge, he gazed below:

> Here was my city, immense, overpowering, flooded with energy and light. . . . And there was I, breasting the March wind, drinking in the city and the sky, both vast, yet both contained in me, transmitting through me the great mysterious will that had made them and the promise of the new day that was still to come.
>
> The world, at that moment, opened before me, challenging me, beckoning me, demanding something of me that it would take more than a lifetime to give, but raising all my energies by its own vivid promise to a higher pitch. In that sudden revelation of power and beauty all the confusions of adolescence dropped from me, and I trod the narrow, resilient boards of the footway with a new confidence that came, not from my isolated self alone but from the collective energies I had confronted and risen to.
>
> I cannot hope to bring back the exaltation of that moment: the wonder of it was like the wonder of an orgasm in the body of one's beloved, as if one's whole life had led up to that moment and had swiftly culminated there. And yet I have carried the sense of that occasion, along with two or three other similar moments, equally enveloping and pregnant, through my life: they remain, not as a constant presence, but as a momentary flash reminding me of heights approached and scaled. . . . Since then I have courted that moment more than once on the Brooklyn Bridge; but the exact conjunction of weather and light and mood and inner readiness has never come back. That experience remains alone: a fleeting glimpse of the utmost possibilities life may hold for man. (*SL*, 130)

Like those mystics who sought to fix the universal relations of the self, Mumford experienced ravishment and fullness of being on one of the commanding passageways of American life. If the experience itself seems too contrived—Mumford's entering a transcendent realm as well as having a place within an icon of American culture—it became, nonetheless, a morally usable event. It warranted, if not sustained, his judgment. A touchstone for what one should experience in the city, this event made incontrovertible what a full, engaged human response to the environment is. Obversely, it emphasized the incompleteness of present city life. In much of Mumford's writings, the insistence upon the "sense" and sensuousness of place remains true to his early revelation. For example, describing his walks through the lower East Side, Mumford speaks of "the absence of space, order, intelligent design, even sunlight and fresh air—

the sense of all the *human qualities* [my italics] that were missing—taught me by contrast, what to demand in every work of humane architecture."[3]

Mumford's writing envisions a city enhancing and being renewed by human nature. This preeminently means a creative, cooperative, and historical self alive to change, possibility, and continuity. Nonetheless, Mumford had few doubts about the practical difficulties of making this a program for the age. The self, he would come to argue, enacts a destiny that is divided and hostile. The city, the grand human artifact, reflects this antagonism. Escaping the legacy of the divided psyche demands a liberating interpretation of the city, a reading that emphasizes the integrative, transforming nature of humankind. Conversely, the less anthropologically inclined thinkers of the city are, the more inadequate their designs.

Members of earlier reform movements, for example, those of the generation of Riis, and the later Progressives had little understanding of this concept of the city and its necessary renewal. They belonged to a generation of pioneers discovering that urban form was being shaped by municipal politics. Their remedies for the slum and its origins dealt with appeals to fraternity, with reform of city government, and with physical improvements in a particular neighborhood. Planting gardens, or restructuring the tenement profit system, or breaking walls to make windows missed what the city was and its actual order: the objective historical development of human powers. The city is not simply the expression of law or economic development or political rule. Instead, it is man in his entirety. It is not simply a location. It is the heart of the region. Clearly, the distance between the *programs* of urban reformers like Riis and urban thinkers like Mumford is vast. "Riis belonged to an older generation than mine," Mumford wrote, and "played no role in my life except as a recognizable name."[4]

II

The city represents and *is* the plenitude of human nature: so Mumford argues. The city is a human project: man making his self. As such, it is an encyclopedia of man-in-general. "The city, if it is anything," Mumford proposes, "is an expression and symbolization of man's wholeness—a representation in building of his nature and diversity."[5]

Early in his career, Mumford argued that the city reflected a dissociation of subjectivity (and by this he emphasizes symbolizing capacities such as language and art that make for self-reflection and sociality) and technics (that activity and its values concerned with mastery of the environment).

The City as Man

Specifically, the subjective, what Mumford calls the "inner world," lost its authority to guide social planning. The good life is confused with a technically inventive one. Rhetorically, the machine and the garden oppose each other. Concretely, this is expressed by the inclination for moral limits, for nurturing, and for valuing the imaginative in opposition to the desire for power, for manipulation, for objectivity and for order. Historically, a convenient point to locate this separation is at the rise of Renaissance science and its denigration of the subjective dimension of experience.

Later, Mumford became intrigued by the city's invariable embrace of fraternity and domination. He would suggest that man's disposition was fundamentally divided between militancy and community. This could be seen in the earliest of cities, junctions of paleolithic and neolithic cultures. The city offers the paradox of human nature. On the one hand, the city preserves the continuity of humanity's symbolizing powers. The city's libraries, museums, and schools are archives. They bring individuals into human history and liberate them from the contingency of isolation. On the other hand, the city is the agent of state power. The contemporary city, much like early imperial cities, encourages a despotism over affairs by multiplying and empowering forms of social control. The city binds myth, theology, and reason to coercion. The city creates a protective, interpretive rationale so that contending renditions of experience and history are suppressed, rendered trivial, or ignored.

In large, then, the city expands man's consciousness of his role in history and nature; it also disempowers its inhabitants, alienating them from their needs and natural environment. For Mumford, authentic urban meditation refuses to accept these oppositions as desirable. His urban writing can be looked at as a conceptual therapy that integrates subjectivity and science once again.

Not surprisingly, Mumford's works deal with political culture in its broadest sense but are unconcerned with specific political events. His attention is given to historical "wholes," to configurations of people and their creations. Occasionally, he talks of his debt to Wilhelm Heinrich Riehl, whose *Die Naturgeschichte des Volkes als Grundlage einer deutschen Social-Politik* made much of the connections between a people, its mores, and technics. Invariably, he writes of Patrick Geddes, his great regionalist mentor, who explored the relationships among an organism's or a community's work, function, and environment. In Mumford's writing there is an attentiveness to an age's characteristic patterns involving the

69

interplay between art and technics. For example, he invariably composes a historical mosaic of energy production, political power, aesthetic creation, and mores.

The relationships Mumford is clearly drawn to are what used to be called representative events, those expressing the characteristic achievements of an epoch—a historicist thesis. His intent is to liberate them from rationales about their origins and referents. For example, his observations on the contemporary city of skyscrapers deal with connections among industrial production, land speculation, energy use, transit systems, demography, and our perceptions of a desirable life. Because subjects such as the city and the skyscraper are often treated as "abstractions" having a logic of their own and an autonomous development that is taken as rational and hence normal, Mumford wants to remake our consciousness of them. In this, his concern is with the historiography and history of alienation.

More to the point, though, is his argument that artifacts represent an interpretable and generalized cultural mind. They are products revealing the gradual alienation of ethical criteria from technics. As a result, his work connects an empirically known object with extrapolated relationships, with what one might severely argue are putative histories of creativity and estrangement. The degree to which artifacts can be so determined is open to question. Yet this sensibility insists that production—whether cultural or material—be restored to its numerous relationships. Objects and events are not seen as fetishes or as autonomous entities but rather as results of man's transaction with society and nature. The reestablishment of the individual at the center of events makes history a study of renewal and transfiguration.

Mumford's sensibilities control his work. He transforms the substance of history into his experience of it. His narrative line is usually a series of observations, often sensuous, capturing the immediacy of a setting. Yet there is more to this: the scale of a building, the perspective created by a boulevard, the smell and soot of coal towns measure man's hopes for the good life against his creations.

Mumford's emotional response to what he describes is affective history. His aesthetic surrender to the situation before him is part of his signature. Brooding upon the qualitative richness of the city, he accedes to it, illuminating for the reader the adequate response. As a result, Mumford's rhetorically sensuous argument becomes moral discourse. It insists that his presentation of a situation is, in reality, an engagement with renewal and that this situation should be shared with the reader. The historical

70

opportunities for a humanizing, balanced culture become occasions for contemporary reflection.

This historical inquiry offers grand hopes. Mumford's books invariably catalog the suppression of "life-nurturing functions." His conclusions, however, are pleas for an attainable balance between art and technics, between the region and its cities. Tactically the historical sweep of each of his major works begins with the village as an ecology; dwells upon the increasing imbalance between human needs and nature, value and technics; and ends with his reading of the promises of a regionalist, "biotechnic" future. This is also his strategy of narration: the development of the book parallels the logic of regionalism; the book's conclusions rescue the regionalist movement, denied by the State, as *the otherwise natural* consequence of human development and historical interpretation.

Mumford's commitments to writing history this way and to focusing on his characteristic subjects account for the distant place his writing occupies within historiography, especially the older Left. His regionalism, he argued, was a basic communism, but this was a democratic communalism. His reading of the psyche's divisiveness and his preference for organicism put his writing apart from analyses of class conflict and discussions of base and superstructure. His presentation of alienation is more intent on emphasizing the moral criteria of integration than upon discussing the mechanisms of capitalism. Moreover, for the contemporary reader Mumford's subject seems too wide, too reminiscent of an unfashionable *Weltgeschichte* that is majestically thematic. Perhaps it is the immensity of his enterprise, one that stands certainly beyond any American historian's efforts to grasp the idea of the city and its history—and in this fashion— that has made Mumford's work déclassé. In addition, his concern with the generalized imagination of a culture, its self-reflection in its representative arts and technics, has been until recently a minority concern. Who, in America, had done this before? Certainly, his affinity for the broad stroke, his inclination toward a universalist interpretation, and his sense of urgency give his work a perspective and immediacy not found in academic writing.

Mumford's prose embodies his inquiry. His style can be described as common American, a rhetoric binding ordinary speech to speculative discourse. Images are drawn from the commonplace; examples are taken from everyday life. Jargon and technical terminology are unusual. This American style was crafted by writers as diverse as Emerson (whose "The American Scholar" is the major call to develop this rhetoric), William

Lewis Mumford

James, Riis, Dewey, Bourne, Lippmann, Farrell, Niebuhr, and Goodman who identified themselves with the making of an American democratic culture that was both popular and critical. These individuals participated in the making of this public culture by forging its language. Problems of common interest had to be grasped by the common reader. Moreover, by choosing this style, writers asserted their place in national life.

To write about the city, Mumford challenged what he felt was the hegemony of professional, specialized historical inquiry. To reconstruct human wholeness he would have to read the city as the experience itself of schismatic human conduct: the drive for unity and the instinct for disorder. He pointed out that his specialty "is that of bringing the scattered specialisms together, to form an overall pattern that the expert, precisely because of his overconcentration on one small section of existence, fatally overlooks or deliberately ignores."[6]

His self-appraisal nicely hints at the development of his urban writing, beginning with an early polemical essay in 1917 ("Garden Cities: Preparing for a New Epoch") in which he argued for the garden city's renewal of life, to his thesis about the conflict between technics and art in *The Story of Utopias* (1922), through his efforts to recover the regionalist agenda evoking a whole human nature in *The Culture of Cities* (1938) and his portrait of the city as the divided mind in *The City in History* (1961), to his meditation, querulous and spirited, on the rise of the State and its ensemble of power in the second volume of *The Myth of the Machine, The Pentagon of Power* (1970). Within this canon are such eloquent studies of town planning and human nature as *Sticks and Stones* (1924); *The Brown Decades* (1931); *The South in Architecture* (1941); and *The Urban Prospect* (1968). In fact, these are only a few of Mumford's works dealing with cultures that through their traditions of art and technics either enhance or constrict human nature. Mumford's works take the measure of human fulfillment— socially, biologically, and creatively—as *the* criterion of adequacy for a civilization.

His ironic sense of being an outsider in a field he helped call into existence led him to appeal to the example of another historian who would write of the chaos of modernity and of humanity's redemption by love and grace. As a young man, Mumford had championed the Henry Adams of Chartres as a critic of architecture: "I doubt if a single 'medieval motif' would appear on a modern building if the architect had read and really assimilated *Mont St. Michel and Chartres*. . . . History, as it is portrayed by Henry Adams, leaves no place for the practice of archeology, either pious or profane; for the more one understands the past, the more one sees how impossible it is to recover by any external device, except as a masquerade."7

As an older man, Mumford invoked Adams as a type. Adams had broken free of the parochial historiography of his contemporaries by offering a more spacious understanding of man and his activities. He had warned his public about the unbridled pursuit of power and of the fracture between valuing and doing. The movement from history as rationale to history as science failed to win acceptance from Adams's generation. Yet working within what he thought was the collapse of his age, Adams had the prescience to speak of mental and physical energies that demanded pacification if the world were not to suffer unimagined disaster. He courageously insisted that man within the realm of "multiplicity" was *the* subject demanding the historian's attention. Adams saw it was necessary to consider the significance of love, of eros, and of grace as part of historical meditation. Speaking of Adams's warnings, of his standing "alone among all the thinkers of his generation, in having made a timely effort to understand the forces of science, technology, and politics that have brought us to the verge of a gigantic and irretrievable disaster," Mumford must have seen himself in Adams's predicament. He must have sensed Adams's legacy of hopes when he (Mumford) pleaded for a recovery of a "countervailing" power, "the energy of life . . . of erotic love, reproduction and creation. . . ."8 Mumford must have also been desperate to champion *this* Adams as a prophetic voice while ignoring Adams the racist and anti-Semite. Yet Adams, too, was orphaned from his patrimony; Mumford, no doubt, richly appreciated the Bostonian's prayer to the Virgin who rescues her children from chaos.

III

By 1919 Mumford felt sure about his subject. Audacious or not, he describes his attraction to large projects and frameworks. "My present interest in life," he writes, "is the exploration and the documentation of cities. I am as much interested in the mechanism of man's cultural ascent as Darwin was in the mechanism of his biological descent" (*SL*, 335).

To a young man coming of age during the tumultuous years from 1910 to 1920, the promise of planning for a region must have been awesome. City planning alone demanded that the world be taken as the case. Urban thinking would be a new and hopeful way of freeing human nature from values indifferent to life, especially the good life. Nothing could be alien, nothing need remain outside the field of study. Moreover wartime and postwar experiments in housing indicated how efficiently and well modern planning could create an envisioned city; planning was no theoretical enterprise. As Walter Moody observed in 1916, "The modern-day city-planner is no longer merely an architect, he is a composite fellow: architect, engineer, promoter, journalist, educator, lecturer, lawyer, and, above all, diplomat."[9]

Mumford was quick to realize that the thinkers he was attracted to and sometimes luckily came across, were part of a new school of urban thought. Taken as individuals, they dealt with specific aspects of the city. For example, they wrote about new public authorities (the specialist in the planning and financing of housing); modern strategies of city building (for instance, siting on a city block); and the city as an ecological unit that must be studied within its region. Moreover, they inquired about the origins of the city and its myths. They also studied its architecture as a clue about the transmission of a humanizing culture. Considered as parts of a whole, these thinkers extended the conceptual and practical boundaries of natural and cultural regions. They changed the way the city would be looked at.

Urban thinkers could now consider the systems of the city (e.g., transit, water supplies, labor force, energy, cultural values) as a totality. The city and the countryside might be more fully integrated. The integrations of building with regional planning, of architecture with technics, of community planning with natural resources, of cultural fables with material innovations—these enlarged the design and scope of any previous planning within or for the city. Moreover, modern planning and building had to be cooperative; an architect would have to rely upon specialists ranging from mechanical and electrical engineers to lawyers and real estate agents in order to build. As a result, planning represented social intelligence. No longer would a building, a neighborhood plan, or a boulevard be simply a property considered by itself or a quick sketch. Urban design would be an enterprise taking into account the nature of the region's resources, its transit systems, its power grid, its schools, and so on.

Not surprisingly, the thinkers Mumford chose to affirm in his works argued that nature was inseparable from culture. This thesis connects such works as George Perkins Marsh's *Man and Nature* (1864); Kropotkin's *Fields, Factories and Workshops* (1898), Nathaniel Shaler's *Man and the Earth* (1905), Patrick Geddes and J. A. Thomson's *Evolution* (1911), and Geddes's *Cities in Evolution* (1915). The study of the destiny of cities and

74

nations demanded a consideration of natural resources. Civilization is a perpetual transaction between people and their environment. The destruction of forests or of topsoil, or the creation of deserts, for example, shapes a civilization's growth. Nature is the text upon which technics writes.

Similarly, the city and its region had to be evaluated in terms of the quality of human life—its valuation of its subjective character. The representation of a civilization's values could be found in its fables of origin and power, in the architecture of its buildings, in the design of the city itself. Readings of the moral values of architecture by John Ruskin in *The Seven Lamps of Architecture* (1849); of medieval and Renaissance cities' designs for sociability by Camillo Sitte in *Der Stadtebau* (1899); and of the political imagination of the Greco-Roman world by Numa Denis Fustel de Coulanges in *La Cité Antique* (1860) revealed aspects of the city that transcended its material artifacts.

The city could not be studied apart from its ecological matrix, the region. In fact, the city expresses the geocultural resources of its river valley. By studying the relationship among the region, its people, their work and culture, the city's present can be illuminated. Its future could be designed.

At the heart of Mumford's own vision of what the modern city, its architecture, and its region are, is the version of the garden city propounded by Ebenezer Howard in his *Garden Cities of To-morrow* (first published in 1898 as *To-morrow: A Peaceful Path to Real Reform*, and reissued in 1902 with its more familiar title). This book, whose thesis was partially realized in the English garden cities of Letchworth (1903) and Welwyn (1919), provided a program for regional planning based upon a limited-growth, cooperative community combining the moral and economic advantages of agriculture and industry. The book was both a response to England's inability to make cities habitable at the height of its industrial epoch and part of the nineteenth-century interest in utopias.

For Mumford, Howard's achievement was his balancing the means and ends of life. Consumption and production, agriculture and technology, population growth and population density did not have to be dramatic oppositions but could be complementary facts. Howard had refused to accept the notion that the Victorian metropolis was worthwhile or that urban planning had to repeat mechanically the plans of nineteenth-century English industrial cities. The garden city was an alternative, offering new living and social arrangements. Mumford called Howard's teaching a "foundation for a new cycle in urban civilization."[10] In Mumford's own work, Howard's book figures prominently, shaping evaluations of town planning and the regionalist future.

Howard planned within the regional context. His garden-city plan, with its maps and charts, is an expanding framework—a series of steps that can be modified through necessity. Its major points are simple. There is a city limited to approximately thirty-two thousand people. As the garden city expands, excess population forms another city. In time, there would be several "Social Cities" connected to a larger city of fifty-eight thousand people. The multiplication of cities creates a cooperative network. Each city would have, for example, a cultural resource—a symphony, a library—that others could share. As a result, there is an interdependent economy within the web of settlements as well as without; decentralization of power and services are facts of this democratic, regional culture.

The city is built in concentric circles and surrounded by a "green belt" (agricultural land). The community is spatially planned; housing density is controlled; industries are sited in particular areas; a human visual and physical scale governs distances, and walking to and from work or shops is possible and interesting. The city owns its land; houses are rented for what amounts to a lifetime lease. As a result, the community receives substantial profits, which fund municipal services, create new amenities, and pay debts. The "Crystal Palace" is a glass-enclosed bazaar on one of the central avenues where competition is regulated and shops are selected on the basis of need. Farms are worked by competitive bid. Moreover, the garden city's government, a "Central Council and Departments," takes efficiency and flexibility as criteria of operation. The garden-city dwellers determine municipal services and payments, the economic character of business (whether profit-making, cooperative, stock-hold), and the agenda of the Council. In short, the spatial and economic arrangements of the garden city reflect each other and are based upon a regard for amenity, labor, and sociality.

Howard's program moderates the urban tensions of capitalism. People can literally buy into a seemingly economically and socially stable community. Their property is their stake in the city. Here they have a voice in their community arrangements, which is different from their often powerless role in the metropolis. In addition, the disparity between the cost of housing and the wages of the lower and middle classes, and the immediate crises of an unregulated economy seem to vanish. The plan also checks a progressive socialism. Its mixed economy of communal and private busi-

The City as Man

ness, actually a community capitalism, balances autonomy with the goals of a planned society. The community dictates what businesses and services it wants. The individual is free to choose how and in what ways to participate in the garden city.

Finally, the garden city, unlike the established city, can carry out its building programs cheaply. This novel settlement does not have to contend with land speculation making renewal prohibitive. It has an already cleared site; inner urban lots do not have to be purchased.

Howard's work is not to be read dogmatically and Mumford invariably insists on this. Howard's book is a plan for a community in the making and should not be read as a cure-all. Clearly, the garden city is not an island; it shares the economy and society of its region and country. Its luster is its recombination of already existing social and economic arrangements that creates a regional life more compelling than what exists.

Yet communities are simply not fabricated by common ownership or agreed-upon services. Communities, in the best sense, are purposeful and cohesive. They are intentional—either driven by a principle or held together by a nourishing way of life. Howard's book is devoted to the mechanisms and infrastructure of the garden city rather than to an elaboration of the contents of life it can make possible. Instead of an intentional community eager for "the good life," the garden city is a good place, certainly an alternative to the metropolis that made daily life frustrating and burdensome.[11] In Mumford's work, the garden city is a remedy for the megalopolis. The modern garden city, made possible by decentralizing mechanisms such as the auto and by electricity, would restore a humane existence to a limited, intriguing version of the contemporary city-state. Fusing art and technics; region and city; people and power, the plan would help make life whole again.[12]

Mumford remembers reading *Garden Cities of To-morrow* in 1916, along with Kropotkin's *Fields, Factories, and Workshops* and Patrick Geddes's *Cities in Evolution*. Howard would remain an exemplar of the best of modern regional planning, that done with an eye toward restoring the balance of life within a new form of community. Geddes would be an inspiration.

As an undergraduate, Mumford came across Geddes and J. A. Thomson's *Evolution*, and then turned to Geddes's *City Development*. The "effect," Mumford recalled, "was decisive" (*SL*, 150). He was soon importing Geddes's lectures from England and by 1917 began a correspondence with this man whom he would later refer to as his "Master." (This is reminiscent of Frank Lloyd Wright's homage to Louis Sullivan: "Beloved Master.")

In spite of Geddes's urging that Mumford become his secretary (they would first meet in 1923), the tension between them was productive enough for Mumford to feel confident about his own pursuits. Geddes was a teacher who demanded to be surpassed. Mumford writes that "in the formative period between 1915 and 1925 Geddes's ideas, but still more his audacious insurgency, left their mark on my whole life. Geddes's greatest gift to me was to deepen and reinforce the foundations that other minds had already laid, while he gave me courage to build an original structure with new materials in a different style: radically different, necessarily, from his own" (*SL*, 158).

Geddes's work confirmed in Mumford a specific sensibility and vision of the city. Like Geddes, Mumford found narrow "specialisms" reductive, destroying the field of the problem. Geddes's ideas about the culture of regionalism, about the importance of a civilization's patterns of energy extraction, production, and social values, and about the need for a regionalist future have analogues in Mumford's thought.

Geddes's own thought deserves mention if only to define Mumford's heritage and originality more fully. Geddes believed that if each science has a singular object and method of analysis, a comprehensive framework for social inquiry is not possible. However, if nature and culture are seen as interpenetrating and interdependent phenomena, a unifying science can be achieved. Causality in nature is not proximate; it extends into the culture of cities. An investigation into this now widening series of events would bind region to people and society to natural history. The regional survey would be this science: it would integrate the conclusions of seemingly autonomous sciences into a program for action. The terms of inquiry for Geddes—environment, organism, and function (the adjustment of organism to environment)—were applicable to all organic activity.

For Geddes, the city and countryside are one. The city functions as the culturally and economically concentrating and transforming agent of the region. The metropolis integrates past and present life through its cultural inventory—the school, the museum, the library. The region draws upon this heritage and helps the city maintain itself through agriculture and resources unique to the area. Consequently, city and country are a whole by virtue of their transactions and by their shared life.

The "valley section," a zone that runs from shore to upland, is the model for Geddes's study. This area is a container populated by types such as fisherman, farmer, and hunter whose lives dramatize the unity of work, place, and function. The survey, then, is an inventory of the region's physical and intellectual resources and their use in everyday life.[13]

The region, in fact, draws upon *histories* existing within the city's present, which are enacted daily. Geddes illustrated this by speaking about a schoolboy's briefcase with its mundane objects—an apple, an examination paper, a reader—which represent the culture of a city as the culture of *the* city. The apple is the fruit of primitive man; the test paper's legacy runs from the imperial tradition in England, back through Napoleonic France, to China; the reader has an immediate history in Diderot's *Encyclopedia* and its antique origin in Greece. In similar fashion, the cathedral dominating a skyline, a bank at the center of the city, and a university campus set against the city streets re-present historically different forms of power. Moreover, institutions such as the cloister, the cathedral, the school, and the university are enclosed spaces transmitting ideas of the sacred and the profane. They are specific places set apart from ordinary life so that it can be, paradoxically, renewed.

Geddes's interpretive exercise is, in small, the regional survey's labor: cataloging the environment, tracing the form of a culture, and arriving at the most comprehensive picture of people and their environment. Although the regional survey's goal seems impossible, the survey refutes the conventional belief that a city's location is limited to its physical boundaries and narrow present; the valley section is better viewed as a situation. The survey extends the area of human possibilities. By fiat, the notion of the region is placed before the public. This area is now given a defined, historic, practical existence. For example, Geddes's classic *City Development* (1904) points out how a well-defined estate-park actually calls for maintenance within the regional context.

Regionalism is marked by popular, local democracy. Political culture is based upon the findings of the regional survey, which indicates how the environment forms the basis for community. The report is, as Geddes put it, applied sociology.

The rise of the State is the regionalist's story of the Fall. It means the erasure of a given history and autonomy, the extinction of a balanced, democratic life. For Geddes, the State is an engine of power and coercion. Centralizing the forms and agents of energy from capital to people, and intolerant of diversity, the State crushes regional independence and mores.

The belief that this is *the* normal form of political existence is a sign of contemporary amnesia. In fact, the State reduces regional culture to folklore; it makes regional politics harmless discussions of local affairs.

The regional survey challenges authoritarian State power. Since it is unable to resist it, the survey does the next best thing. It points out how a better life comes about. Summarizing his suggestions for park planning in Dunfermline, Scotland, Geddes speaks of the need for unity. His solution ignores the State: "Place, work, family—region, occupation, life—geographic, industrial, and social well-being—these are but varied wordings of the threefold unity of life, work, and surroundings—organism, function, and environment—which we are seeking to realise in this our own good town."[14]

A question worth asking is: Are these terms clear? It is hard to say at what point Geddes's talk about organicism and place becomes metaphorical, though he certainly believed in an ecology formed by nature and society. Late nineteenth-century scientism gave social thought and history a vocabulary drawn from the natural sciences, especially physics and biology. And not surprisingly, Geddes was given, by background and profession, to draw upon organic tropes when talking about topics ranging from the nature of learning ("the leaf-molds of earlier cultures from which our advancement of learning draws its sap"), to the specializations of the city ("we are inclined to think that many ganglia may be needed to maintain the health of so vast and multi-radiate a body politic"), and to urban growth ("What really matter nowadays the divisions between innumerable constituent villages and minor boroughs whose historic names are here swallowed up, apparently for ever, like those microscopic plants, those tiny plants and animals, which a big spreading amoebe so easily includes, so resistlessly devours?").[15]

It is certainly not novel to point out the tyranny of analogies like organism and state or to question the different functions words like "growth" and "organic" play in historical inquiry and natural science. Nonetheless, the regionalists seemed drawn to them because they re-presented a unified nature and culture. Moreover, these terms defended the vibrancy and integrity of life in an age of polluted, choked cities. Even though Mumford, for example, argues that his use of organic tropes is nothing more than illustrative, his insistence upon such terms emphasizes an order of life that validates moral judgments.

Clearly, Geddes's regionalism is a politics of ecology. The regionalist movement's valuation of the "organic" as the criterion of a culture's integrity had little place in political theory concerned with class antagonism or the history of institutions. Regionalist writing saw such theorizing as given to categorizing and abstraction. The relationship of civilization to environment was ignored. The integration of city and region, the balance between energy and production, art and technology, city and countryside, the regionalists argued, lead to a new politics. The regionalist movement speaks of these relationships as having a functional unity so that each maintains the others, each works to a common end with the others: the model of "organic functionalism."

What was amiss in the early regionalist movement was its own lack of reevaluation. For regionalists, the laws of organic functionalism validated their program. The valley-section and its settlements were *the* model of geosocial organization. Organism, function, environment, or work, place, and folk (the last three, terms of social analysis employed by Frederic LePlay, the French sociologist whose influence on English regionalists was deeply felt) remained regionalist "givens." The theses of regionalism, however, could be dismissed or minimized while the advantages of planned, small cities and various types of regions (administrative, geographic, or industrial) could be maintained, some as workable fictions and others as economic realities. Decentralization, new forms of transportation, "instant" cities, and mass migrations, for example, challenged the utility of the river-valley paradigm with its almost sessile population and its informing powers of place. The "organic" certainly means more than filiation and ecological balance, but how warranted was it to transfer its putative values to the human community?

It is instructive to look at Geddes's own judgments of European history, if only because Mumford would find them useful, to see how the concern for the "organic" sweeps away, for instance, a reading of politics as a category discussable in and of itself: witness, for example, Max Weber's eminently differing work *The City*, which examines the development of the metropolis in terms of political economy. Geddes placed the Europe of his day in the paleotechnic age: the epoch of coal mining that devastated both the city and the countryside. Coal is mass, dirty energy; it encourages overproduction, centralization of labor, waste, and ruination of nature. The city becomes a filthy, sprawling slum, a kakatopia. Life is mechanical and dull. Imperialism and war are normal.

Opposed to this is the promise of the neotechnic age: nature is conserved and seen as a conservancy. Energy is clean and decentralizing. Communities are designed to live within rather than on the environment;

housing is planned for adequate light, ventilation, and gardening. Association, adaptation to the environment, cooperation, and limits to growth and production mark this eutopia.

For all the ambiguities of his thought, and for all its contentiousness, Geddes remains a teacher to our times. His ruminations about the geographic and historical importance of place and his belief that the city had to be experienced to be studied serve as weapons against intellectual aridity. His insistence upon assessing a civilization in terms of its physical and cultural relations widens our understanding of the dimensions of daily life. Geddes, Mumford wrote, "taught me how to take in the life of cities, both from inside and from outside, both in time and in space: not as a mere spectator or as a collector of statistics or a maker of abstract models, but, to begin with, as a citizen and a worker, participating in the total life of a community, past, present, and prospective" (*SL*, 155). [16]

The hope of regionalism as a reconstruction in politics after the murderous nationalism of the Great War was attractive. Geddes and his circle drew Mumford to London from his heady position as an associate editor for the *Dial*. Geddes had invited Mumford to join him in Jerusalem and then follow him to India. Victor Branford, a collaborator with Geddes on a number of monographs dealing with the projected regional future, offered Mumford a position as editor of *The Sociological Review*. This opportunity was more concrete than Geddes's and was less constraining; Mumford would not be Geddes's amanuensis. In 1920 Mumford traveled to London to assume his own role within the Branford-Geddes circle.

Unlike the American expatriates in Paris who felt that the crassness of America was foreboding and stultified their talent, Mumford was pulled back to the American landscape. He stumbled across Van Wyck Brooks's pieces on American culture. Writing to Brooks in 1942, Mumford spoke of the intellectual tug of Brooks's "Reviewer's Notebook" which appeared in *The Freeman*. "Your words," Mumford offered, "made me come back to America when I read them in London in 1920 . . . they settled my fate for me and made only one decision possible: to return." [17]

Brooks's pieces were part of his assessments of an American culture that justified materialism as the good life. In his celebrated "On Creating a Usable Past" (which appeared in the *Dial* of April 11, 1918) and his meditations on the American present, such as *America's Coming of Age* (1915) and *Letters and Leadership* (1918), the history of American literature became the tradition of failure. American men-of-letters, if not surrendering to materialistic values, at least favored them. The chance for a mature life and a heightened self-consciousness was thwarted. Without a sustaining community and a place to make a full life real, writers were powerless to critically distance themselves from their culture and impotent to transform a public.

The historian's task is cultural renewal. By mapping the "tendencies" of failure in culture and self, creativity would be possible. Brooks wrote:

> Knowing that others have desired the things we desire and have encountered the same obstacles, and that in some degree time has begun to face those obstacles down and make the way straight for us, would not the creative forces of this country lose a little of the hectic individualism that keeps them from uniting against their common enemies? And would this not bring about, for the first time, that sense of brotherhood in effort and in aspiration which is the best promise of a national culture?[18]

In "A Reviewer's Notebook" written during Mumford's London period, Brooks continued to think about the national conditions of the artist's defeat and replenishment. For example, in assessing the characteristic failure of promising American authors such as Stephen Crane, Bret Harte, and Ambrose Bierce, Brooks argued that the popular canons of success prevented them from achieving a maturity of craft and personality. He contended that "for half a century no one in America has spoken of greatness . . . no one has asserted that literature, philosophy and art represent values of transcendent importance."[19]

Brooks's version of a tragic American past helped prepare the way for a *Kulturgeschichte* of alienation, for discussions of the estrangement between the writer and the environment. An affirmative national literature could represent only a dull rapprochement with a culture hostile to creativity.

Brooks can be credited with doing more than guiding Mumford to America. His essays suggested that literature would be one major clue about a people's relation to place. A study of native literature could illuminate the regionalism of the past and its chances for a future.

IV

By the early 1920s, Mumford had achieved his intellectual independence. Although the themes that increasingly occupied him came from Brooks, from Geddes, and from Howard—the rise and fall of the culture of regionalism—he labored in a field almost his own. Moreover, he refused to become entangled with the dogmas of urban planning. He remained independent of the political Left and Right.

Lewis Mumford

"The exploration and documentation of cities," his stated vocation in 1919, stretched beyond the confines of urban history and the regional survey. He would contend that the city is an embodiment of human nature itself and that the traditions of American regionalism are those of the experimental temper.

Mumford came to argue that tracing the course of failure in America as Brooks had done was a blindness of its own. America had an age of exuberant inventiveness and community design: the golden day, the regional New England culture. The spirit of this epoch was not forgotten but was buried. The problem for the writer, in fact for the American public, was how to make use of it.

But what is a region? For Mumford, this was the human region. In a 1931 symposium, the "Round Table on Regionalism" at the University of Virginia, he pointed out that in "natural regions, certain modes of life have arisen in adaptation to fundamental conditions." A public is defined by its location and shaped by the activities that zone makes possible. "A common background" (food, air, water, resources) is natural and supports the cultural (customs, interests). The region, therefore, "as it is disclosed by the modern geographer, has a natural basis and is a social fact."[20]

This notion of region entailed a corresponding idea of the city. Mumford began to write about the city as something more than a simple container, as more than a casebook in political development and economic struggles. He envisioned cities as regional transmitters of all that is distinctively human. The city is a series of continuous, ever-present stages of symbolizing activity and interpretation. It makes available the traditions of human creativity and production. Rediscoveries of the city by Fustel de Coulanges, John Ruskin, Camillo Sitte, and Patrick Geddes uncovered an earlier, more integrated urban life than our own. The values of this "other" city ranged from a high aesthetic order to regional balance and cooperation. These examples suggested that modern city and regional life could be remade.

In order to be humanizing, the city had to belong to its public. The city, Mumford argued in what might be called his urban policy statements, is a common trust controlling its land. Unfortunately at present, land speculation controls the shape and development of city resources. Regionalism is a pathway beyond the city: it leads to the universal community.

Mumford's early pieces show him as a man of what he took to be *his* age. His writing starts to define a program that exists, for the most part, outside mainstream American politics: a program that first looks at the possibility of re-creating regions as economic and cultural entities. By doing this, local democracy would revive. Moreover, the region's preservation of history enhances the opportunities of citizenship—the right to be part of the culture of humanity. Human nature, much as Emerson propounded in "The American Scholar," would be integrated: valuing and doing would not be disparate. Technics would be judged by humane criteria—is it good for people? For the region? Is it needed? Does it enhance life?

Brief pieces, for example "A Very Royal Academy" (1920), "The Adolescence of Reform" (1920), and "Abandoned Roads" (1922), sketched the malaise of the present. An earlier generation had simply wanted things to go; the triumph of the practical meant a diminished understanding of the fullness of life. Experience is devalued and the idea of the good life is what is routine. The good community, however, furthers human wholeness. It makes possible "a more lively appreciation of the human adventure, a more adequate conception of human potentialities."[21]

The regional survey is the most adequate scheme for a genuine universalism to emerge from the First World War, so Mumford's "Il Faut Cultiver Son Jardin" (1920) proposes. The survey makes us aware of the nature of other regions whose traditions seem strange but whose common humanity is masked by the aggressive features of the State. Internationalism becomes possible when the life of nations is replaced by cooperation among regions.

For Mumford to write about regionalism was one thing; he could argue that it had a respectable ancestry. But it was more difficult for him to demonstrate that it had a viable present. Was there really an American public familiar with its makers? Could regionalism be disentangled from grandiose utopian projects? Was it a viable alternative to the State itself? Mumford began to publicize regionalism's saving tradition, its modern founders, and its current projects. He wrote about regionalists who reminded their audience of what the city once had been and should become. Titus Salt, Ebenezer Howard, Patrick Geddes, and William Cobbett were figures who ought to have a place in *the* urban tradition.[22] Their work proved that cities had satisfied and could continue to satisfy human needs. Light, space, proper sanitation, cultivation of the land, and visual interest had given, for example, the medieval town, city, and region their value as settlements.

Further, Mumford argued that modern city planning was opportunistic, neglecting the regionalist lessons of the past. What city design took seriously the values of conservation of nature and culture? The transition from American town to sprawling city and from locale to state ignored the physically and symbolically continuous nature of urban life. As the city lost its regional character, so it lost its distinctive features. The Chicago World's Fair and the City Beautiful movement dramatize this confusion: they glorified irrelevant, inappropriate monumentality, pacifying a crowd without transforming it into a public sharing a time and a place. "It is in terms of a lapse in political functions," Mumford wrote, "through the historic change from the town system to the state system, and the increase of city populations without the effort to develop new political controls that the state of American cities materially and spiritually before the civic renaissance must be gauged." Citing the "cultural attributes of Periclean Athens . . . the political controls of fifteenth-century Bristol . . . the social qualities of Dantean Florence," Mumford insisted that the values of an urban humanism guide modern urban reconstruction.[23]

Demonstrating that regional planning was a practical, contemporary affair, Mumford turned both to the intentional communities of Palestine and to American regional planning. In "Nationalism or Culturism? A Search for the True Community" (1922) and "Herzl's Utopia" (1923), Mumford saw regionalism—not a state—redeeming communal life. Central to his argument, one that depends on the autonomy of the regional culture, is the particularity of the Jewish people. They had maintained a culture in the diaspora; a civilization had been transmitted through local communities within alien lands. A spiritually rich existence was possible, therefore, both within and outside the State. Now that immigration to Palestine had given it a distinctive Jewish presence, the question remained whether the Jews would succumb to the history of others and create a state or whether they could draw the regionalist conclusion from their survival. Jewish utopian aspirations, Mumford argued, could be realized through a regional culturism: local communities that are free to form wider associations. This is not any state but a state of community. Jewish life, surviving statelessness and diaspora, "depends for its existence upon the activities of the local communities."[24] In America, however, the Jew is swept by the tide of nationalism.

The importance of new Jewish community plans is found in Herzl's affirmation of association rather than State development. His *Altneuland* overcomes the political limitations of his earlier *Jewish State*. Herzl's championing of the "Association," which makes cooperation and development things apart from the State, is worth taking seriously because the "Association" can be achieved, avoiding an authoritarian nationalism.

The City as Man

For Mumford, Herzl was a garden-city thinker, Herzl's visionary tract "resembles very closely that put forward and actually carried out by . . . Howard and his associates in the First Garden City; in fact, the Garden City Association, as first conceived by Mr. Howard and earlier by Mr. J. S. Buckingham, is precisely a *Genossenschaft* in Herzl's sense of the term."[25] Clearly, Mumford felt that a community experiment was first an experiment in community: new social arrangements are critiques of earlier social and economic life. Though Herzl and Howard seem strange coregionalists, both *Altneuland* and *Garden Cities of To-morrow* deal with a redemptive, designed present.

No less important, Mumford's writing began to draw upon the plans and achievements of the Regional Planning Association (later known as the RPAA). During the 1920s, Mumford's association with the RPAA gave him the chance to explore the eutopian imagination in modern America.[26] He had never planned a community but he was now with individuals who had. They were practical, successful, and visionary. The RPAA was a loose organization whose major task was the development of a coherent regional agenda countering city sprawl that prevented decent, humane living. (It is worth noting that Patrick Geddes was present at the first weekend meeting of the group in May, 1923). The RPAA, the *American Institute of Architects. Journal* announced, "proposes to assist as far as it can in contracting the present haphazard growth of cities in America." The regional plan "calls for new population centers, where natural resources will be preserved for the community, where industry may be conducted efficiently, and where an adequate equipment of houses, gardens and recreation grounds will ensure a healthy and stimulating environment."[27] In the twenties, members of the RPAA worked on projects such as Sunnyside Gardens (1923) in Queens, New York (where Mumford lived for several years); Radburn (1929) in New Jersey; and the plan for the Appalachian Trail, a project Benton MacKaye proposed in 1921.

Mumford's championing of regionalist projects at home and abroad is of a piece with his studies focusing on acts of physical and symbolic transformation. Whether writing of William James, or of the mass manufacture of objects whose forms are inappropriate, or of the architectural mistake of surrendering to past styles, Mumford described a narrowed creativity in which convention limits response. In the same spirit, Mumford lauded those individuals who enlarged the possible. He praised Geddes for advocating regionalism and Dr. Rubinow whose work in Palestine helped community life. An essay he wrote on the functional value of early American building and a study of Henry Adams's architectural vision complete Mumford's early contributions to regionalist thought. [28]

V

By 1931, Mumford's work assumed a characteristic breadth and unity. He had written about utopian literature (*The Story of Utopias*); the role of American planning within an industrializing culture (*Sticks and Stones*); an interpretation of America's regional past (*The Golden Day*, 1926); the opportunities facing modern communities ("Regions to Live In" and "The Fourth Migration" for the *Survey Graphic*, May 1, 1925), and assessed the often-forgotten talents who survived the crushing of regional culture (*The Brown Decades*). These separate works represent a single interpretation in progress. Each text extends the last, so that architecture, urban design, American fables of individualism, and early national community experiments form a *eutopian* meditation. [29]

This period is also the beginning of Mumford's experiment with a rhetoric conveying the value of the organic, balanced community and the portent of a mechanistic, exploitive society. Metaphors of the garden, the flower, and the cell contrast with those of the mine, the slag heap, and coal. Space in which growth has a natural limit contrasts with space that is finally "dead." Mumford is creating an interpretation of culture in which these two perspectives come to define each other, but he is also arguing that both order our experience of nature and society.

As early as 1925, he was talking of working within an immense intellectual pattern. Seeming nonchalant, he wrote of his ambition to "describe what has happened to the Western European mind since the breakdown of the medieval synthesis, and to trace out the effects of this in America." [30]

Mumford conceived and wrote *The Story of Utopias* from February to June 1922. Buoyed by optimism, he believed that the work could help prevent that "calamitous miscarriage of human effort"—another Great War. [31] *The Story of Utopias* remains a graceful reading of several plans for the city. It also defines the *eutopian* (good place) imagination as opposed to the utopian aspirations of the industrial age. The book is Mumford's reading of a culture through its imagination, in this case through invented cities rebelling against conventional patterns of life.

As Mumford described them, utopias are systemic, cultural themes. They are often identical with city designs that see human nature as invariable, as if dogmatic social blueprints were plans for a community in the

The City as Man

making. As a consequence, the utopia is categorical, abstract, and rigid. Yet, the utopia is the writer's reflection upon a society unable to change. As a result, the literature of this genre revives languishing values that cannot be presently realized.

Mumford's interpretation of three major cultural images from the Renaissance onward—the Country House, Coketown, and Megalopolis— defines either a society's dedication to the paleotechnic or its failure to create an organic culture. For Mumford, these three cultural images integrate notions about labor and leisure, autonomy and centralization, habit and behavior. Ironically, the power of the image lies in a sense of insufficiency; the image paradoxically offers what is missing in life.

Mumford recognized the problem of writing a history based on tropes that are overdetermined—as if they could reveal the complexity of social problems—and in 1922 mentioned this to Geddes:

> In the treatment of Coketown and the Country House I am going to suggest that each great historic period has a real, and to a certain extent, a realized Utopia, implicit in its habits and its institutions and its experiments; a Utopia which is . . . the pure form of its actual institutions, and which may therefore be abstracted from them and examined by itself. To write a history of these pragmatic Utopias would be to present the historical "world-within" and thus supplement the conventional historian's account of the world-without.[32]

The image is made with an end in view; both are understandable and accessible to the historian, just as they are understandable in their own epoch. This is a common-sensical argument but also a protective strategy. Interpretation has to begin somewhere, and for Mumford this somewhere is the continuity of human understanding; man speaking to humanity in general. The "world-within" is, for Mumford, something akin to a cultural subconscious that formally becomes a public rationale. He tells Geddes that "until psychoanalysis claimed the field [of history] we did not sufficiently realize the importance of the world-within . . . we did not see that it had a directive function."[33]

The Country House is a repository for goods gathered elsewhere. It is aregional: its architecture and building materials are not native to the region. Isolating the individual from the community, it is a product of rapture, not communion. The autonomy of the house proclaims its owner's freedom from society. In fact, the house is a series of estrangements: personal achievements and enjoyments are separated, just as contemplation and appropriation are divided.

Coketown, the triumph of the technical mind, ignores the qualitative, subjective dimension of life. Laid out in a gridiron pattern, Coketown's life is uniform and tedious. Schedules are planned around factory production. Streets are patterned upon mathematically determined lots for speculation and efficiency of transport. Coketown manufactures waste. Its products are made to wear out and to break so that the town's economy will not slack. The rubbish heap is its fitting monument.

The National State enfolds these images. The State destroys regional life by running artificial boundaries over natural areas. It impoverishes local democracy as regions are absorbed into administrative departments or zones. It imposes a way of life originating in the capital and not in the locale. To paraphrase Paul Goodman, people become personnel. The major city of this political unit is Megalopolis: an inchoate, monstrous city that centralizes activity. For Mumford, this is a city of paper and credits: activity here involves the acquisition of paper.

In these grand utopias, science and the "inner life" are divorced. The distinctly human contribution to experience is devalued. Art and technics, the self-generative and manipulative characteristics of man, confront one another as different cultures. Eutopias, on the other hand, are commitments to their integration; they are projects for the full life. *The Story of Utopias* becomes, obviously, Mumford's eutopian work sketching the unity of a modern, satisfactory civilization.

"The cultivated life is essentially a settled life," Mumford pronounces. The democratic community, not the authoritarian State, flourishes in the region. In turn, regionalism leads to the universal community. The world is now "open"; shared experience is a fact. He writes: "For the first time perhaps in the history of the planet our advance in science and invention has made it possible for every age and every community to contribute to the spiritual heritage of the local group; and the citizen of eutopia will not stultify himself by being, let us say, a hundred per cent Frenchman when Greece, China, England, Scandinavia and Russia can give sustenance to his spiritual life."[34]

Mumford's reading of utopias is polemical. The book's major assumption is that much about a civilization can be gathered from its utopian imagination. The literary utopia is reductive, however, and to read it as Mumford does simplifies problems about both the subject and its narrative conventions. Nonetheless, by dismissing the major utopias of Western literature as betrayals of the longing for utopia, Mumford still left behind him the seductions of the utopian imagination—the visions of ideological cities.

Tethering science to what seems practical (community problems) uneasily ignores a science that now will not critically examine its own hypotheses; we can keep our myths, Mumford insists, but now we must "infuse them with right reason." In fact, Mumford's proposals are closer than he knew to a positivism he disliked, and a pragmatism he was suspicious of. He saw science as a problem-solving activity, but one arising out of local affairs. As he described it, science should be a community project: it is "brought to bear upon the conditions in a particular community, in a definite region."[35] There is a social economy to this kind of science; it is *interested* intervention. Its importance resides in the security it offers: it meets the "essential needs" of the community. The regional survey, an example of a "local synthesis of all the specialist 'knowledges,'" unifies art and technics by presenting to a public the history of its culture and suggestions for the control of its environment.

Mumford had to demonstrate that regionalism had been suppressed because it opposed the State. As the continuation of an authoritative experiment that had been abolished from official history, regionalism would be rescued from charges of impracticality and eccentricity. Eutopian thought would become regional policy.

Sticks and Stones is the first step in Mumford's historical reconstruction of regionalism's importance in American life. This book turns away from the written utopia and looks instead for an American future in which "Home, meeting-place, and factory; polity, culture, and art" are united.[36] This fusion, Mumford contends, is one of "the fundamental tasks of our civilization." The isolation of "life and art" can be overcome.

The abandoned, forgotten community is the motif of *Sticks and Stones,* and it guides Mumford's reconstruction of American culture. Architecture is the key to this history. For the sake of interpretation, a building, a village, a city are public and accessible in a way that utopian writings are not. Architecture is an ever-present, tangible reminder of the dialogue between tradition and innovation.

Mumford's examples of worthwhile community plans range from Greek cities to sixteenth-century English villages. The lost regionalist community is seen as part of the classically urban as well as the noteworthy, struggling modern-city tradition. Whereas Mumford interpreted regionalism as a history of the whole man, he was also fashioning a historical evaluation of the city that protected regionalism from its failures. Regionalism would be a program to be achieved although it was one that had not been continuously realized.

Early American settlements maintained their distinctive values by limiting growth, having like-minded members, and providing for the well-being of their population. Agriculture was an exercise in conservation, indicating how carefully the village strove to balance its needs with physical resources. But this, for Mumford, is only one model of a community that can be readapted to any age because it renews the spirit through cooperation and adjusts the means of life to its ends.

Strikingly, Mumford does not draw upon the literature of *gemeinschaft* for a different reading of a hoped-for community nor does he make much of the pathology of New England's theocracy and its authoritarian disposition. Instead, he calls attention to the *devices* that make for community. As he describes it, the shape of the settlement embodied its organic nature. The garden city is prefigured. "All the inhabitants of an early New England village were co-partners in a corporation; they admitted into the community only as many members as they could assimilate." When the settlement becomes too congested and affairs consequently become unwieldy, "the original settlement throws out a new shoot."[37] The community determines production as well as land use. Differences in sizes of plot are based upon domestic status and family life. Uniformity of plot is uncommon.

The transition from the regional community to the capitalist state marks the decline of the authentic community. Capitalism and its new market values liberate the village from its dependencies upon the immediate environment, a system of ecological balances, limited resources, and local fraternity. At the same time, Nature is transformed from a system of relationships into commodities.

In terms of architecture, means and ends become maladapted. Building material is gathered elsewhere and without regard for fitness; a structure either is unsuited for its site (creating heating, lighting, and ventilation problems) or destroys it; there are problems with sanitation, congestion, and water supplies.

Mumford's theme here and elsewhere is modern capitalism's coercion of sensibility. Life is controlled by the schedule of production. In turn, production transforms the city into a vast human hive of labor.

The modern city centralizes capital; it pulls people away from the countryside; it turns adjacent communities into commuter suburbs; it monopolizes cultural resources and fatally weakens community invention and independence. The metropolis becomes a place to work but not to live. Moreover, the skyscraper remains a building without a community. Its form concentrates people and the need for services (power, water, transportation), draining city resources. It enforces an anonymous design because the architect loses control over siting, lot size, and development. Rather than educating our sensibilities as does the eutopian city or the early settlement, the modern city tends more and more to a mechanical, tedious form. As the city expresses the imagination of industrial capitalism, so does it make *eutopian* projects seem impractical.[38]

This argument is elaborated in *The Survey* of May 1925, an issue devoted to the RPAA's proposals. These were pronouncements. Clarence Stein, Robert Bruere, Benton MacKaye, and Stuart Chase, among others, spoke about the American future. American cities had their infirmities diagnosed and remedied in regionalist terms. Our cities, Clarence Stein propounded, are dinosaurs: maladapted to the environment and dysfunctional.

The shape of cities, many of the contributors argue, is determined by energy use, extraction, and transmission. The coal mine, railroad tracks, rail head, and power station transect the city and control its growth. At the heart of the urban energy source are smokestack industries, railroad yards, and coal dumps. Coal pollutes; its radius of energy transmission is short. Consequently, the city's energy sources promote congestion and filth as production is intensified. Paradoxically, the economic success of the city increases its density, its waste, and its erosion of a region's resources. Decentralizing modern energy—electricity—breaks the form of the paleotechnic city, Rober Bruere argues in "Giant Power—Region Builder." The city no longer has to be the nucleus of the energy system. In "From Coals to Newcastle" Stuart Chase points out that urban congestion and reliance upon railroads are related and unnecessary. Benton MacKaye, in "The New Exploration," contends that the regional frame of planning highlights the wastefulness of the urban, self-congesting economy and its transportation system. For example, raw material is shipped back and forth in order to make a finished product; areas are drained of their produce and have to import the same raw material from other regions.

Mumford's essay "Regions—To Live In" complements these studies by arguing that the city is inextricably part of the region. Urban planning that is not regional in scope is muddled. The flight to the suburbs, in fact, is an escape from a city losing its ability to satisfy the needs of its population: this migration contrasts with the contentment of the garden city.

Mumford's "Fourth Migration" is the jewel of *The Survey*'s special issue. American migration across the continent and the subsequent back-flow into the cities are seen as a pattern formed by settlements, conservation of energies, and social values. His explication reaches back to Shaler, Marsh, and Geddes; it also looks forward to his championing Henry Adams's prognostications about the energy of authoritarianism. Mumford's reading of migrations emancipates his work from what might have been a narrow discipleship in regionalism and its theory of the river-valley civilization. From this point on, his meditations see the fables and symbols of a culture as if they were directives guiding the culture rather than conserving it.

"The Fourth Migration" discusses two Americas: one settled, the other moving. The migrations reveal what kind of society is in the making and its valuation of the whole person. The "America of settlement" did not partake of the movements west and then back. It sustained its characteristic ecologically minded existence until the mid-nineteenth century. Industrial and agricultural life were balanced: Mumford cites waterwheels, mills, and farms. A "fine provincial culture" was created through the web of universities, lyceums, churches, and schools. The figures of the American renaissance emerged from this time and place: "Motley, Prescott, Parkman and Marsh . . . Emerson, Thoreau, Melville, Whitman and Poe."[39]

The migrations themselves overlapped, indicating how the past use of land, energy, and cultural creation molded the present. The first migration (1790 to 1890) recklessly cleared the land, exploiting its resources. The covered wagon is the characteristic image of this epoch. Its mobility and shelter represent "a rapacious, migratory society. The second migration (1830 to 1910) "worked over this fabric a new pattern of factories, railroads, and dingy industrial towns. . . ."[40] The city is now made for work and business. The third migration (1870 onward) is composed of those leaving farmlands and villages and moving to the city. The countryside is drained of its resources as the city centralizes capital, people, and culture. Prosperity is the sign of a decent life.

The fourth migration is based on the decongesting potentials of the gasoline engine, the telephone, the radio, and electricity. An overconcentrated urban population can be dispersed without loss of work and culture. Regional planning could achieve its goal to make a "vivid, creative life throughout a whole region—a region being any geographic area that possesses a certain unity of climate, soil, vegetation, industry and culture."[41]

Throughout this issue, the regionalists opposed the achievements of the modern city. Decentralization, community planning, the regional framework, the garden city with its superblocks, green boundaries, and limited size constitute the new community. Yet *The Survey* contributors ignore the implications of their plans. With the stretching of the power grid and the dispersion of people across the countryside, the metropolitan public's physical, critical mass is diminished. A democratic public depends on numerous, differing communities of interpretation making city life an expanding conceptual and economically innovative environment. This public is, in the regionalist argument, devalued and lost. For the regionalists, the daily shared, pluralistic character of city life would occur through disembodied voices on the radio, or within the limited population of the garden city, or in the workplace. The accessible, urbane neighborhoods making for grand cities would be replaced by the village dependent upon technologies rather than people. No less important, the regionalists had their own naive faith in an electric-borne culture. Unless access to media is truly equal, decentralization merely increases the radius of controlled information.

Blindly, *The Survey* writers dismiss the excitement of the city. There is something dogmatic about a plan that equates a settlement of nearly thirty thousand (though this is usually a flexible number in regionalist writing) with the practical, good community; about arguing for limited growth while dismissing the conflictful, educative city; about intimating that regional values have a permanence rooted in human character whereas the contemporary city does not. Form may have no clear consequences for a community; the decentralizing power grid may not make for a public.[42]

For Mumford, however, the conflict between a regional plan and a purely metropolitan one is also a struggle between the idea of the city as an organism and the concept of the city as a thing. "There is no compromise," Mumford warns, "between these two points of view for the inorganic is as different in quality and function from the organic as a cinder is from a flower." The city could be compared to a cell in mitosis. An older concept of urban growth is accretion. The contemporary notion of development is "organic"—or "growth by fission." When the city reaches a functional limit, it "divides up, as a cell divides, and forms another city, with its own nucleus of civic institutions and its own norm of development."[43] The city not only has vital signs; it is itself vital. This metaphor is a method: organisms deteriorate if they exceed their metabolic rates. "Each city," Mumford writes, "is a living entity, with qualities of its own; that, like all organic bodies, it has a norm of growth beyond which it can only go by forfeiting or weakening its valuable qualities."[44]

This imagery could have easily been derived from Geddes or from any number of nineteenth-century thinkers who reduced the order of culture to the laws of a various Nature. It would be unjust to fault Mumford for his rhetoric, though not for his confusing metaphors with ideas. For someone who grew up in the paleotechnic era, controlling images like the cinder and the flower were eloquent summations of the gritty life of cities and the regionalist future. The early settlement and the trading post, the garden city and the metropolis, the flower and the cinder compose a vocabulary of ecological opportunities for modern civilization.

Mumford would invariably be drawn to images of and analogies for the city. They enriched our sense of the city as a network of meanings as well as testifying, paradoxically, to its irreducible essence. They also suggested how the desirable city appeals to our sensuous nature, unlike the urban gridiron map or photographs of metropolitan skyscrapers. In "The Sacred City" (1926), an essay discussing Hugh Ferriss's new urban iconography and Willy Pogany's "vast colored transparency," Mumford writes about both artists' fascination with monumental, overbearing buildings that obliterate the qualitative aspect of experience. These works are homages to abstraction and reification. On the contrary, Mumford's city attends to the "things that would still matter . . . birth and death and falling in love and marrying and giving in marriage and fine living and high think-ing. . . ." Humane cities, Mumford argues, have existed: "the activities they enshrine are part of man's permanent heritage as man. . . ."[45] The good city is good because it makes a complete self possible. Social crit-icism, therefore, is philosophically reactionary, preserving the "organic" vision of people and city.

In *The Golden Day,* Mumford as much invents as meditates upon an age and place in which the "permanent heritage" of Americans is found. The ideological and scientific currents that washed away the European commu-nity—and here Mumford cites the Protestant spirit, the centralizing State, and the progress of quantifying sciences—are found now in *seemingly* American types whose limitless ambitions made a spiritual and physical wilderness of America.[46] Interested only in mastery of the physical en-vironment, the pioneer and the trader extended the area of settlement by ravaging whatever was in their way. The difference between the eastern and western settlements is ethical. The pathos of American history is the defeat of the ordered, limited community by those who live without and beyond moral and social boundaries.

Mumford's history has regionalism falling victim to the capitalist imagi-nation rather than having a *natural* development of its own. Mumford isolates the short life of intellectual New England by refusing to connect it to the economic and political dramas of the West: the two areas could be two different nations. In fact, between 1830 and 1860, the "old culture of the seaboard settlement had its Golden Day in the mind" whereas the other America of migration "had up to 1890 little more than the boomtown optimism of the Gilded Age to justify its existence."[47] Paradoxically, regionalism is done in by years of plenty. Ignoring the Jacksonian legacy with its extension of law and economic opportunity, Mumford focuses instead on the struggles of a New England literary culture. Neglecting the formation of an American political culture and the creativity it made possible is a strategy as well as an almost fatal weakness, for it is only by quarantining letters from their social conditions that Mumford is able to talk about the two Americas and about the figure of the solitary artist existing apart from political affairs.

The avatars of the period, Hawthorne, Emerson, Thoreau, and Whitman, lived the principle of "nakedness." Trusting their own judgment and relying upon their own experience, they created a present that did not recapitulate the past. Wanting to break free of the habitual nature of conduct, they paradoxically had to undergo the spiritual crises of their intellectual ancestors. Intellectual history is made by rebellion: the freedom of each generation is enacted and yet undone by the children of the next.

Political allegiance, Mumford intimates, has a human scale; it is a loyalty to the region one feels part of. Hawthorne had argued that New England was as large a piece of land that could claim his allegiance. Thoreau found that New England was his world of concern. Civic regionalism such as this is the apogee of Mumford's history. The Civil War and its aftermath put an end to this sensibility that made an American humanism possible.

"The promise of regionalism" became, for the American politician, the "menace of sectionalism." A culture that balanced the imagination with labor and production with need was eradicated. As a result, subsequent American thinkers were victimized by industrial culture. They were unable to conceive of a different and more satisfying existence than the one immediately in front of them. They trekked to Europe or hid in a sentimental past. "For the dominant generation of the seventies," Mumford notes, "the new personalities that had begun to humanize America did not exist. . . ."[48]

Mumford's enchantment with the characters of the "golden day" is based on their self-illumination which somehow made for a community of other enlightened selves. "Nakedness" is the uniquely American character of autonomy. How "nakedness" could be transmitted is a question that should be asked. This concern, however intriguing, ignores the development of America through its institutions and political conflicts. Mumford is not concerned with "mass" or "public" experience. Historians like Frederick Jackson Turner and Theodore Roosevelt spoke of the passage from the eastern seaboard across America as a commonizing and communalizing process. For Mumford, studying this odyssey of ambition ignores what the authentically transfiguring nature of American life was: in other words, the self-renewal made possible by American regionalism.

The new politics that Mumford calls for begins conceptually. It must. There are no state institutions transmitting regionalist hopes. The visionary politics *The Golden Day* espouses "is nothing less than the effort to conceive a new world."[49]

Mumford's unwillingness to widen his historical framework and his empathy with the figures he depicted were, paradoxically, strengths. They allowed him to rediscover the isolated, almost forgotten, creative figures of industrial America's "brown decades." Their projects, ranging from engineering to painting, defined the possibilities of integrating the arts and technics of their time. The golden day had not been a memory. Its significance was its renewal of the next generation.

The Brown Decades pays little attention to individuals whose work was fruitful because of the contradictions of industrial capitalism, whose labors were not necessarily buried by it. The founders of American pragmatism who could call Emerson the father of them all are ignored; the pioneers of American literary realism and naturalism are passed by. Mumford's eye was on other things, especially the paradoxes of American civilization. On the one hand, the book is an elegy for America's paleotechnic culture; it is a graveyard. On the other hand, a different tradition of needful invention and creativity has survived. Losing sight of lost artists of that time, we weaken "the sense of solidarity that a continuous tradition, actively passed on from master to pupil or disciple. . . ."[50] *The Brown Decades* preserves this history and by doing so becomes part of it.

For Mumford, who sketched his theory about this period in "The Buried Renaissance" (1930), the experimental, balanced mind lay behind the brown decades' explosion of inventiveness. It defended the older, regionalist promise of life threatened by mass industrialization. Yet the brown decades' insuperable love of mechanization checked the hope of the "golden day."[51] The transition from a life of reflection to one of making things damaged the American character. A vital critical spirit (the "nakedness" Mumford had earlier described) assessing an individual's judgment of experience in the face of social convention was lost. The individual was now driven by an empty progress. A tidal wave of objects and mechanical schedules flung him about. Indeed, the impulse for invention, Mumford argues, was never brought within "an harmonious system of concepts and feelings. . . ."52

The insurrectionary spirit of the golden day is found in transfiguration: for example, in the relationship of mentor and pupil, or in architecture's demonstration that there are yet better ways to live. Few of Mumford's contemporaries saw that John and Washington Roebling, the makers of the Brooklyn Bridge; painters Winslow Homer and Albert Pinkham Ryder; the designer of landscapes F. L. Olmsted; and architects H. H. Richardson, John Root, and Louis Sullivan—to name just a few—belonged together as artists creating an American vernacular, a contemporaneous form, modern in achievement but permanently human in value. Louis Sullivan is the "first American architect to think consciously of his relations with civilization," Mumford asserts, and adds that Sullivan "knew what he was about, and what is more important, he knew what he ought to be about." Winslow Homer's importance "lay in the fact that he embraced the life about him and made what he could of it. . . ."53 Frank Lloyd Wright nourishes the experimental tradition.

The architects that Mumford presents as luminous, Richardson, Root, Sullivan, and Wright, are individuals who reconceived the relationship of form and function. In the largest sense of their achievement, Mumford's founders of American architecture made tight the knot of function, environment, and people in an epoch that benignly tried to unravel it. Their works integrate material means and humane ends, becoming models for renewal. However, *The Brown Decades* ends with a lament for a "culture of things," the present age of "monstrous cities," a time of the "regimentation of men."

Mumford had to bridge the tradition of the brown decades' experimentation and modern times. Otherwise, the regionalist experiment would remain a closed historical episode. The bridge is human nature itself. Throughout the book Mumford grandiloquently contends that human nature attains its maturity within the ordered, experimentally inclined region. "The bridge, the garden, the ploughed field, the city," is Mumford's Homeric invocation to "The Renewal of the Landscape"—the second section of *The Brown Decades*. These objects compose the settled life of place. They take us from the crossing of natural boundaries to the limits of domestic gardening to the large field and to the bounded city. Mumford lists them serially, indicating the significance of the whole they form: expressions of man as maker, progenitor, tiller, and citizen. Here, the isolated act is a fiction. Categories of life, such as husband, wife, citizen, laborer, thinker, lose their significance. In their unity they are, in Emersonian fashion, Man.

Contesting this description are the consequences of the brown decades. Profoundly moral, they confront us physically as dead cities, coal heaps, polluted air and rivers. They are the chosen future; they dramatize commitments to waste, imbalance, and destruction.

The problems Mumford selected to write about in *The Golden Day* and *The Brown Decades* characterize his later work, which speaks about the nature of renewal. For Mumford, human nature is fundamentally self-generative and willful. People will to create, to symbolize, and to manipulate. A history that addresses this issue deals with humanity's pertinent struggle. It can focus on self and social geneses as invariable historical possibilities.

Mumford was not reticent about this project. His previous work prepared him for a bolder venture. "Everything else," he wrote to Van Wyck Brooks, "that I have attempted has been a side-issue, or rather, has been like a spring or a brook or a rivulet, significant only in so far as it has converged on this main stream. . . ." (It is worth noting the importance of the simile: *The Golden Day* was originally to have been titled *Running Streams.*) This new project that Brooks heard about was tripartite. The first work, as Mumford sketched it, would examine the role of machines, "which covers incidentally," Mumford casually writes, "the major problems of economics and of politics and morals as related to that"; the second work would be a study of cities and would deal with culture and politics; the third, on "Personality" would "bring everything together" but concentrate on "philosophy and education and marriage and what not."[54]

Mumford's essays, even before this announcement, had been verging on a planetary theme, namely the integrated life within world cultures. If this seems like an impossible project, his reviews of Spengler's *Decline of the West* shed light on what he believed to be within the grasp of the regionalist tradition. Spengler, Mumford asserts, is the "first philosopher of history, with the exception of . . . Geddes, to carry over into social life and its movement through time the fundamental concepts of biology." Spengler "feels the unity and continuity of life."[55]

The failure to explore this unity, Mumford writes, results in a "sociology which ignored the fundamental instrument of humanization in society, the city; we have had an economics which never recognized the final stage in the productive process, that of creation, the stage expressed in art and thought and culture. . . ."[56] Experience is no longer man experiencing.

Every act, he asserts in "What I Believe" (1930), is "organically conditioned by its environment"; politics, as a reading of human affairs isolated from nature, is parochial. Instead, one acknowledges the powers of life. Our dispositions constitute, at first, our affairs with and within the world. As Mumford put it, "One begins with a world of values and only as a result of persistent inquiry and experiment does one reach such a useful concept as that of a physical universe, considered as self-existent and separate from these values." We do not confront the world as an object; rather, it emerges as such from our activities in it. Consequently, "organic" wholeness is the valuable basis for human growth. That it *can* be lived is found in Mumford's praise of Geddes who "showed that a conception of life, unified at the center and ramifying in many interrelations and comprehensions at the periphery could be rationally lived. . . ."[57]

By the early 1930s, the "organic" emerges more and more durably in Mumford's writing as a concept embracing filiation and interdependence in and between nature and society. Mumford's idea of the organic did not permit "laws of nature," as fascist apologists would have it, to speed up or direct political culture.[58] *Technics and Civilization* (1934) advances Mumford's claim that an "organic balance" can be known and politically achieved. Man's working upon and in response to nature is the dialectic of human history. "All our really primary data are social and vital," he writes. "One begins with life; and one knows life not as a fact in the raw but only as one is conscious of human society. . . ." The organic is purposive and cooperative. This is evident, Mumford argues, in the "life-sustaining" physical structure of nature. A new science of history that is concerned with the embodiment of filiation is necessary. This science dislodges hypotheses about a mechanical universe indifferent to purpose, whose elements are unrelated. Instead, "Form, pattern, configuration, organism, historical filiation, ecological relationship are concepts that work up and down the ladder of the sciences: the esthetic structure and the social relations are as real as the primary physical qualities that the sciences were once content to isolate."[59]

Our past is composed of a series of imbalances because our use of energy outstrips our ethical control of technics. For technics is not technique; it is a choice about the way human will imposes itself upon nature. There is no quarantine of technics within civilization, just as there is no human domination of the environment without an ethical end in view.

Technics and Civilization is the logical prelude to *The Culture of Cities* because it connects the structure of society with the gross ecology the regionalist argues is our environment. A regionalist "knowing" and practice are now historically necessary and socially logical. In complementary fashion, *The Culture of Cities* seeks to restore the city to its rightful cosmopolitan and ecological status. By doing so, the book argues for a city drawing upon the resources of the natural environment and the culture of nations.

Whereas these claims have their roots in Mumford's earlier short pieces, the book's originality is undiminished. What American book contemporaneous with Mumford's affirmed the city as a historical, cultural, *and* physical human ecology? What regional plan or city scheme tried to evaluate the culture of the city as a function of its use of resources? Excluding Wright's urban jeremiads, it is fair to say that until Paul and Percival Goodman's *Communitas* (1947), American planning schemes were not concerned with a reevaluation of what human nature may be in a new city. Looking backward, Mumford's regionalist propositions seem to become eminently workable alongside the creation of the TVA and Greenbelt towns (though these last were far from garden-city experiments).

The Culture of Cities is a twilight book written against the background of European fascism. The attending themes of contemporary Western letters—the rise of mass man, the public and radical nature of evil, the birth of the modern totalitarian state—make their appearance in this book as the megalopolis comes to dominate historically life-giving communities. Continuing Mumford's plea for a redemptive future sketched in *Technics and Civilization, The Culture of Cities* examines the evolution of the city in relation to the democratic, regionalist, and decentralizing life of the "bio-technic" epoch.

As the "Introduction" to *The Culture of Cities* makes clear, Mumford saw the need to decompartmentalize life as an urgent task opposing contemporary rationales of power. The traditions of experimentation that make life full and cooperative are the legacy of mankind. Humanity must be written about in the network of its activities, rather than outside them. Mumford's point of critical departure is not life that is sterilized by theory but "life as it was lived in the concrete." He epically invokes Geddes's typology of the valley-section—"regions and cities and villages, in wheatland and cornland and vineland, in the mine, the quarry, the fishery."[60]

The City as Man

This is a modern shield of Achilles, and figuratively presents a natural region in terms of self-containment.

In an elaborate rhetoric opposing the symbiotic and cooperative to the parasitic and mechanical, Mumford writes in a section that must be quoted in its entirety, that to

> scorn one's roots in one's own region and admiringly to pluck the paper flowers manufactured and sold by the metropolis becomes the whole duty of man. Though the physical radius of the metropolis may be only twenty or thirty miles, its effective radius is much greater: its blight is carried in the air, like the spores of a mold. The outcome is a world whose immense potential variety, first fully disclosed to man in the nineteenth century, has been sacrificed to a low metropolitan standardization. A rootless world, removed from the sources of life: a Plutonian world, in which living forms become frozen into metal; cities expanding to no purpose, cutting off the very trunk of their regional existence, defiling their own nest, reaching into the sky after the moon: more paper profits, more vicarious substitutes for life. Under this regime more and more power gets into the hands of fewer and fewer people, ever further and further away from reality. (*CC*, 255)

The contempt for an existence without enlandisement comes close to the fascist typology of the cosmopolitan and subhuman. A culture of the soil, of family, of church in the service of the State, however, was far from Mumford's point. His description degrades the State. The opening and closing phrases bracket the development of civilization from its contempt of the sources of nourishment ("roots") to its psychosis—alienation from the only order there is ("from reality"). The balanced rhetoric suggests the narrator's distance from contemporary metamorphoses and the hypnosis they exert. Mumford presents a culture that turns itself into its goods and in which the highest obligation is consuming ("the whole duty of man"). The running metaphors function as a junkyard inventory of urban planning Mumford dislikes—ranging from Le Corbusier's cellules to the Russell Sage Plan for New York's growth. Elsewhere in the text, commenting upon his use of botanical tropes, Mumford contends that "these are of course figures of speech: but they are means of counteracting and truing up analogies that are even more abstract . . ." (*CC*, 295).

The city is preeminently a teaching: Mumford reminds his readers that "Mind *takes form* in the city." The city is nothing less than projected, decipherable reason. Education by the city is communion. As one is perpetually called to the seeming "otherness" of the city, so the city as "mind" is drawn into one's conduct. The city is a literal agora for humanization. It fuses the order of nature (filiation, cooperation, functionalism, and individuality) with cultural creation. Consequently, city planning must account for the breadth of life. It is *the* new human science. The city's pedagogy is about the full sensuous life in which reason and eros shape existence; in which individuality and the historic community enrich each other. Mumford writes: "Life has, despite its broken moments, the poise and unity of a collective work of art. To create that background, to achieve that insight, to enliven each individual capacity through articulation in an intelligible and esthetically stimulating whole, is the essence of the art of building cities" (*CC*, 484–85).

The Culture of Cities measures well-being under this aspect of community. Mumford's argument conjures up grand cities—Rome, Athens, Paris, and Florence—whose buildings project or elicit human concerns; whose piazzas and squares bring people together; whose institutions, such as churches and universities make people aware of their creative patrimony.

The difference between Mumford's scheme and the good city's completion and decline found in classical urban meditation is Mumford's focus on the conservation of energies rather than on a polity made possible by the highest good's apprehension. Urban development passes through six stages, Mumford propounds, expanding Geddes's categories so that there is an eopolis (a village culture); a polis (a cluster of villages within a general area); a metropolis (one city dominating smaller settlements); a megalopolis (a city of unbridled wealth); a tyrannopolis (a city controlled by one group); and a nekropolis (a city in destruction). This rise and fall parallels classical thinkers' political elegy about the decline of reason. In Mumford's scheme, the fall of the city is due to man's failure to live within an ecology formed by nature and culture.

Mumford's interpretation of the city often depends on the city's inability to make a moral rather than a habitual use of its past, on its failure to make a creative rather than a routine deployment of its opportunities. As a result, *The Culture of Cities* is attentive to appropriate urban form: the ensemble of an "inner life," energy, and technics meeting new situations.[61] At its best, the city shapes activity so that individuals are endowed with multiple examples of renewal.

Mumford was not inclined to accept the inevitability of decay, the return to the feral state which is the threnody of social meditation. This was a possibility but more likely a misreading of human experience in general. History is not the same as historiography and for Mumford who writes of a "saving remnant" humankind is full of surprises. The past is a tenuous fulfillment of impossibilities. Contingency is a motif of the historical imagination. Consequently, Mumford can write, albeit clumsily and badly, about the unpredictable as "mutations" and "early processes or rejuvenating reactions" (*CC*, 293, 292).

The biotechnic age is a promise kept alive within modernity. Philosophically conservative and politically radical, regionalism is this pledge to sustain nature *and* history. Whereas Mumford writes of the biotechnic city as *"the chief instrument of education,"* he finds the region to be, "like its corresponding artifact, the city. . . . a collective work of art" (*CC*, 367). The preservation of the inherent possibilities of experience by this "collective" fabrication conquers the urge for a final form, a singular rendition of life. In city meditations, the rhetoric of generation must challenge that of the fixed. "Our cities," he writes, "must not be monuments, but self-renewing organisms: the dominating image should not be the cemetery but the field, meadow, and parkland . . ." (*CC* 439–40).

In a decade in which thinkers on both the Left and Right argued for political change rather than for the need to maintain existing social arrangements, Mumford's suggestion that the regionalist program could enhance, even rediscover, human satisfactions is not an unusual point. What is striking is the suggestion that a functional society, a whole, could be ordered by rearranging historically fragmented pieces. As he put it: *"what distinguishes the biotechnic community is not the introduction of any essentially new institution so much as their adequate organization and incorporation as an elemental, indispensable part of the whole"* (*CC*, 477). Adequacy of function is the criterion for this holism; cooperation and economic efficiency are its measures. "No act," he writes, seeming to disregard the absolute valuation he places on it, "no routine, no gesture will be devoid of human value, or will fail to contribute to the reciprocal support of citizen and community" (*CC*, 484). Mumford's imagination was not utopian. He refused to bleach dissonance and political demonism from a history fabricated by people. The city promotes a genuine public by encouraging contending communities. Carrying on the associative structures that Mumford first located on the microorganic level, the culture of cities becomes "ultimately the culture of life in its higher social manifestations" (*CC*, 492).[62] The new city can embody as well as minister to human education: this education is also an education in needs.

Mumford could confidently argue that despite an "uphill battle," regionalism and the biotechnic settlement were no longer theories. *The Culture of Cities* points to the achievements of Howard's garden-city proposals found in Letchworth and Welwyn in Great Britain, in Hilversum in Holland, in Ernst May's satellite communities in Frankfurt-am-Main in Germany, and in Radburn, New Jersey.

Yet it is difficult to say how palatable the book was to its contemporary audience. In the preface to the 1970 edition of *The Culture of Cities,* Mumford writes of the book as seeming "remote"—in the eyes of city planners—from practical affairs. Nonetheless, the book was given a hard reading by those who were hostile to the idea and politics of the organic. Meyer Schapiro, dismissing Mumford's methodological and conceptual vagaries, contended that the book depends upon a "Mysticism of the Organic" in which polar terms, the "organic and inorganic, are often nothing but heavily weighted homiletic counters. . . ." James T. Farrell, who was a friend of Schapiro's and had raged against the Catholic authoritarianism of his Chicago youth, was invariably opposed to a social program based on a justification of hierarchy and order. The "organic," he proposed, let Mumford smuggle in authoritarianism. Mumford's rejection of the dynamics of Marxism illuminated his sense of reform: the organic, functional model of society erased the historical character of class conflict. "The hypothesis of economic determinism," Farrell argued, was removed from its place in historical analysis. Instead, Mumford presents the reader with a picture of a self-regulating, ordered whole rather than a form composed of "productive relationships and economic interests."[63]

Throughout his career, Mumford refused to be drawn into an argument that contested the ecological basis of culture and the possibilities it gave for human development. Marxism had ignored the former and hence misread the latter. Its American proponents were not ready to deal with the regionalist thesis in terms other than class conflict. Mumford's defense of the garden city, his restatements about modern housing and planning, and his growing meditations of urban form that reached into a speculative past and forward into a catastrophic future asserted the organic basis of his urban discourse.[64]

What he would increasingly refer to as a "megamachine" and the "Invisible Machine," a mass, urban society coerced and militarized, became the major chords of his later work, giving it a timeliness and, for some, a political eccentricity no other contemporary city thinker brought to the public. Certainly, his own early calls to fight Nazism rather than accommodate it, his arguments that liberalism had failed to gauge the irrational nature of humanity, and his disgust with the temporizing of American intellectuals on the Left for their failure to encourage intervention in Europe strengthened his argument that the contemporary city had failed part of its essential educative task, namely to realize the democratic spirit. Society had become dreamy. Official history was narcotizing state history; it was a soporific confirming the mechanization of life.[65]

In "The Nature of Our Age," written in the aftermath of the war, Mumford speaks about the crises of empire, notably Rome: sleeping and awaking became metaphors for the apocalyptic. Two classes of people, those asleep and those awake, represent respectively a surrender to the State or the affirmation of life. "A wholesale 'conversion,' a deep change of attitude is essential," he pleads, for we have to "reject what is disintegrating, e.g. the power of the sovereign state, the divorce of scientific knowledge from moral responsibility. . . ."[66]

People can transcend a limiting, nationalistic culture to consider the integrated man as species-man. The transfiguring imagination drives this history of renewal. For example, Jesus, as Mumford depicts his mission in *The Condition of Man*, sabotages a life of habituation. His subversion of political institutions, his giving dignity to those who lived outside the narrowly conceived circle of moral law and legality, his deliberate identification with the totality of the human community make him the model of realized humankind. By arguing that a moribund, institutionalized Judaism gave birth to Christ's teaching, which was transfiguring, Mumford offers us personal and social renewal as the significant, central fable of Western civilization. Transformation challenges the historian to attend to human inwardness, to give weight to those changes in and by individuals that are not ascribable to empirically observed causes.[67]

VI

From the 1940s onward, Mumford's interpretation of the urban past and future became darker. The war had crushed the politics of liberalism; it had cost Mumford his son, Geddes Mumford, missing in action in Italy. Totalitarianism was, as Hannah Arendt suggested, a new form of political association. The self-renewal Mumford hoped to make into a political strategy could not be a public policy. Moreover, the war made cities into tombs. Who could or would plan a building or a neighborhood without taking into account, in even the slightest way, a future inferno? Cities were now being planned for evacuation. The divorce of technics from value was now a shibboleth, the "two cultures" in C. P. Snow's words.

Mumford continued to see urban planning as still the most important, practical means of discussing the humane life and creating it. He was, as always, concerned with the social content of the city's form and the balance of regional life. Yet he began to argue boldly that the city itself embodied the struggle between fecundity and aggressiveness. A regionalist history could speak to the resurgence of life-nurturing values. As he had done some twenty years before, he invoked the makers and accomplishments of regionalism: F. L. Olmsted, Ebenezer Howard, George Perkins Marsh, Patrick Geddes, Victor Branford, Clarence Stein, Henry Wright, Benton MacKaye. He held before the reader projects such as Welwyn and Letchworth, Sunnyside Gardens, Radburn and Baldwin Hills. He referred to groups such as the one at Le Play House in London and the RPAA.[68]

City Development: Studies in Disintegration and Renewal (1945) is the best example of Mumford's commitment to regionalist projects. Summing up the themes of his early city pieces from 1922 to his then contemporary essay "The Social Foundations of Post-War Building," Mumford argues that the form of buildings and sites are signs of man's estranged powers. Again, this is not new. But what is, is the devastation of war. There is an actual, urgent opportunity to act.

Paradoxically, destruction frees the city from its past. Utopian city design is encouraged. Mumford's own assessment of the city of the modern age, found in the aforementioned ambitious essay, "The Social Foundations of Post-War Building," is important because it spurns monumental designs and civic grandeur. Mumford argues instead that the city and its region must be planned for the cycle of our natural and social life: from birth to death. Moreover, urban design had to account for everyday existence. Mumford writes of a "purposeless society, in which the parts were neatly articulated and ordered, while the whole made little sense to the common man in terms of life-satisfactions and life-fulfillments."[69]

From the new age emerges the "balanced" individual "in dynamic interaction with every part of his environment, one that is capable of treating economic experiences and aesthetic experiences, parental experiences and vocational experiences as the related parts of a single whole: namely life itself."[70] Mumford's contention that the desired balance integrates thought and work ("We must expect more manual work from the intellectual . . .") is shrewd as well as naive, based upon an apparent distrust of attaining the worthwhile life in economies of abundance. Work seems like an obvious common denominator to someone insistent upon creating a society out of cooperative, shared experiences. The city becomes a setting for a community that by labor and life does not siphon the countryside of goods and people but restores an earlier equilibrium.

The City as Man

Nowhere else does Mumford write so succinctly about the importance and form of the region. Now, it is the natural setting of the human community. Again, this is worth reconsidering, if only because the valuation of region in an epoch of new federalism seemed so demonstrated (given the TVA) and so necessary, and yet was perceived as so impractical. "If the first place to achieve balance is in the family," Mumford suggests,

> where the human personality is nurtured, the co-ordinate pole of planning is the region, for it is against the natural setting of hill and river and sea, of soil and climate, of natural formations and man-made landscape, that the human community defines itself . . . there is one characteristic of a region that must underlie every geographic or historic reference: it must combine the primeval, the urban, and the rural as part of the daily setting of life.[71]

While vigorously restating the regional pedagogy that he developed early in his career, Mumford now emphasizes that the city and its region make the authentic self possible by nurturing the individual within the permanent *settings* of human transformation. Regionalism evokes the wide, undetermined nature of experience that parochial cultures pacify. Nonetheless, this is also a millennialist argument: bombing has deprived the city of its protection and its freedom, two of its rationales for existence.

VII

Mumford's version of regionalism had a dawn but no day in contemporary America. The experiments with greenbelt and "new" towns, and plans made to coordinate resources such as water on a regional basis were not programs for the good life or chances taken to enhance human nature. They were, often, chessboard strategies recombining urban and environmental pieces in the face of the megalopolis and strained natural resources. The rethinking of the city was still—significantly—found in books ranging from Frank Lloyd Wright's discussions of the city to the Goodman brothers' *Communitas*.

The City in History could hardly have changed American or European urban planning, especially if one accepted fully its basic thesis. Cities had an order conferred upon them more by the limitations than by the possibilities of human nature. *The Culture of Cities* informs *The City in History*, but it is a daring redaction of the earlier work. *The Culture of Cities* pointed to the threatening future of the metropolis. *The City in History* argues that the city—if its form is correctly translated—expresses destruction itself. The framework of *The Culture of Cities* is now expanded and

109

given a different background. In the earlier text, the medieval city marks a high point for the satisfaction of wants. The later work traces the city's origins from approximately 2500 B.C. to its contemporary megalopolitan form but, crucially, the city is seen as enacting its early psychological legacies. *The City in History* speaks openly, albeit guardedly, of human nature endowing the city with the attributes of fecundity and destruction. City life transcribes this struggle of the psyche pitted against itself as a permanent human characteristic—though the consequences need not be inevitable. Mumford's assessment of the city, therefore, as the shape of human nature dismisses the studies of mass culture, small towns, and public arts that progressive social thinkers of the forties and fifties saw as indices of national life. Whereas *The Culture of Cities* spoke at length of the regionalist movement, *The City in History* developed its consequence (one never far from the concerns of Geddes's circle)—"One World" man.

Discovering *the* form of the city unearths the core of human dreams that gave it birth and that, in turn, it nurtured. The city not only is a projection of mind but also is its mirror. On the one hand, the city objectifies consciousness. On the other hand, the city's form re-presents the struggle of the militant temper against fraternity. Mumford's work now accounts for the city's present in terms of urban origins. "Can the needs and desires," Mumford asks, "that have impelled men to live in cities recover, at a still higher level, all that Jerusalem, Athens, or Florence once seemed to promise? Is there still a living choice between Necropolis and Utopia: the possibility of building a new kind of city that will, freed of inner contradictions . . . enrich and further human development?"[72] Mumford's choices of cities are set pieces, yet each of the cities he deals with here and elsewhere (and intriguingly, he does not deal with Jerusalem) has been the home of a new man who transcended the customs of an older, habitualizing culture.

Whereas Mumford writes of the urban heritage as one that is pushed back beyond the second millennium B.C., he tantalizingly suggests the enduring character itself of the city and the unresolvable crises of the psyche. For example, asking whether the New World reproduced or offered a cluster of forms that were related to Western cities, Mumford writes "Was this New World urban complex due to an original predisposition toward urban life carried in the genes?" or was it confirmation of an archetype or the result of dispersion (*CH*, 91). His answer is a reluctant "one cannot answer; but one should, I believe, keep an open mind" (*CH*, 92). Yet his argument that there is a general form for cities emphasizes that

The City as Man

urban life is the most complex form in which a generalized psychic drama is enacted.

Mumford's point of reference is "homologous" culture, the historically invariable, structured colonies of insects which exist outside a time of becoming, the realm of transfiguration. Unable to discern the present as a point of futures, they are devoid of possibility but not of durability. They are the book's model of urban arrest. The choice of insect colonies to measure human organization is a classical one (witness Plato's and Aristotle's bees and wasps) and suggests Mumford's desire to link his reevaluation of transformation with eutopian thought. Insect societies are not deprived of experience but they have no interpretations of it that modify conduct.

Cataloging the features of insect colonies similar to those of humans, Mumford makes it plain that "this is an example of parallelism and convergence." The relationship of the hive to the city is illustrated by the monarchial city, the capital city. There is an "Insectopolis" with a specialized military force whose raison d'être is the protection of the queen. Analogously, the royal city (with its enclosure, hierarchical order, and identification with the monarch) produces a collective self not so much hostile to autonomy as it is incapable of it. For human and insect, the disposition of space *is* a disposition. The elaborate though never-changing insect colonies emphasize that the city alone reflects what is human: the capacity for renewal.[73]

The history of the city is found in its form that embraces domination and fecundity. They appear as theologies and politics of power and fertility in architecture and implements. The city's history is inescapably part of its life: a combination of the necropolis, the early village, paleolithic and neolithic cultures. Neolithic village phenomena (the agora, the shrine, the house) and the aggressive paleolithic hunting culture (with its implements of war and its mythology of male power and violence) give the city its characteristic tension and, Mumford intimates, its creative energies.

The city exists paradoxically. Neolithic rites of fertility are placed in the service of paleolithic culture. As a result, the neolithic reverence for life survives through the irony of its new form. For example, human sacrifice parodies the neolithic sacrament of balance while dramatizing the paleolithic value of conquest. The changing urban form expresses the changing values of social control, from the circular early city evoking maternal nurture to the later city expressing male power in its deployment of the obelisk, the tower, the citadel. The village was "woman writ large," and its

Lewis Mumford

secular and religious life were defined. In contrast, the city enshrines the king as a deity. The relationship of the sacred to the profane is altered as the shrine and the stronghold become one, just as the king and the ruling deity lose their separate identities and partake of each other's powers.[74]

The City in History, therefore, focuses on the patterns of human self-objectification expressed by such phenomena as housing, city walls, neighborhoods, street lengths; by the concentration of capital, division of labor, and military power. The city is a "materialization" of its politics in the broadest sense of the word. Mumford explains the growth of the city in terms of this rhythm of "etherialization" and "materialization":

> etherialization: the concrete structure, detaching itself through a human response, takes on a symbolic meaning, uniting the knower and the known; while subjective images, ideas, intuitions, only partly formed in their original expression, likewise take on material attributes, in visible structures, whose very size, position, complexity, organization, and esthetic form extend the area of meaning and value, otherwise inexpressible. (*CH*, 113)

Space and idea project each other. For Mumford, the Greek city was symbolically and physically formed around space. The Socratic dialogue climbs toward abstraction within the agora. The movement between idea and form dramatizes renewal: "But to overlook the place of dialectic in the polis is to overlook the city's main function: the enlargement in human consciousness of the drama of life itself, through whose enactment existence discloses fresh meanings, not given by any momentary analysis or repetitious statistical order" (*CH*, 178).

Rome and Athens are polar examples. The "pathological overgrowth" of Rome wars against a decent life. Its past controls its future. It suffers from "megalopolitan elephantiasis." The "precedents of Rome almost automatically revive," Mumford observes, and catalogs the penchant for tall buildings, dense housing, and mass entertainments that make life frantic and choked. Contrast this with Athens, a "conception of urban unity." The city can be seen as a whole; its form is a commitment to a human scale.

Athens is a typological city. The medieval town, the Dutch village, and the garden city continue Athens's tradition of "balance" and renewal. As in *The Culture of Cities*, they are examples of an affirmative order of life. Yet they are buried under the architecture of State power and its technics of domination. Surprisingly, Mumford does not examine the relation between city form and slavery as practiced in Athens or the use of "public-making" spaces such as the piazzas of medieval and Renaissance cities for the persecution of minorities and heretics. Just as the fortress and the shrine became proximate during the development of the city and occupied the city center, so in the age of power the Bourse and government buildings are at the urban core. The architectonic of space and idea that sustained the apprehension of the good in Athens, in the modern city becomes the creation of places for public control and State power.

As in *The Culture of Cities*, in *The City in History* Mumford opposes the ecologically mindful to the wasteful. The contrast is between subjectivity and technics. The mine, the railroad, and the machine create a city that is industrial in standard. Whereas agriculture and the pastoral sensibility have been pushed out of the urban framework, they make a sublimated appearance as the landscaped park offering the city a sheltered space as well as a critique. For example, Olmsted and Vaux's New York's Central Park is a haven in the city as well as a lesson in planning.

Yet Mumford returns to Howard and regionalists such as Stein and Henry Wright, thinkers who invoked the saving traditions of human communities. Mumford's discussion of Howard's role is worth looking at. Mumford's rethinking of the garden city and its promise as compared with their earlier presentation in *The Culture of Cities* is certainly proof of what he believed the modern city to be. In *The City in History*, Howard's plan is significantly reinterpreted. There is less emphasis upon the traditions of city planning that Howard drew upon and much more commentary on him as a city thinker—someone who sees the city as a steward. Crucially, the set of functional balances characterizing the garden city in *The Culture of Cities* is here seen under the aspect of the organic. Mumford now reads Howard's work as a hopeful undoing of the paleolithic legacy of aggression, imbalance, and specialism. Howard's program is rhetorically couched in terms reminding us of the virtues of neolithic life with its celebration of a community ecology. This is possible once again.

As Mumford puts it:

> His [Howard's] genius was to combine the existing organs of the city into a more orderly composition based on the principle of organic limitation and controlled growth. He began, not with the inertia of disintegration, but with an analysis of the life-maintaining human functions as related to the urban and rural environments. . . . what was radically new was a rational and orderly method for dealing with complexity, through an organization capable of establishing balance and autonomy, and of maintaining order despite differentiation, and coherence and unity despite the need for growth. (*CH*, 518)

By affirming biological normalcy as a political value, the garden city challenges political thought to become ecological and regional in character. Howard is now less of a city planner designing the apparatus of a settlement and more of a naturalist regulating vital relations. Mumford is certain about this. He contends that Howard "brought to the city the essential biological criteria of dynamic equilibrium and organic balance: balance as between city and country in a larger ecological pattern, and balance between the varied functions of the city . . ." (*CH*, 516).

This generous reading of Howard's work with its underscoring of eco-systems and an implied metaphysic goes beyond Mumford's previous explication of Howard, especially that in *The Culture of Cities*. There Howard had been presented as someone mostly concerned with over-crowding, decentralization, and ownership. Witness Mumford's more aus-tere interpretation of Howard's achievement in the earlier text. His "con-tribution was to see the problem of city building and housing as a regional one" (*CC*, 396). As a literal regionalist, Howard would have been unable to address the deeply structured psychological crises of cities. Now a mem-ber of the regionalist enlightenment, he could be viewed as someone speaking against the paleo-militaristic settlement. Mumford is concerned with renewing the nature of "nakedness": in this case, with individuals like Howard whose significance lies in their empowerment of the regionalist tradition.

The City in History remains Mumford's preaching against the inade-quate life of the times. Cataloging a fall from coherency (natural and ethical) expressed by the modern city, Mumford declaims, "The loss of form, the loss of autonomy, the constant frustration and harassment of daily activities, to say nothing of gigantic breakdowns and stoppages—all these become normal attributes of the metropolitan regime"(*CH*, 544). "Total extermination" is the character of the megalopolis. Challenging the modern city demands breaking the knot of megalopolitan culture. This becomes nothing less than an assault upon the human disposition to both create and yield to the "myth" of the imperial State. Historically, however, renewal is a fact. Transfiguration is the preeminent condition of being human. The city-as-hell can be replaced by a city that is as truly cos-mopolitan as it is decentralized. For Mumford, the physical nature of decentralization embodies its moral value: resources and production, cul-ture and technics can be matched so that a world culture, fraternal and unimpoverished, can truly make man a species being.

The evolution of the city points to new opportunities. The city can be "etherialized." The electric grid, not the city as container, can be the environment. The city can become a world center whose now unique form transcends its former walls.

The City as Man

Mumford's last meditations on the city are tightly bound to both this wish and the tragic urban past. These reflections, of which "Utopia, the City and the Machine" and "City: Forms and Functions" are good representatives, look back to the catastrophes envisioned in *The Culture of Cities* and forward to the dire, two-volume work, *The Myth of the Machine* (1967, 1970). A speculative regionalism, now pushed into the fog of the neolithic, is an epoch whose sense of affairs can be regained. Cooperative communities and agriculture represent the harmony of settlement and nature. An idyllic life is swept away by aggression, a startlingly newer form of confronting others. The city is its product: its ruler incarnates a god; its work force labors for a theocracy; its crafts turn on the use of metals; its social life is regimented and specialized. This is the seedbed of the "Invisible Army" (a post–sixteenth-century phenomenon, one that would be labeled "megamachine" by Mumford) controlling human affairs. Mumford is aware that this drama is a historian's optative past—a candid, generous concession that hedged a good part of *The City in History's* early chapters.

What is intriguing about this reading is not its utopian character in which the past as the past is seen as something still to be achieved. Rather, there is a need to authenticate historically and naturally the paradox of the modern city with its spiritually enriching culture warring against a coercive politics and civility. Without the rise of *a* city becoming the rise of *the* city, Mumford is deprived of the basic explanatory mechanism for the megalopolis. Nonetheless, his argument for the fundamental antagonism between transformation and power is, perhaps, a fable of its own—much like Henry Adams's Mariolatry in the face of a future morality-become-police. In *The Myth of the Machine,* Mumford insisted upon the reality of the megamachine: the convergence of science, technics, and political power as a unified community of interpretation rendering useless and eccentric life-enhancing values. Subversion of this authoritarian kingdom begins with that area of human contact with the world that cannot be successfully repressed—one's feelings about one's self. Everyone has access to this manner of knowing; it makes the self, not the State, the center of judgment. Whereas engagement does not immediately challenge the efficiency or productivity of the megamachine, it seizes those terms themselves and rereads them. As Mumford puts it:

> We now come back to the basic idea that underlies this book. If we are to prevent megatechnics from further controlling and deforming every aspect of human culture, we shall be able to do so only with the aid of a radically different model derived directly, not from machines, but from living organisms and organic

115

complexes (ecosystems). What can be known about life only through the process of living . . . must be added to all the other aspects that can be observed, abstracted, measured. [75]

VIII

Mumford's early works, reflections upon the balanced life that the garden city made possible, are halcyon. The commercializing spirit of the 1893 World's Fair, the loss of an American native community design, and the apparent normalcy of metropolitan growth could be offset by regionalist plans. Modern cities, as he pointed out, were not modern at all; they were maladapted to the hopes and promises of available technologies. His studies of the regionalism of the pre–Civil War and the consequences of industrialism are prefaces to renewal. They challenged what he believed to be an empirical rendition of experience that could not substantiate the roles of wish, desire, and eros within the world.

His later works, written in the face of the war and its aftermath, presciently gauged the machine as an expression of a denaturalized and alienated life. Mechanization had not only taken command, it also had choked the ability of people to renew themselves and their societies. Cities had become machines. Mumford's reliance upon organic models, organic rhetoric, organic judgments, and organic economies—each with its own area of meaning—is an appeal to the buried self, one that can affirm its own sensuousness and, by doing so, turn cities into something livable again.

In his last works, Mumford universalizes the drama he believes is enacted by and within the city. This is the capacity of the nurturing settlement to withstand the city of war: more fundamentally, the war human nature wages against itself.

Mumford's writing urgently and insistently offers us his reading of the democratic city. If the city's transmission of the heritage of renewal is not made accessible to everyone, urban culture is authoritarian civilization. If the opportunities of city life are not made available to all, the city disempowers rather than confirms the good life. If the city and its region are not envisioned and planned for as a public trust, the city is no longer a habitation for humans but a marketplace.

It is tempting to see Mumford's work as a vast illumination: a secular city in which transfiguration and self-fabrication are patterns of life but in which the organic and the mechanical have become city walls themselves.

The City as Man

In fact, the concepts of the organic and mechanical have become tyrannical. But why should there be any reserve about this? Mumford's autobiographical reflections and his letters make much of cities that had changed before his eyes: from the early regionalism of Boston to the "metropolitanization" of New York, from the imperial cities of the West to the sprawling cities of America. Rhetorically countering this deterioration, Mumford depends upon a series of images suggesting the permanent possibility of renewal and the pathos of urban degradation. The garden and the mine, the flower and the slag heap are, finally, irreducible universes. To those who have not lived in drab, filthy soft-coal cities, the concepts of organic and inorganic lose their "feltness," their concreteness, and become, without loss of meaning, metaphors in a tragic ecology.

Mumford's writing remains true to the ambitions of historians of civilizations—ranging from Hesiod to Geddes, from Pausanias to Spengler—who argued that history is man in all his powers. In this sense, Mumford was clearly from but not of his generation of American writers. His quest for an adequate city history went beyond describing the customs of the New England village, the ascendancy of a specious liberalism, and the rise of technocracy. Freeing ourselves from the tyranny of the past depends upon our reading of history as both a summary and a critique of choice. Regionalism is that summary and in America, who, except Mumford, had so sustainedly undertaken the regionalist labor? No longer could city life be portrayed in narrow conceptual fashion and be accepted as the city we know. How could the city and the totality of its life be separated? How could its history not chart the possibilities of the future?

Clearly, Mumford broadened American urban inquiry so that an account of the city had to include, if not be, an interpretation of the city's preservation and transmission of what he broadly termed art and technics. Thinking the city meant, above all, considering how human symbolizing had created this grand artifact transfiguring those within its influence, liberating them from a solitary present.

"A truly modern design for a city must be one that allows for both its historic and social complexity, and for its continued renewal and reintegration in time," Mumford writes.[76] This is a project for generations, and it is possible that Mumford remembered Randolph Bourne's dictum that the past is not yet over.

Paradoxically, an author who had faulted Mumford for his hierarchical organicism and who was committed to examining society exclusive of regionalism dramatized the urgency of Mumford's teachings about the democratic city. James T. Farrell depicted the specific ways in which the city transmitted the legacy of renewal. He devoted most of his fiction to evaluating how the culture of the city becomes accessible to its youth. By culture of the city, Farrell meant its liberalizing agencies; by youth, Farrell meant the young he had grown up with.

Like Riis and Mumford, Farrell believed that a public had to be created so that individuals could transcend their particularistic commitments and participate in the democracy of the city and the culture of humanity. How else could intelligence become social? How else could community and civility be achieved? And again, like Riis and Mumford, Farrell chose to write about the city as *his* city: he described the Chicago of his youth and the New York of his adulthood from the ground up—in the terms that he experienced it. He found sociology too narrow and sterile to describe the city: it was unconcerned with human beings as fully human. It quarantined facts from their significance. His fiction refocused attention on what he believed was the way people really do come to appropriate the meanings of the city, and on the ways they tragically do not.

Chapter 3

James T. Farrell:
The City
as Society

NO NOVELIST of our time has so persistently identified the substance of his fiction with the teachings of the liberalizing city than James T. Farrell. His novels depict how characters make use of the city's commitment to build a public through shared, rational experience. His narrative strategy has been to present in great detail the often unnoticed and small ways these democratizing occasions are made possible. As a result, his writing often deals with the means by which a community or group helps widen an individual's understanding of self and others. His fiction, generally autobiographical, is so deeply implicated with *this* pattern of events that it is, by now, a commonplace to argue that Farrell's writing is not only what he experienced, but what *only* he experienced.

This is true, but qualifiedly so. Farrell's novels and short stories are concerned not simply with a specific community, but rather with it as a generalized community trying to understand the city. Influenced by his reading of John Dewey and George Herbert Mead and by his understanding of the accomplishments of the Chicago school of sociology, his fiction minutely, even tediously, dramatizes the "incremental" nature of choice as part of the culture of democracy.

The uses Farrell made of *his* city are found in his fiction. In 1927, he was twenty-three, putting himself through the University of Chicago by working in a gas station. One day, he picked up a book of poetry to read while waiting for customers: He wanted to be a writer. Chicago, his native city, had no special meaning for him. Decades later, he recollected that as a youth Chicago had been for him a "city to study" and that he had dreamt "of love and adventure elsewhere." Reading Carl Sandburg's "Chicago," Farrell discovered his vocation: he would be a novelist of the city. "I was beginning to find in myself," he recalled, "to feel in myself, and to feel into all that I had known, and was getting to know, day by day, in Chicago, a significance which was material for head, heart and imagination." Sandburg's poem, he wrote, "lifted me with excitement . . . whipped me into impatience." "Chicago" he added, "acquired size in my imagination, and what happened there, and what people did, that was of human meaning; it was the stuff for literature."[1] In fact, he had already chanced works dealing with the people and scenes he would later be drawn to: a novel set on Fifty-eighth and Prairie; an autobiographical novel dealing with his school days, influenced by Sherwood Anderson's *Tarr*.[2] In his writing Farrell would move beyond his fascination with how Chicago youths inherited their city to a concern for how they interpret their social heritage. For Farrell, this heritage is the idea of the democratic city.

This social meaning of the city was, for him, a live issue. Farrell believed that his life was intimately and irrevocably bound to his urban past. His fiction almost obsessively deals with the poverty of his parents, the cripping parochialism of the South Side's Irish Catholicism, and the suffocating middle-class pieties of the relatives who raised him. Yet these themes also serve as a prologue to his novels that deal with the liberation he saw promised by what he believed was the city's culture of democracy. His novels would focus on the ethical crises of his protagonists, usually radical and progressive writers in Chicago and New York, as they tried to find how their present accommodated the *meanings* of their past and their hopes for a chosen future.

II

Mentioning that he would later "do some work" on the nature of Chicago, Farrell began to describe to Richard Wright the role Chicago played in America. Remembering in 1942 the Chicago of his youth, Farrell emphasized the contribution the University of Chicago made to American thought. The university provided America with a critical intellectual perspective necessary for social inquiry. Several members of the university's faculty were studying the processes that made for a democratic community. "At that time," Farrell reminisced, "there was a really democratic if naive attitude prevailing—the notion that through education, through utopian methods, through knowledge, you could develop the good society." Jane Addams's Hull House had "real hopes" behind it, and the "whole idea of doing something for the people was implanted" in Chicago faculty such as John Dewey, George Herbert Mead, and Thorstein Veblen. In fact, Chicago was on more intellectually familiar terms with Europe than New York was. What was striking, however, was the sudden end of this city's influence. The literary renaissance, for instance, "folded up. The writers went elsewhere. Most of them suddenly found that they had nothing left to say."[3]

Elsewhere, Farrell amplified this theme, most notably in a letter to Stanley Pargellis about Chicago and its place in American culture. Farrell contended that late nineteenth-century Chicago became a world capital through the efforts of Chicago bankers; from 1880 to 1910, this dream of empire had been realized. Chicago "was one of the centers, as it were, of the American dream." Early Chicago industrialists saw the city as a monument to their hopes for grandeur. A "feudal pride" for their city did not prevent them from exploiting their workers, yet they were not deterred from their task of "building a great city." In a more optimistic reading of the brown decades and their consequences than that given by Lewis Mumford, Farrell pointed out that Dewey, Mead, Jacques Loeb, and others "concentrated" the tendencies of that era and helped make possible a progressive basis for civic action.[4]

Nonetheless, in the same letter Farrell observed that he was a child of a meaner, dispiriting age. "I came at a later period," he wrote, "[and] I grew up inside of the city of Chicago, and after the city had passed its period of greatest hope." Chicago's progressive spirit and grandeur had perished at the beginning of his generation. The city of his youth could only point to a past swelled by civic dreams and intellectual movements. He felt that his work was written in isolation and deprivation: he had a "lonely road" ahead of him and he spoke of how he "accepted its origins."[5] The wasted lives around him revealed the need to revitalize the city's liberal heritage by creating again a genuinely urban culture.

Chicago remained his pole star, even after he settled in New York. It defined his fiction and his life. In his letters and notes he would compare it to New York or Paris. He would jot his impressions of the city when he returned to it. He invariably wrote of his alienation from it. In a fragment obviously trying to capture the city's epic richness and yet its inviolable, frustrating claims upon him, Farrell called it "my home town, my native city, my natal city."[6]

Farrell's Chicago and family had immense literary uses. Chicago, the "American" city, reflected the emerging "tendencies" of the nation. Writing in 1942 to Saul Alinsky, Farrell discussed the literary task he had formulated a decade ago. It was a "project or programme of books" that would deal with "The American Way of Life." Its focus is concrete; it would discern the "patterns of individual destiny." Chicago assumes a major role: in the main, the project "will be Chicago up to the depression."[7] Farrell believed that Chicago, a city connected to the broad stretch of American life rather than closely tied to international trade served as a "rather concentrated focus of the social life of modern America."[8]

His family was "a mirror of a whole American social genre."[9] It is fair to say that Farrell described his family as an *agent* of urbanization enacting the tensions of the city. As a result, his identification with a city that he saw as commandingly American and with a family that he believed represented a significant national and urban theme invested his own struggle with an importance far beyond its individual nature. Moreover, his attraction to the city—first Chicago and then New York—is bound up with an equal fascination for his success and for his becoming the kind of progressive American that his past and place could not predict.

His maternal grandparents were illiterate Irish emigrants from County Westmeath. Their achievements ironically point to the impasse a city can reach in widening its inhabitants' lives. John and Julia Brown Daly immigrated during the Civil War and, after living in Wisconsin, settled in Chicago. John became a teamster whose life, if we trust his grandson's fiction, was hard—punctuated with frustration but sweetened with dreams of Ireland. His wife's peasant superstitions and religious rituals seemed to insulate her from the city she lived in. Like many immigrants, they remained anonymous and untouched in any transfiguring way by the sweeping opportunities of Chicago. Nonetheless, their five children were upwardly mobile: moderately successful and mainly "Americanized."

Unlike the Dalys, Farrell's paternal grandparents do not appear in his major fiction. They evaporate from his work and judging from their disappearance, make incomplete his novels' understanding and portrait of his self. James Farrell, however, was hardly anonymous. Coming to New Orleans from Ireland, he was first a slave master, later a soldier with the Louisiana Tigers, then a sewer sweeper, and finally, moving to Chicago, a teamster. An example of rugged individualism, he no doubt passed on the opportunity for the same kind of work to *his* son who, less opportunistic and less flexible, got teamster jobs for James T. Farrell and his brother.[10]

For both sets of grandparents, the American experience was not as diverse as it might have been. The men ended as teamsters—and this work becomes, for a while, a family vocation. The women are tied to the parochial aspect of Irish Catholicism. The tug of the Irish past makes America somewhat uncomfortable and offers no affective politics of idealism. These interweaving phenomena insulated them—as they did so many immigrants—from being part of a larger public. What is significant is that this pattern of isolation broke during Farrell's boyhood and became a major element of his story of America. He bore witness to the difficulties of making an immigrant past comport with the American present.

James T. Farrell was born in 1904 in Chicago's South Side. His neighborhood, he stressed, was a working-class one, but it was not a "slum."[11] German and Irish by composition, it marked waves of immigration and mobility. In 1907, his parents were forced to send him to the Daly household: too many children and grinding poverty were the reasons. Except for brief periods, Farrell would now live with his grandmother, his Uncle Tom, and his Aunt Ella until he was twenty-seven. The distance from his parents was only three or four miles but for all practical purposes the two households were connected only by sentiment and kinship. His uncle earned at least ten thousand dollars a year. His aunt worked as a cashier in a downtown Chicago restaurant. This family moved to a seven-room apartment near Fifty-eighth Street, across from Washington Park. Ring Lardner, as well as the manager of the Chicago White Sox, lived in this neighborhood.[12]

Unlike his brothers and sisters who remained with his parents, Farrell became a child of privilege. He enjoyed steam heat and indoor plumbing. He was spared the diphtheria that caused the death of a brother (Farrell believed that his parents' poverty ensured the outcome). He did not hold odd jobs, he remembered, but worked for a regular salary throughout his youth. He would not have to become a teamster. Poverty would not decide his future. Coached by his uncle in the superficial nature of genteel conduct and succored by fables of upward mobility and American success, Farrell acquired a richness of urban experience that would not have been his by birthright.

His two families were examples of the extremes of urban life. One family was bound to an impoverished neighborhood, to jobs that were physically exhausting, and to a local culture that acted as a barrier against the progressive ideas that the city preferred. (It should be noted, however, that Farrell's siblings also escaped the poverty of their parents.) The other family could move at will and acted upon what was seen as the advantages of city life. The Daly household was not tied to one neighborhood, nor— judging from Farrell's writing—to the tight cluster of families that often made working-class life cohesive. Individuals could pretend to some autonomy and choice.

These two families suggest what used to be called the theme of two nations. The psychological and cultural conflicts Farrell witnessed critically shaped his response to the substance of fiction. The relationship of everyday life to the context of capitalism fascinated him. He wanted to assess, as one of his fictional alter egos asserts, the cost of moral choice under capitalism.

Farrell's emotional closeness to his father, a man who would remain distant from, if not alien to him; his empathy with a class that he had, in many ways, risen above and would, by virtue of his writing, always remain apart from; his rightful appraisal of the laborer's struggle for dignity as a universal theme—all suggest the intensity of his identification with his parents' struggles. Writing for a Back-of-the-Yards dinner, Farrell spoke of his nearness to the international worker. The work laborers do, he wrote, "forms the basis of our entire civilization." He added, "I think of my father, of his fierce love of his family, his determination to keep his head high: there are thousands, millions and millions of men like him."[13]

He disliked the banal, self-seeking lives of the Dalys who had lovingly and generously rescued him from an almost certain desperation. It is fair to say that they gave him the means to write. Talking of the maleducation of immigrant children who had been deliberately instructed to equate culture with manners, Farrell noted that the outcome is their finding "their idea of what the good life is in a hotel, and that is a mixture of an idea of good manners and being rich." He continued, "I'm talking about certain relatives of mine who got their idea of an expanded life, their idea of what is manners . . . from being associated with hotels, either by working in it or being salesmen."[14] This double estrangement, from his natural parents and from a family that smugly interpreted what it believed to be the version of an upward American life was enduring. Farrell's fiction takes this tension as *the* characteristic drama of the family.

Farrell received an intense parochial education. His early letters and jottings indicate that he was a spirited, bright boy, though unremarkable in his interests—usually sports. When he attended De Paul University for a semester in 1925 and then transferred to the University of Chicago that year, he broke out of the limited future his education had seemed to ensure. He tested his freedom by leaving the university in 1927, making his way to New York where he worked as a cigar-store clerk and later as an advertising salesman. He returned home broke but ambitious. He was going to be a writer.

James Weber Linn, his creative writing teacher at the University of Chicago, was occasionally filling his column, "Round About Chicago" in the *Chicago Herald Examiner,* with Farrell's New York observations, and his sketches about the life around him. Chicago proved to be attractive for the budding writer. Farrell reflected years later that the "streets and neighborhoods of Chicago" were one of his universities, and he recalled that much of his work was an "effort to describe the poetry and the poverty of these streets." He turned a number of compositions in for a course at the University of Chicago but was told to write about something else. "Thinking of this now," he wrote, "I recall the advice which my father gave to me again and again: 'Always remember—you are the son of a working man.' "15

His writing about the Chicago scenes he knew was given a comprehensiveness by the shock of self-discovery, if we trust the narrator of Farrell's short story "Studs" (1929). His self-discovery was a kind that made sense to Farrell: a recognition made possible through others.

The crisis that caused it was a death. In 1929 Farrell went to the wake of his friend "Studs" Cunningham, whose life seemed banal and without promise. The scene jolted Farrell. It made palpable his estrangement from his South Side past. An opponent of the Catholicism of his family, a reader of Veblen, Dewey, and Mead, and a student at the University of Chicago reviled by the teachers of his youth, Farrell had undergone a sea change. He had migrated from the world of his past. Poignantly describing this shock of recognition, Farrell wrote in his introduction to *Studs Lonigan* that his "attitude" toward Studs was a "simple one: 'There but for the grace of God go I.' "

He no longer thought he had a life or future in common with his earlier friends. Describing them, Farrell's narrator speaks of their spiritual deaths: "All the adventurous boy that was in them years ago had been killed. Slobs, getting fat and middle-aged, bragging of their stupid brawls, reciting the commonplaces of their days." They are creatures of boredom. Their lives are increasingly narrow, and withdrawn. The pleasure of their day is a "hexagonal of whores, movies, pool, alky, poker, and craps."16

Earlier, Farrell had discovered the setting and people of his fiction, the South Side of often illiberal Irish Americans. Now he had a theme explaining the relation of his characters to their place. Individuals enacted the culture of their place. Their character was forged in the clash between the parochialism of their group or neighborhood and the open future offered by the surrounding alien city. Farrell rendered this struggle as an individual's understanding of the *meanings* the city transmits of its culture.

Farrell's major writing deals with this tension between heritage and prospects. His novels and stories indicate that his obsession with the making of self is *the* force that drives his fiction. His novels depict the chosen destinies of South Side Irish Americans from the early years of the twentieth century to the closing days of the thirties. His characters morally rise or fall by virtue of their willingness to commit themselves to what John Dewey called problem-solving activity.

Farrell's commitment to have his fiction raise these problems *is* his literary development. This accounts for his being called, often unimaginatively, tediously honest or sincere. He did not define his work in terms of hard, deterministic naturalism, a tradition his critics, who often read his fiction as a study of the authority of mass culture, find important in understanding his rendition of characters. In fact, those who most deeply influenced him—Dreiser, Joyce, and Zola—and who could be seen as philosophically conservative precisely because of their experiments with naturalism, were seen by Farrell as insurrectionaries. Their opposition to a culture of fixed meanings and their struggles to break the limiting repertoire of conventional literary explanation were Farrell's literary tradition.

Farrell saw himself as a writer outside the company of contemporary writers and yet part of a community of men of letters who worked in the face of hostility. As a young man, Farrell admired Dreiser's defiance. His example, as Farrell put it, "his strength, his persistence in the face of opposition, the sympathy and depth of feeling in his writings—all this had encouraged me." Similarly, Joyce "rejected religion; he had launched forth against the 'rabblement'; he had asserted his views and his determination to be independent."[17]

Joyce, Farrell observed, was "the first Irish writer to arise, after a national literary regeneration had begun, who introduces the city."[18] Dreiser became the great novelist of America's epoch of urbanization, finding unassimilable the "cultivated traditions of Europe, the culture of New England, the culture of Victorian England."[19] These men were writers of the city, announcing the significant themes of the modern artist's development: the individual's struggle against the conventions of the public and, paradoxically, the individual's attempt to appropriate the culture of the city.

Farrell's reading of the tradition of struggle, a struggle he saw as pitting urban plebeian writers with enriching, iconoclastic imaginations against an arid literary establishment, is his version of literary creation. Certainly, this was not the only interpretation of creativity he talked about but it was one that he believed was his. Functioning as a measure of authenticity, the struggle indicated how the writer as an outsider established an original, perhaps visionary, relationship with society.

Ironically, Farrell's work is victimized by the environment of his past that he interpretively transformed. His past became the terrain he knew best and he believed that returning to it would somehow prove insightful: it would remain an enduring subject for fiction. He writes in 1939 that "I have not exhausted its [the neighborhood's] possibilities by a darned sight. There are plenty of new emphases to be drawn."[20] His writing remained inseparable from the psychological circumstances of the time and place of his youth. His novels and collections of short stories (which number well over sixty), however, could not sustain what he called the story of "America as I knew it" because, finally, there was so little of then contemporary America in the works themselves. Reworking again and again the same events and the same pattern of moral existence made his fiction repetitive and categorical. Farrell understood this but pointed out that writers "can only deal with so much. The world is bigger than anyone. And one has to take certain types, moods, problems, conditions, eras, social areas and then try to explore them thoroughly. So on 'Can All This Grandeur Perish,' they [the critics] say—he has said all this."[21]

Clearly, though, he did not believe he had said "all this." Even given his insistence on exploring the formation of a democratic public, his fiction became aesthetically privatizing and narrow. He had written all this before; its variations had meaning only for him. Sadly, and finally, it was less a meditation and less a chronicle. It became, simply, a report.

III

For Farrell, the city is an environment of socially created meanings in process. The range and variety of urban encounters offer opportunities for individuals to see themselves as others do, as well as to understand the experiences of others. From the home to the school, from the street to the church, from play to conversation, an individual is forced to reassess and to partake of another enlarging interpretation of experience. This gradual and finally cooperative process in which we identify ourselves with a common good as well as an interested one, creates a public. That is, democratic life enables us to understand ourselves by means of others. Doing so, we share in and control a common destiny.

For Farrell's characters, fate is the summation of their choices. The individuals he portrays create themselves by thinking, choosing, and acting *within* the possibilities of their society. His fiction's unrelieved attention to the commonplace captures these slow, incremental acts that are finally seen as a destiny. As Danny O'Neill, one of Farrell's fictional selves puts it,

> I am thinking in terms of destinies. Destinies are made up of the happenings of a life. These follow one after the other, the phrase to use is "in serial order." . . . They do not add up, but they accumulate . . . in a tendency, a direction, and they are like the "cometogether"—currents that compose the current of the wind. A life is blown by a wind called destiny, and that wind is controlled by the mind as much as by circumstances. [22]

As Farrell himself explained: "I seek to answer the question: what happens to people? I hold a functional conception of character, viewing it as a social product embodying the reciprocal play of local influences on the individual and on society. I am concerned with the concrete process whereby society, through the instrumentality of social institutions, forms and molds characters. . . ."[23] Farrell's success is just this. He is not an ideologue but rather an ideational writer, one who depicts the *situation* of ideas and their perceived function in the lives of his characters.

Farrell brought to his fiction the liberal promises of his coming of age. And these were the possibilities of the democratic city articulated by such figures as Mead, Dewey, and members of the Chicago school of sociology such as Robert Park, E. W. Burgess, and Frederic Thrasher. Given the evidence of his fiction, these are *his* Chicago school. These men wrote about what he believed he had lived through, understood, and escaped. Their writing confirmed for him the significance of his struggles.

Farrell's thoughts about sociology, including the Chicago school of sociology (and in his letters and essays he usually identifies this with the work of Park, Burgess, and Thrasher) were not always generous, even though its influence on his writing is obvious. He had a distaste for what he saw as sociology's dry work. Its inclination, he felt, was with abstraction robbed of significance, so he argues in 1929.[24] By 1931, he is soured. His concerns were with understanding how a self is formed by its interplay with society, and he argues that sociologists had cordoned off a "fact" from its network of relations and meanings. "University Sociology fact finders," as he calls them, ignore what the artist knows: that "life has meanings" and that

The City as Society

"there are values, and that for human beings these values are the most important things." In contradistinction to sociological theory, he claims the best definition of culture he had read is Tyler's, whom Dewey quotes: culture is "that complex whole of knowledge, belief and morals, custom, and any other capabilities acquired by man as a member of society."[25]

He acknowledged, nonetheless, that the members of the Chicago school affected his writing. In "The Story of Studs Lonigan," he wrote how Studs's experiences were "concrete and specific" and pointed out that he "made sociological analyses of the neighborhood in which Studs lived, applying conclusions and hypotheses from the studies of University of Chicago sociologists. . . ." He did not do this, he added, to confirm their theories but to "clarify" his own understanding of the material of this fiction.[26] Thanking Frederic Thrasher, author of *The Gang: A Study of 1,313 Gangs in Chicago* (1927) for his Introduction to *Young Lonigan*, Farrell tells Thrasher that his personal copy of *The Gang* is now missing. Farrell mentions that in *Young Lonigan* he was only "somewhat" conscious of the things the sociologist mentioned but that what Thrasher has to say about change in Studs's neighborhood will be clearly developed in a later novel. Five years later, Farrell asks E. W. Burgess if he would help defend *A World I Never Made* from antivice crusaders. Pointing out their common vision, Farrell notes how his fiction correlates family type and urban area.[27]

Park, Burgess, and Thrasher helped Farrell envision the city as a series of settings, each representing the facts of transformation and the values attributed to such changes by the public. Their work explores the creation of the urban community within human ecology, the spatial patterns of urban migration, settlement, succession, and competition.

The Chicago school was attracted to a model of urban development that was concentric and zonal. The city's growth, land use and value, and area of settlement could be plotted and understood as enfolding urban rings. In "The Growth of the City," E. W. Burgess identifies the generative core of Chicago's growth as the Loop. This central business district is encircled by an area of and in transition, whose concerns are light manufacturing and business. Surrounding this ring is yet another, populated by workers wanting to live near their jobs but also escaping the decaying second ring. The final ring or zone is residential.[28]

The metabolic phases of the city are organization and deconstruction. Rapid expansion displacing people and industry from their respective zones disturbs a fragile social equilibrium. Crime and vice increase, which register, Burgess argues, causes of urban change; they are not causes in themselves. Nonetheless, where mobility—"a change of movement in response to a new stimulus or situation"—is greatest, and where there is a loosening of primary social control, areas of psychological and social conflict are created.

A public based upon an understanding of others could be formed out of the diversity of the metropolis. The neighborhood, the fundamental unit of association, had to be brought into the civic sphere. A social ethic must bind, in some way, the differing and private minds of the city. Public knowledge, in this case, would be a shared understanding of how the city functions and grows, of how neighborhoods and areas of work interpret and re-present the city for individuals. Institutions and agencies such as the school and the newspaper would overcome the parochiality of environment and make a public.

For example, by understanding how the competition for land and economic opportunity downtown creates the illiberal community, individuals could grasp how their own attitudes were formed. There would be a rational basis for civic intervention. Racism, taking an explanation Farrell found useful for *Studs Lonigan,* was caused by migration outward from the expanding city core. As one population was forced from its zone and invaded another, competition for land and land values increased. Prejudice serves as a rationale rather than as an explanation of hostilities. An understanding, therefore, of events no longer encompasses proximate cause but links economics, demography, and urban form.[29] This relationship could be generalized and in a crude way used to evaluate and at times predict urban areas in crisis.

Human nature, these sociologists believed, was considerably shaped, but not determined, by the environment. The city, in a general way, correlates opportunities with zones, character with area. Nels Anderson's *The Hobo* (1923), Clifford Shaw's *The Jack-Roller* (1930) and Harvey Zorbaugh's *The Gold Coast and the Slum* (1929) might have made the city seem more deterministic and less open to improvisational conduct than it is but they did point out how certain groups, for example, the gang, are attracted to specific activities and parts of the city.

Frederic M. Thrasher's *The Gang* and his observations prefacing Farrell's *Young Lonigan: A Boyhood in Chicago Streets* (1932) explore the relationship between Farrell's characters and their neighborhood. An interstitial area, the South Side was losing its white middle-class composition and becoming a multiethnic and multiracial rooming-house district. As the

South Side changed, the attractions of an easy opportunistic street life challenged those stabilizing, traditional values of the church and school. The conflict weakened the family's chances for control of its children. City streets *do* educate children but they often do so, Thrasher argues, by opposing the values of the family with those of the saloon and brothel. Given the weakness or absence of any authoritative public institution to challenge the lure of the street, children become demoralized; their lives are constricted. This "process of informal education," as Thrasher calls it, does more than erode the promise of youth. It is a substitute "for what society fails to give," he writes in *The Gang*. "In this background," Farrell explained in 1929, "I intend to treat a number of boys who grow up, and who, mainly, drift to the poolroom and its complements as the only outlet of their impulses for the romantic and the adventurous."[30]

George Herbert Mead and John Dewey helped Farrell understand how social psychology is part of cultural meditation. Unlike the Chicago sociologists, Dewey and Mead discussed how consciousness becomes social, allowing the self to share in the meanings of experience generated by the large community. The self's passage from a sectarian environment fixing the *meaning* of experience into a society responsive to the *meanings* of experience is the movement toward an ethical, democratic life. Our knowledge of ourselves is made possible through our knowledge of others; our understanding of experience is contingent upon our appropriation of the viewpoint of others. Farrell's lavish concern with how characters liberate themselves from the parochialism of their social group or accept as normal the frustration of their lives is part of these thinkers' influence. Looking at Farrell's work in this light makes the substance and form of it intellectually engaged with the significance of urban democracy. What must have struck Farrell as central to his own interpretation of the South Side parochial community was its quest for certainty in a world of novelty. In what ways could a social legacy or a community opposing the interpretations of experience the city conveys diminish the movement toward freedom?

When Farrell matriculated in 1925 at the University of Chicago, the influence of "the Chicago School of Philosophy" remained in "full force."[31] In a letter dated 1931, he praised Mead's explication of the scientific method and scientific thinking. He reviewed *The Philosophy of the Present* in 1932. By 1939, Farrell summed up what he thought was Mead's achievement: going beyond Dewey's *Human Nature and Conduct* in exploring the social genesis of mind and self.[32]

Before Farrell had expanded the short story "Studs," describing the wake of his friend, into the *Studs Lonigan* trilogy, Farrell had read Dewey's *Human Nature and Conduct, The School and Society, Reconstruction in Philosophy, The Public and Its Problems, Individualism, Old and New, The Quest for Certainty,* and *Experience and Nature.*[33] Later in his career, Farrell emphasized that he was a "philosophical naturalist in the John Deweyan sense. . . . I take facts from all kinds of sources, but they're not just piled up to build a case for environment. The environment and the people more or less come together."[34]

Farrell did not want to extrapolate a psychology from culture. Dewey suggested how our transactions with experience should begin with the physiology of response and end with actions that renew our relations with others. For these reasons, *Human Nature and Conduct* is central to Farrell's work, and he pointed out its importance by noting that

> shortly after I began working on Studs Lonigan, I happened to be reading John Dewey's *Human Nature and Conduct,* and I came upon the following sentence which I used as a quotation in *Young Lonigan:* "The poignancy of situations which evoke reflection lies in the fact that we do not know the meaning of the tendencies that are pressing for action." This observation crystallized for me what I was seeking to do.[35]

Human Nature and Conduct asks what an adequate moral life is by inquiring how intelligence (in this case, one's awareness of self and others) intervenes between response to stimuli and habitual behavior. For Dewey, conduct expresses the relationship between our experience of an environment and our shaping social heritage. Individuality and acculturation have as their crises our physiological and psychological abilities to respond in new and provisional ways to novelty in order to understand and control what is around us. We can exert our will within the world.[36]

For Dewey, inquiry takes place when habits, an individual's conventionalized response that now frees the attention, are thwarted. The interplay between individual and environment is, in a sense, broken or incomplete. For Dewey, the "moral correlate of liberated impulse is not immediate activity, but reflection upon the way in which to use impulse to renew disposition and reorganize habit."[37] Impulse guided by thought reorganizes habit so that it can deal with the problematic character of experience. This improvisation assesses futures, possibilities for action within the present.

When habit becomes what Dewey terms "habituation," we do not react to the unsettling current of experience. Activity seems monotonous: our response actually is monotonous. Consequently, when "habits persist

while the world which they have incorporated alters," we do not respond
to experience so much as we ignore it. The good is the thoughtful renewal
of engagement. The good is the felt consequence of action. If rival impulses are suppressed, or if impulses are consistently denied, engagement
is impoverished, routinized. Frustration and boredom characterize this
impasse.[38]

Thinking is humanly transfiguring. "The thing actually at stake in any
serious deliberation" Dewey writes in a section central to Farrell's understanding of character, "is not a difference of quantity, but what kind of
person one is to become, what sort of self is in the making, what kind of a
world is [in] the making."[39] Education is, finally, education in becoming a
self. Individuality *is* a relationship to and with society. We exist within and
by pasts made accessible to us. We live, in other words, by communities of
interpretation.[40] Self and social knowledge, therefore, implicate each
other, a point Farrell's novels invariably develop.

Dewey's naturalism makes education a progressive inquiry into this-
worldliness. Dewey's intent to liberate the meanings of the contingent and
unique from parochializing interpretation and his emphasis on growth
deeply influenced Farrell, and he recalled, years later, how he was drawn
to expound these ideas.[41]

It has been said that George Herbert Mead was the hub and Dewey the
circumference. For Farrell, Mead provided the core of the explanation
about how a self became social. In his diary entry of August 16, 1936,
Farrell speaks to his and Mead's notion of the social function of knowledge.
It seems likely that Farrell was recalling his own adolescence with its
promised future of an intellectually isolating yet common life. Mead,
Farrell comments, "makes it so clear that there is an absolute necessity for
a community where there are many rational men. What good does it do for
us to have knowledge if we cannot share it with others? What is the value of
our knowledge if it is to be locked up within our own minds? So Mead
would reason."

Mead's argument that there are multiple meanings of the past arising
from a problematic present also spoke to Farrell's own continuous reconstruction of the past, *his* "story of America." A carrying of relationships into
the present, to paraphrase Mead, is precisely what Farrell was doing.
Writing in 1939 to a friend about Sidney Hook's manuscript on Dewey,
Farrell explains Mead's theses as follows:

Mead says that the locus of an event is the present. The distinctive character of
an event is that it is an emergent and in its emergence, it has about it an aspect of

133

novelty. The event, located in the present, is a product of a system of the past. At the same time, as it were, this event, belongs not only in the system located in the past out of which it has emerged, but also in a new system which is necessary by its emergence and by its characteristic of novelty. By placing it in the new system, the meaning of the past changes, and in a sense, grows. In other words, while the past is irrevocable, it is not, when viewed from the present, settled and unchanging in its meaning. In this sense, new pasts are always rising before us. . . . Mead deals . . . with the manner in which we reorder the past because of new discoveries.[42]

The "sociality" of the emergent, its being "several things at once" as an event "both in the old order and the new which its advent heralds," defines Farrell's programmatic commitment—or obsession—to turn again and again to his background. He is creating a body of historical fiction in which the conditions of knowing are inseparable from the reconstructed subject.

For Mead, the passage from a private, isolated consciousness to a consciousness that can adopt the perspectives of others traverses an ethic and a politics. Self-reflection, the self becoming an object to itself, is possible only through the importation of the consciousness of others. "Rational intelligence" (the conduct by which an individual adopts the attitudes of a group) is contextual. Mead explains that "a social object [is] one that answers to all parts of the complex act, though these parts are found in the conduct of different individuals. The objective of the act is then found in the life process of the group, not in those of the separate individuals alone."[43]

The construction of shared meanings is accomplished by language, making shared experience possible. Composed of significant symbols understood by the community, language elicits the same response in self as in others. Bringing the perspective of others to the self allows the individual to consider his actions through the attitudes of others.

Growth involves imitation and response, what Mead calls a teleology of gestures, knotting the self to others and terminating in a recognition of self through others. The order of maturation is the order of socialization. Self-consciousness, a reflexive act, makes the individual an object accessible to himself; he comes to see himself as others do. For example, in "play" a child adopts a variety of roles and responds to the stimuli that he himself has generated. In "game," the child comes to adopt the attitudes of a group, a "generalized other," and he controls his actions in relation to this. Throughout this elaborate interplay that distinguishes a genuinely participatory community life, there arises a continual sense of self and self-otherness.

The City as Society

The continuous process of socialization is quickened by the interplay of individual and communal response; between what Mead calls the "I" (the temporally defined present of the self) and the "me" (internalized community attitudes). The "I" often responds uniquely and unpredictably to situations. The socially conserving dimension of character, the "me," is habitual. Through the transactions of the two, a functional self exists making past and present comport.[44]

The encounter between self and other has a tyranny of its own; a rigid response to a social symbol can be limited and limiting. The repertoire of meanings a symbol provokes is reduced; the "generalized other" eliminates generalized others. In a passage that could easily be the heart of Farrell's own work, Mead writes that "any self is a social self, but it is restricted to the group whose roles it assumes, and it will never abandon this self until it finds itself entering into the larger society and maintaining itself thereby."[45]

Mead's presentation of sociality leads to the adequate social object, the democratic community. Its politics make accessible the meanings of experience through its contending communities. As a result, a democratic society guarantees a continuous, rational adjustment of self to others. Nonetheless, Farrell was skeptical about Mead's optimistic version of the community as humanity and about Dewey's interpretation of a democratic culture. The highest good may be shared experience but this did not practically account for social conflict or for those occasions that did bring people together but prevented them from cooperating.[46] Elsewhere, Farrell argued that Mead "emphasizes integration in society without seeing disintegration. In other words, he fails to give due position to the class struggle."[47]

The theses of the Chicago thinkers gave Farrell's work its urban perspective. The city was not simply a physical presence to be described in terms of its appearance; it incarnated social intelligence. It could be described through a character's enactments of the culture it transmitted. The urban crises of class and racial antagonism were, in reality, failures of civility. The democratic city paradoxically exists through its conflicting, sectarian and shared life. The city extends one's comprehension of self, others, and experience into that of the enlarging community. The influence, if not inspiration, of the Chicago thinkers upon Farrell's work is ultimately found in how his characters *think* the city and in how they choose to act upon this. And again, the significance of the Chicago school is found in his notion of functional writing—fiction as shared experience, as participation in a common understanding. As Farrell put it, "if we read books honestly, and do not try to repress ourselves, it is likely that we will identify ourselves with all that is human."[48]

IV

If Farrell is known for any work, it is *Studs Lonigan*. Composed of *Young Lonigan: A Boyhood in Chicago Streets* (1932); *The Young Manhood of Studs Lonigan* (1934); and *Judgment Day* (1936) the trilogy is a natural and social history, akin to the epics of French naturalism rather than the smaller portraits of the urban family found in American literary realism. *Studs Lonigan* is given almost wholly over to what its characters conceive of as society. This, in fact, is ironically self-limited, for all they come to know is what they believe is unique and valuable to their neighborhood— their race, class, and religion. Their unwillingness to act upon curiosity sums up, for Farrell, the rational style of their background. Yet their past is that of mass culture in which education, whether from the pulpit or by the press, is a protective rationale for power or tribal preservation. Perhaps Farrell's sense of fortuitously escaping a similar fate and Dewey's injunctions about the will for renewal became an insistence that Studs's life could be different if he only wanted to make it so. In fact, the novels dramatize Randolph Bourne's litany of the deindividualizing agents of an unreflective culture in his study published in 1915, the year before *Studs Lonigan* begins: "the American culture of the cheap newspaper, the 'movies,' the popular song, the ubiquitous automobile."[49]

Against this background, the trilogy concerns the slow and deliberate process by which Studs evaluates the possibilities of his time and place. Like other novels portraying the failure of democratizing politics in a closed part of the city almost wholly given over to the values of sentiment and conformity (the studies of fascism in the works of Moravia, Doblin, and Isherwood, for example), *Studs Lonigan* is swollen with missed opportunities for creating a civic culture. What is omitted is important: the daily expectations and acts that make for a democratic society. Whatever hope Studs has to know something about life beyond what he receives from his friends and family, and whatever desire he has to be a part of a city that he grows to feel has a destiny for him are slowly denied. The books, Farrell writes, were "conceived as the story of an American destiny in our time" and deal with the "making and education of an ordinary American boy."[50] Studs is, in small, America's fate from the optimism of the Woodrow

Wilson years to the hopelessness of the Depression. *Young Lonigan* begins on the day that Wilson is renominated for the presidency; a peroration on the promises invested in an American boy who, his father believes, might even become president. *Judgment Day* ends with Studs's death in 1931. Wracked with fever and tormented by a nightmare gathering up his past, Studs and the nation collapse.

Studs Lonigan is a portrait of the city. At first, it seems to be a rather conventional one, so much so that it is hard to imagine what Farrell portrayed that was different from earlier, urban fiction. Indisputably, Farrell's city *functions* differently from those depicted by earlier European and American writers. His is a city of immense and churning growth, making diverse mores and values accessible to everyone through *public* institutions. The library, the university, and the church combine with the immigrant memories of characters and indicate how this city sustains multiple allegiances to sectarian pasts and a universalizing present. The city's promise of civic life transcends its narrowing communities and their defined territories: so Danny O'Neill, Farrell's alter ego, discovers.

Studs's civic limitations seem ironic, given Farrell's portrait of the city. Clearly, Chicago fables are enthralled with the ease of beginning again, of reinventing the burned city to suit its idea of itself. Farrell's casual references to the architectural landmarks of a new robust Chicago emerging from its past of ashes—from White City (the 1893 Columbian Exposition), to the skyscrapers that nurture Studs's dreams of success—emphasize how unnecessary historical memory is. Yet as *its* poet declaimed, "the past is a bucket of ashes." The tradition of Chicago *is* rebirth.

Farrell prefaced *Young Lonigan* with four epigraphs that complement his rendition of the city's legacy. They suggest how much Farrell wanted to place the Lonigan novels in the largest tradition of city writing, from popular songs to classical meditation. The first citation from the song "East Side, West Side" captures the poignancy of urban childhood. It also plays upon the divided city Studs inherits, the city of islands and snares. Adventures "all around the town" are, at first, of *all* the town. Later, they are trips to the city's brothels and dives.

Farrell follows this stanza with Frank Norris's dictum in the battle over American social realism. "A literature that cannot be vulgarized," Norris declaims in *Salt and Sincerity*, "is no literature at all and will perish." *Studs Lonigan* is part of the vulgar canon, a literature its partisans felt was authenticated by its plebeian, urban subjects. This body of letters "vulgarizes" or brings to the reader what other literature ignores. Farrell's work becomes the experience of the mundane. The book's diction, flat and unprovocative, is Farrell's presentation of Studs's consciousness. "I set as my aim," Farrell explained, "that of unfolding the destiny of Studs Lonigan in his own words, his own actions, his own patterns of thought and feeling. I decided that my task was not to state formally what life meant to me, but to try and re-create a sense of what life meant to Studs Lonigan."[51]

The dissonant voices of the progressive city are rarely heard. The Lonigans and their friends compose the social chorus of the book. Their talk is conspiratorial, insulating them from the city as *the* generalized other. The absence of different styles of conversation and commentary and Farrell's refusal to provide an intrusive narrative make a shared culture difficult for the Lonigans (and the reader) to comprehend. Transmitted as a convention, culture is an unbroken, inviolable interpretation of events. Because the Lonigans' isolation is, finally, from the comprehensiveness of civility, they have little or nothing in their lives that can transform them.

The third epigraph comes from Jowett's translation of the *Republic:* "except on the case of some rarely gifted nature there will never be a good man who has not been used to play amid things of beauty and make of them a joy and a study." The irony of this statement is that Studs has chosen to make his city barren. The connection between the city and civility, between the capacious dialogues about the good offered by the democratic city and the lives of the Lonigans, is broken.

Human Nature and Conduct provides the last quotation. "The poignancy of situations that evoke reflection lies in the fact that we really do not know the meaning of the tendencies that are pressing for action." In a large sense, the task of education is to make reflection and action adequate to situations. Throughout the trilogy, Studs's grasp of what a live choice actually is, diminishes. First presented as a raffish, spontaneous boy who casually acts upon what he gathers are the lessons of his mentors, he dies as someone who distrusts thinking itself. He becomes, crudely, his past. The pathos of his life is not that he is a victim of schools, of church education, of mass culture, but that he is their triumph. As a child he is given a neighborhood. As an adult he chooses his environment, one devoid of significance.

These epigraphs speak to the union of city and self. Not surprisingly, they easily lend themselves to the Chicago "tradition" as Farrell knew it. In this trilogy, isolation from the public quarantines one's nature. The common daily examples of Studs deriding what is around him, only to be baffled by others or to feel belittled and shoved aside, are dramatized in

The City as Society

Farrell's depiction of Studs's quest for belonging. For instance, with the announcement of the armistice, an immense, reeling crowd floods the city, and Studs is put at the heart of it. Compressed into this throng, Studs feels that his own youth has been tried and failed. He is simply an unnoticed, humiliated adolescent. Or as a young man hoping to be inducted by the "Christophers," Studs finds that he is unable to speak about what he has seen; he can't, in fact, use a language depicting himself vis-à-vis others.

Replete with Thrasher's Introduction explaining how the city educates its children, *Young Lonigan* came with a publisher's caveat: the book is "limited to physicians, surgeons, psychologists, psychiatrists, sociologists, social workers, teachers and other persons having a professional interest in the psychology of adolescence." For a book promoted as frankly as this, with its hints of adolescent steaminess, sales must have been disappointing. Fewer than 533 copies were sold. Moreover, *Young Lonigan* had an odd formal appearance, as if Farrell was just as interested in writing his own *A Portrait of the Artist as a Young Man*. *Young Lonigan* has no quotation marks. Dialogue recedes into narration. A small debate followed about whether the book was too frank, too clinical, or even a novel.[52] *Young Lonigan* begins Farrell's meditation on the social uses of adolescence. His sketches of boyhood are about the all too common snare, as Jane Addams called it, of preparation: the sapping of the instinct for change. *Young Lonigan* opens in 1916, upon Studs's graduation from St. Patrick's grammar school. On that day Woodrow Wilson is renominated for the presidency and Will Orpet is tried for homicide. During that day, Studs pretends he's tough. His father, Paddy, muses about the circumstances in life that make one man a saint and the other a sinner. Father Gilhooley delivers a commencement address dealing with death, judgment, heaven, and hell in terms relevant to the closed South Side parish, which hates Jews, Negroes, communists, atheists, and liberals. For all its artifice, this is a prologue to the future, emphasizing deliberated choices and interpreted pasts. It is to Farrell's credit that this present is gradually decomposed into smaller, less momentous choices.

Studs has his childish pleasures in the city, and Farrell writes sentimentally about how much an urban childhood is a mixture of local pride and wonder. The nostalgia old man O'Brien has recalling Washington Park race track, Studs's happy identification with his native place when he points out the O'Callaghan house as one of the first in the neighborhood, and his swelling hopes of taking Lucy to White City are instances of a naive and moving civic patriotism.

James T. Farrell

Opposed to his pride are the actual circumstances of his youth. His neighborhood is presented as the single acceptable community. Studs is expected to defend the racial and religious values of his place—that is the message of his parents' homilies and his teachers' lessons. Paddy Lonigan, for example, believes that the test of *his* manhood is his support of neighborhood mores. Its reality, for him, is his fear of the city's otherness. "When he'd bought this building, Wabash Avenue had been a nice, decent, respectable street for a self-respecting man. . . . But now, well, the niggers and kikes were getting in and they were dirty, and you didn't know but what, even in broad daylight some nigger moron might be attacking his girls."[53]

Like any perceptive social novelist, Farrell is interested in things that now cannot happen, in sensibilities hostile to novelty. Whether roleplaying in order to dramatize his manhood or rehearsing lines that deaden his responses, Studs is driven by anxieties about loneliness whose significance he lets others interpret for him. Pathetically, he accepts his frustrations as normal. He sees himself fulfilling the limiting expectations of his group. For example, his posturing gradually becomes inseparable from his character. Dramatizing Mead's theory of behavior, Farrell writes: "People paraded to and fro along Fifty-eighth and many turned on and off of Prairie Avenue. . . . Studs vaguely saw the people pass, and he was, in a distant way, aware of them as his audience. They saw him, looked at him, envied and admired him, noticed him and thought that he must be a pretty tough young guy."[54]

In the last episode of *Young Lonigan*, Studs wanders through Washington Park. Coming across the rotting body of a fish, Studs understands that one day he will die. He hears the wind wail "like many souls forever damned." Thinking of Lucy, his childhood sweetheart, he is confused—shaken by love and responsibility. Ending on anxiety is a nice touch, and we are reminded that Tillich later characterized it as a fear expressing our self and yet the call to be a self. Certainly, Studs does not know what his emotional response portends about his courage. Nonetheless, Farrell's depiction is more artful than it has to be. After all, Studs is still a child. More relevant is Dewey's thesis: "It is one of the penalties of evil choice, perhaps the chief penalty, that the wrong-doer becomes more and more incapable of detecting these objective revelations of himself."[55] As in the beginning of the book, Farrell raises the issue of the deliberated life. If Studs does not have the courage to be himself, this failure is no prophetic occasion for a young boy. What is, though, is his gradual alliance with a neighborhood that disempowers him.

The Young Manhood of Studs Lonigan turns Studs's encounter with mortality into that of his death-in-life. The fish of *Young Lonigan* is now Melville's leviathan as well as Hobbes's. An epigraph prefacing the book has Fleece, the *Pequod's* cook in *Moby-Dick*, talking to sharks. Hectoring them for feasting on the carcass of a whale, Fleece declaims that their hunger is not to be blamed; that is their nature. He preaches, "No use goin' on; de willians will keep a scrougin' and slappin' each oder, Massa Stubb; dey don't hear one word; no use a-preachin to such dam g'uttons . . . till dere bellies is full, and dere bellies is bottomless; and when dey do get 'em full, dey won't hear you den; for den dey sink in de sea, go fast to sleep on de coral, and can't hear not'ing at all, no more, for eber and eber."

For Farrell, mass man *is* brutally interested in the city—hardly indifferent to its challenges as Ortega argued. The vocation of reason that Socrates spoke of as rooted in a childhood of beauty becomes a violence against its demands for purification. For aggression in *Studs Lonigan* is either against others or, more intriguingly, against self-reflection.

Now a teenager with no unusual capacities, Studs accepts the partitioned city of ethnic neighborhoods. He used to walk *his* city: now he observes it. The windows of poolrooms, a view from a park bench, or an alley, or a street corner are vantage points cultivated by Studs's mentors, who range from poolroom hustlers to parish priests. All of them agree that these scenes are *the* city.

The Young Manhood of Studs Lonigan begins and ends with the sudden fury of the powerless and betrayed. Lee Cole's rage opens the book: "I'm glad to go [to war] and take my chances. I've been a shipping clerk for a whole goddam year, and I'm fed up with it and that goddam bitch of a wife . . . and that squalling brat. I'm fed up, and want to see the fun."[56] The novel closes with a New Year's Eve brawl. Drunk and splattered with vomit, Studs collapses on a Fifty-eight Street fireplug. These incidents aesthetically bracket the thwarted self. Enraged at their anonymity, Farrell's characters strike out at anyone. They are bewildered by their helplessness; the future of the city, they feel, has turned against them. Vignettes swell the novel formally presenting the disjointedness of Studs's life. He lives on random scraps of experience confusing what he knows with what there is. The world and his wishes are one. He patriotically slugs a child named Stein because he is German and Jewish; he believes that he

James T. Farrell

is Private William Lonigan, Doughboy Lonigan, and close to a decade later, Yukon Lonigan. He invests his sense of failure with cloistering, nationalizing fantasies of rugged individualism because he has been educated to believe that this speaks to the best in American life.

What has educated him now surrounds him, literally closing the distance between reflection and culture. This novelistic strategy lets Studs appear as entombed and trapped, even if only by his own choices. The church, his family, and his friends persistently drown the voices of the other city. In fact, this cluster of influences becomes more significant than the city itself. Acting out the drama of urban expansion by unknowingly identifying politics with territory, the Lonigans and their community lose the chance to understand their own situation and that of others. Seemingly free-acting, they think their futures originate solely with themselves. (For example, Father Gilhooley's new church will, the parishioners hope, drive up real-estate values and check black migration into the South Side.) These attitudes are overwhelming, so much so that Farrell has Studs wander into a meeting of the "Bug Club." Like the Chicago sociologists, John Connelly explains the connection between racial prejudice and urban development. He speaks of aspects of the city's

> growth which were relevant to the question of race prejudice in Chicago. These factors also were not mere hearsay, but plausible ideas presented by members of the Department of Sociology at the University of Chicago. . . . He explained that the City of Chicago could be divided into three concentric circles. . . . When the city expanded, it expanded from the center. In Chicago, thus, expansion spread out from the Loop. The inner circle was pushed outwards causing corresponding changes in the other concentric circles. The Negroes coming into the situation as an economically inferior race, had naturally found their habitation in the second circle. . . . The pressure of growth was forcing them into newer areas. . . . With their economic rise, the Negroes sought more satisfactory housing conditions. . . . All these factors produced a pressure stronger than individual wills, and resulted in a minor racial migration of Negroes into the white residential districts of the south side.[57]

In contrast to Studs's ignorance of the social origins of his conduct, Danny O'Neill wants to be a writer and "purge himself completely of the world he knew." *"Some day,"* O'Neill thinks, *"he would drive this neighborhood and all his memories of it out of his consciousness with a book."*[58] Whereas Studs identifies his future with the chauvinism of what he has been taught is America, O'Neill, in his own tendentious way, wants to create an open future. An adolescent aspiring to be a "savior of the world" or a destroyer of the "old world with his pen," his dreams of the future are provisional. His commitment, however, to interpret and to make use of what he understands about his past is enduring.

The New Year's Eve party is an explosion. Its violence running from rape through brawling is a blind, furious assault upon self-created and socially given limits. Strategically, the party spills from closed rooms into city streets, from the prison of the past into a now mystifying city. Drunk, lying on a street corner, Studs completes the cycle of parochialism in the city. His collapse is a turn to the walled community. Farrell saw this as a theme in the sectarian education of youth. Caught within this pattern, individuals became social types. Farrell speaks of this destructive legacy by closing with a new migration to the South Side. Coming down the street is "black . . . woolly-headed, fourteen-year-old Stephen Lewis" dreaming of the day that he would be "big enough to stand on the corner and shoot craps for real money."[59]

Judgment Day is Farrell's lamentation for Studs, his community, and a dyseducative American culture. Studs's death can and should be read as the figurative end of capitalism. Farrell, shaping an allegory out of the trilogy's realism as if the novel's data alone was insufficient for his theme, catalogs the diseases ravaging Studs's friends. Deploying Marxist tropes about the rotting body of capitalism, Farrell argues that Studs's death sums up the minatory culture he enacts.

The psychological vastness of the alien present controls the book, from its portrait of the flat plains of the Midwest to the immensity of Lonigan's final nightmare, containing his friends, the personae of national myths, and the demons that haunt him. Yet the physical city reminds him of how small and ineffectual he is. The book opens with the unfolding of a perspective seen from a railroad train; Studs is gazing at Midwestern villages and their desolate setting, the core of national fables about agrarian virtues. The trip tests geographic and moral boundaries. Returning across the Indiana plains from Shrimp Haggerty's funeral, Studs turns away from the grime of the small towns he sees to think about how his allegiance to his neighborhood has tyrannized his own life. He is reminded that the world "was full of places and things he had never seen and would probably never see."

Yet love pushes him across the city. In a touching way, his passion makes him aware of the richness of city life. Catherine, his fiancée, prates about her boss wanting to have Chicago beautify itself, and Studs begins to dream of having a destiny as looming as the city's architecture. Gazing with

Catherine at Memorial Stadium and at the buildings on Michigan Boulevard, he feels "their soaring suggestions of power." His life can be a public one, and the city buildings speak to his need to be a person of importance.

His ambition, given what he sees and hears, is not unusual. What is though, is his sudden loyalty to the city's spirit. He feels at one with the Chicago of resurrection; this city will empower his new life. He has looked, this evening, at the spectacle of Buckingham Fountain and the Art Institute, at the success represented by the buildings on Michigan Boulevard, and he is "stimulated by the sudden and surrounding sense of the city's growth which he was experiencing." Imagining that "in all those buildings . . . there were men with money and power and everything they wanted, men with names that everyone knew and respected," he tells himself "that from this night on, Studs Lonigan was starting." But he suddenly becomes "weak and limp with the let-down from his thoughts."[60]

How can we not help thinking of *this* twist in urban letters: the city boy afraid to raise his fist at this sight, unable to vow to conquer it. Unlike the French realists and naturalists who conferred upon their characters a hunger to appropriate the rewards of the city, Farrell does not endow Studs with the fury produced by a marginal background. Yet this *is* Farrell's point: Studs thinks he already possesses the sensibilities the city can give him. There is no disparity between his wishes and his background.

More and more stridently proclaiming the immensity of capitalism's dreams, the city overwhelms him. He is pictured as manipulated, or belittled, or adrift. Convinced by the swell of rumor and by the declamations of Solomon Imbray that Chicago will have an "unprecedented development," Studs invests his money in Imbray stock. It becomes worthless. Similarly, the controlling institution of his place, Father Gilhooley's church, is unable to defend what the past has meant. The church is poor; its school is black; Gilhooley has been assigned to another parish. The neighborhood, more so than before, has succumbed to the city's growth and diversity.

No matter how much he depends on movies or the radio or newspapers to make his situation intelligible, Studs is a man without a place. Whether with Catherine, or surrounded by crowds, or walking through the city, he is a figure of almost oceanic isolation and anxiety. He

> became light-headed, and thought of what a big place the world was after all, and he was sort of lost in it. He felt that he had always been like this. Ever since he had been a kid, he had wished and waited, and there had been no change except for the worst. . . . He had met lots of new people, become almost thirty years

old, lost his health, and now he was getting married and going to have a kid of his own. And what change would there be after he got married? . . . He was just a goddam chump trying to figure out too much.[61]

He is agoraphobic and lonely for the past. Attacking a liberal mayoral candidate wanting racial equality; agreeing with Stan Simonsky about the danger of foreigners; and feeding on the anti-Semitism of Father Moylan, Studs equates the city with his neighborhood's fear of it.

He feverishly plods his way across the city, hating those who have deprived him of what he believes is his rightful place. His journey now takes him from a cheap burlesque show out toward Van Buren Street and its sleazy businesses, onto the Loop, and then home to bed, from which he never arises. Cutting through the concentric zones of Chicago to its disintegrating suburbs, his trip maps the city whose changes he has never understood.

As Studs passes into a coma, Paddy wanders the streets of *his* boyhood. His wandering is abruptly halted by a labor parade demanding an end to the capitalism that has made his own rise possible. Confronted by the solidarity of the marchers, Paddy is bewildered. He, too, has traveled full circle back to the unredeemed promises of his youth. The parade is the urban correlative of Studs's bad dreams and brings Paddy face to face with what he has feared and been unable to pacify.

Juxtaposing the marchers' communion to Studs's feverish nightmares parodying American dreams of success, Farrell refuses to separate the promise of the city from its parochial interpretation. Tormented by dreams of the city's culture, Studs dies, literally surrounded by a family that has pitted itself against that same city.

By the time the trilogy was finished, Farrell's rendition of the city—for all its monumental presence in *Studs Lonigan*—seemed thin, too unaccommodating to the paradoxes that make the city aesthetically rich. His functional conception of character rinsed the city of its historic commitments to embody myth and ritual, of its abilities to transmit that fullness of a life transcending its material conditions. In contradistinction, Henry Roth's *Call It Sleep* depicts the transcendent answers the city gives to those who question its merely physical presence. Dahlberg's *From Flushing to Calvary* absorbs its characters' portentous struggles into an unfolding polytheism. Mumford's *The Culture of Cities* speaks of the city's preservation of the sacred and profane.

Farrell's rendition of the city, however, was personal and strategic. Personal because Farrell never thought of the city and the culture it transmitted in terms other than naturalistic ones; he had little sympathy for explanations that were not, finally, secular and causal. Strategic because he is not concerned with the arational imagination; he is, however, by the antirational. He saw his characters in terms of their Irish-Catholic background that disabled them. They cannot put their traditions of education and culture to any use except preserving their community's isolation from the larger city.

Studs's death seals Farrell's obsession with epic portrayals of closed lives and communities. Farrell's depiction of characters would now focus on those liberated from their past by the nature of the democratic city. He would write about how his protagonists reassess their past in the light of the problems the city confronts them with. Unsurprisingly, his characters are writers drawn to the question Farrell asks: How is the self formed? How does it transform its environment?

The Danny O'Neill books (*A World I Never Made*, 1936; *No Star Is Lost*, 1938; *Father and Son*, 1940; *My Days of Anger*, 1943; *The Face of Time*, 1953) continue Farrell's depiction of an American education. In these novels, urban education is close to the Chicago thinkers' notions of it. Danny's curiosity is stimulated by whatever is unsettling. His attention to others, as he passes from group to group, makes him socially self-conscious as he accepts uncertainty and doubt as normal.

Danny grows up in a city of various ambitions and ethics that have and are being lived. He first understands that the meaning of the city is found in the lives of two families: the O'Neills and the O'Flahertys. As in Farrell's own case, Danny's parents can't support him. They have too many children. He is raised by his aunt, uncle, and grandmother. Consequently, his education is a matter of families as well as their futures.

The O'Neills are trapped by poverty. Jim, a teamster, and his superstitious, devout wife, Lizz, find themselves in a city that is secularizing yet protective of the sacred. Her faith in a world divinely ordained and his sense of the tragedies of his class pit them against each other. She gives his money to the church; he can't support his family. His work makes him look for this-worldly explanations of things. Her piety is, finally, her acceptance of a life out of control.

In contrast, the O'Flahertys are urbane. Al and his sister, Peg, are, respectively, a shoe salesman and a cashier, refashioning their Irish heritage to comport with their present. Al quotes Lord Chesterfield, hoping that Danny will become a gentleman. Peg identifies morality with social class. Al and Peg are city creatures imitating the fashion and manners of

146

what they see around them. The city, for them, is a bazaar. Their behavior is shaped by the market.

The novels study how language rooted in class empowers an individual by identifying possibilities for autonomy and mobility. For Danny, language will allow him to enter into the city denied to his families. He will identify himself with writers who have committed themselves to humanity in general. His fiction, he promises, will war against suffering and degradation. The richness of language—writing, reading, talking, listening—gives him his sense of self.

The O'Neills' speech is shaped by, and announces, catastrophe, conveying the invariable helplessness of Farrell's poor. The novels are saturated with Lizz's prayers, her cries to saints, her colloquys with the dead, and her curses, as well as with Jim's outrage at how his family suffers. The self-dramatizing stories of Danny's aunt, the banalities of his uncle, the folk wisdom of his grandmother are also invocations—but to power and the rationales of success. Al and Peg equate morality with their relentless affirmation of capitalism. What Danny hears are, then, tales of the culture of the city: the dizzying chances for urban businessmen, the steadfastness of Catholicism in a dissolute city, and the private tribulations of the bourgeoisie. Farrell makes the point that he had made in *Studs Lonigan*, that O'Flahertys and O'Neills are citizens made by what they encounter and talk about.

These voices of despair and ambition present, at first, the urban environment Danny knows. They make him aware of the conflictful, pluralistic city in terms of antagonism: between the sacred and the secular, between the Irish-Catholic community and the city, and between the middle class and the poor. To a great extent, these multiple conflicts shove Danny to the margin of the large society: unable to participate in one tradition, he starts to share many.

A World I Never Made presents the city as a collage of attitudes. This form is tactical in that Danny, throughout his life, will struggle to make sense of what he grasps about a public culture offered to him in bits and pieces. His parochial schooling and the incuriousness of the O'Flahertys barricade him from others at first. Yet his freedom comes through and by the community he insists is rightfully his, as he passes from the instruction of his school years to a politics examining the axioms of everyday life.

As Farrell pushes Danny to the foreground, the city's promise is focused. Insistent upon giving boredom and monotony their due, Farrell argues that an American urban childhood is almost too rich, too swollen with minute choices, for the novelist to slight. The book begins with Danny as a literal public figure, carving his initials in wet cement near a theater. Wanting to put his mark on the city, Farrell argues, is ambitious and natural.

In opposition to this childish appropriation is poverty's destructiveness. Farrell depicts the spiritual retreat from crises that powerlessness creates. City thinkers have argued how the city itself presents a democratic, pluralistic life through its characteristics: apartment houses, department stores, mass newspapers.[62] Farrell makes a different point: the city also offers rationales for those who have no opportunities to rise. The city not only protects the sacred but also encourages faith so that life is endurable. Doing the laundry, Lizz O'Neill gazes through her tenement window at St. Martha's. The contrast between earthly grime and spiritual existence reminds her of her chosen fall. She denied her "call" to become a nun and is fated to suffer. Living in hopeless poverty, she believes that God would have given her miracles to perform if she had only consecrated her life. Her regrets are confirmed by her isolation in the city.

These two vignettes of mother and son organize the presentation of urban life. Farrell portrays this as a struggle in terms of orders of belief and knowing that make the city open or closed. He writes about the techniques of control that the O'Neills and the O'Flahertys transmit. For these contending houses are among the contrasts "in human destinies as they unfold in common scenes of life," Farrell explained.[63] In *Father and Son,* these "destinies" tear Danny apart. His father wants him to be true to the working class; his uncle wants him to be mannered; his parochial education pushes him to the priesthood. Each demand would be a commitment to a particular kind of endeavor, ranging from the profane to the sacred. Danny has sampled all of these commitments, wanting none of them. Nonetheless, he is burdened by what his relatives make of their lives and the limits they accept. He launches himself grandly beyond their ambitions by rejecting their idea of proper station and deportment.

Pointing out how easily these characters might respond to the novelty of the city and to a chance for a different life were it not for their own habituation, Farrell describes the surprises of the familiar. Danny's father, Jim, now a supervisor with the Express Company, comes home early one morning and is astonished by what he sees. "There was something mysterious about the deserted street. A hidden meaning seemed to be lurking in it." Gazing out a window, Danny's Uncle Al sees people strolling through Washington Park. They "seemed to be so at ease. They seemed to be living in another world."[64] The point Farrell makes, casual enough to be buried in a welter of detail, is that the city *is* more various and unique than the meaning given it by any one person. If only for an instant, the novelty of the city breaks one's way of looking at it.

It is Danny who believes that the world around him can be read. Naive or not, this loyalty to interpretation is the writer's claim, urging him to invoke the essence of things so that he can make us see them in their freshness through and in—paradoxically—prose. After Jim's death, Danny revealingly and clumsily compares his father's life to a book, but clearly this reminds us of the poignancy of the book Farrell is writing. O'Neill thinks: "Death was a kind of fact that closed a book. His father's book was closed, and all the might-have-beens now were inside that . . . locked book."[65]

Jim's wake is balanced by the novel's last scene, the routine of Continental Express's call room. Mechanization—the batteries of telephones, the endless flow of schedules, the rote work—has buried Jim's struggle for individuality. Watching the company's workers, Danny resolves not to "end up the same way."

In *My Days of Anger* Danny rebels against the waste of human dignity that he has seen. Unlike the characters in much proletarian literature, who come to ideological consciousness after discovering that they are the politically disinherited, O'Neill becomes political after discovering that he is *culturally* disempowered. He will triumph over the illiberal city; his writing will be part of the progressive human community.

The book's rage for the possession of a culture was clearly Farrell's. While writing *My Days of Anger* in 1942, Farrell recalled how he had left Chicago to come to New York fifteen years before. "Having heard," he wrote in his diary, "of Balzac's character shaking his fist at Paris and saying I will conquer you, I wanted to do this, and I did it in my own mind, riding through the Bronx on a hot night." Now, when walking through New York, he noted, he was brought back to his early days there. "They are to be re-created," he added, "in *My Days of Anger*."

The novel opens and closes upon the theme of the loss of a transforming language. Al, vacationing on a steamer, wishes he knew Latin so that he could describe the mountains around Lake George "in the great dead language." The book ends with the by-now predictable talk of the Continental Express workers. Language has become trivialized and, in turn, diminishes experience. But throughout the book, Danny yearns for a transfiguring rhetoric and discovers how it can free him from his past by representing his will within history. As a result, he can battle for the future of others through writing. As Danny describes it,

> Her [his grandmother's] sorrows, the sorrows of his father, his people, the sorrows of the past lay on him. His people had not been fulfilled. He had not understood them all these years. He would do no penance now for these; he would do something surpassing penance. . . . He would do battle so that others did not remain unfulfilled as he and his family had been. For what he had seen, for what he had been, for what he had learned of these agonies, these failures, these frustrations, these lacerations, there would never be forgiveness in his heart. Everything that created these were his enemies.[66]

This incantatory passage wards off what he has known about his history. It has been set in a city of spiritual and physical dryness: the middle-class banalities and comforts of the O'Flahertys, the express wagons, the tenements, the junk, the poverty of the O'Neills. Knowing how easily this can become his future, his writing is a compulsive purge of this possibility. Replying to Professor Saxon's critique of his work that "all of humanity doesn't live in the gutter. You've almost swamped me for ten weeks now with stories and sketches about whores and pimps, stealing in gas stations . . . poor workingmen, miserly immigrants. . . . prejudiced Irish Catholics," Danny asserts, "I didn't make unhappiness. I didn't invent Chicago. I'm only trying to describe Chicago as I know it."[67]

Chicago held Farrell's youth; he did not come to maturity in it. Chicago represented a deferred progressive dream. New York, the city he spent later years in, was for him a city that exceeded the imagination. In 1943 Farrell remembered the city he had encountered some twenty years before. Quoting a friend, Farrell recounted how New York in the twenties was a "suction pump, drawing . . . the most intelligent, spirited and adventurous boys and girls of America. . . . There is so much talk of Paris, and its role in American life these days. But it was New York that was the magnet. Ambitions were poured into this city."[68]

The Bernard Carr series, spanning 1927 to 1936, is Farrell's study of a young writer (for all practical purposes, an older Danny O'Neill who is Farrell himself) who wants to have a freely chosen future. Breaking the backbone of a deterministic phenomenology, in this case the mechanical, commonplace Marxism of the thirties, Carr comes to accept a version of history and politics emphasizing the ambiguous, unfinished nature of meaning.[69]

In May 1943, Farrell was talking about a "boy of promise in terms of his milieu." This new character, a writer, would leave Chicago for New York and fall in with a group of young writers "dreaming of the future." The protagonist's career is to be charted "through the mental climates of New York"; the book encompasses the "waste of a literary generation." New York's literary culture and politics, its publishing houses, its art galleries, its places like Union Square were material for fiction. "None of this," Farrell added, "has been done right, done in the right way. And it is all the scenery of many tragedies." What were these tragedies? Farrell argued they were social in nature: "social in this sense—all this energy, all this spirit, all this sincerity, all this talent . . . has been squandered." In fact, the project would be a "Studs Lonigan on a higher plane."[70] Unlike Farrell's initial sketch, Bernard does not fail, as others around him do, by succumbing to the authoritarianism of ideology.

The Carr trilogy studies the legacy of two cities. It is reminiscent of the works of nineteenth-century continental writers such as Balzac, Flaubert, Stendhal, and Zola in which cities are presented as tests of their protagonists' ethical imaginations. What does it mean to aspire to the putative culture and social triumphs that a grand city makes possible? And what are the penalties for realizing this dream, as if the city itself was the temptation of the modern spirit?

The Carr novels are a meditation on the need for an informing tradition of inquiry. Chicago's South Side is Bernard's dogmatic past. New York is an invitation to the future. Obviously, both cities are less important in themselves than they are as Bernard's ideas of them. Bernard is inseparable from the claims he believes each makes upon him. New York is the subject of his "geographical fantasies and hopes." The city is explored through his desires (going to a prostitute, he thinks "Here would be an aspect of the mystery of New York, of life") and ambitions (he wonders if he could succeed in New York as Eugene O'Neill did). Yet New York makes his understanding of his Chicago life possible.

Farrell had an eye for the vagaries of urban life, especially for its often garish hangers-on in cheap hotels and for employment lines. Carr becomes one of the small people of the city, clerking in a cigar store, and later selling advertising space in Monahan's *Blue Book*, a fictional yellow pages. His sales route is Farrell's human anatomy of the city's economy: people speak about their chances to make a living. Yet Bernard's urban knowledge is about the petite bourgeoisie caught in the web of transactions and commodities. Controlled at every point by the market, those he meets spur him to find out how free he really is.

His spare time in New York underlines this issue. Just as Studs was depicted as being overcome by the city, so Carr is portrayed within the grand institution of human culture—the library. His reveries about libraries as linguistic cousins of liberation are cut short by a pretty face. This is a nice rendition of Bernard's naivete, but that Bernard takes it (as does Farrell) with seriousness indicates the fundamental, almost puritanical, unease of character and author about any detour from their vocation, the making of a writer.

This deadpan portrait is redeemed by the idea behind it. Can one be fully human without a commitment to human betterment? Must writing be a political act? Or can it avoid being political? The library represents a sanctuary from the mundane; Union Square represents a rallying point in the battle against injustice. Farrell's portrait of the two defines the solidarity of cultural appropriation and political justice. Bernard joins Sacco and Vanzetti's death-watch crowd in Union Square. This is a space, sacramental in his eyes, set apart to transfigure the normal city. Bernard describes the scene as "quiet as a cathedral." He can compare the silence only to that "of a church when the priest approached the sacred parts of the mass."[71] Later, the square is again compared to a cathedral, but to one lacking altars and mysteries. Overlooked by buildings housing the Communist party and the Yiddish daily *Forward,* the square opposes by virtue of Farrell's sacred imagery the life that profanes inquiry and justice. Bernard is revulsed by the complacency of people ignoring the vigil and asks "was this humanity walking on Fifth Avenue?"

The library, Union Square, his sales route in Queens are more than geographic signposts. They make plausible Bernard's driving inwardness against the background of the city. They are his landmarks reminding him of his allegiance to self and others. "I am a young man," he notes, "in search of a biography." His question leads him to raise Mead's argument for the diverse yet unified self made by society. Bernard asks "what was he other than a human biped . . . ? What was he, as distinct from what he had in common, biologically, with all men? A salesman! A would-be writer! A lonely youth wanting friends and a girl! Somebody in revolt against family, the mores of family, home, society! Sometimes a drunkard. Sometimes a coward. . . . And so, what am I? Answer: a collection of somebodies wanting to be a synthesis of somebodies. . . ."[72] His love for Eva, a married woman, dramatizes how *literary,* how desirously artful his wishes are. Admitting the truth of her claim that she loved him more than he did her, he decides to write about her, making her literature: in actuality, to make his sensibilities literary. This is a callow decision, even as is his tendentious claim that Washington Square is *"the setting for that sad love*

story [James's *Washington Square*]. *And it was the stage for Eva and me."*
The novel closes with his letter to Eva. Bernard explains that his departure
for Chicago is a necessary one. "On the surface of things," he writes,

> it looks as though I have failed, and that by leaving I am running away, running
> back to everything from which I have tried to escape. But I am going back to
> Chicago with more confidence than I really had when I came. The whole
> meaning of my trip here was that I was seeking to discover myself. And that is
> why I want to be a writer. I want to know and discover myself, because if I do, I
> will know other people. And that is what I really mean in wanting to be free.[73]

His letter, at once personally revelatory as well as conventional, is his
claim to have achieved in the city, the vast community of otherness itself,
his identity.

Bernard Clare ends lyrically: Bernard's voice rises against the city. *The
Road Between* is dramatic; Carr is submerged in the chorus of New York
literary politics. Coming back in 1932 with his wife, Elizabeth, he wants to
believe in something, to commit himself to some transcending experience.
The Communist party, personal rapture, a visionary politics—these crowd
him but they reveal an urgency about his craft. He wants to be sure about
things and certain about himself.

His writing, *his* portrait of a thoroughly urban artist, gives itself over to
the conflict between the parochial and liberal traditions. Bernard wants to
discover how the family understands the surrounding city: how the family
constructs *its* city, and how the individual emerges from this. His first
novel, *The Father*, is itself this problem. As Bernard puts it, "I wanted to
write about values, what some of the values and commandments of the
Church mean concretely in actual life. And I wanted to deal with a typical
and prosperous family in a neighborhood like the one I grew up in."[74]

Told of his father's death, he reluctantly returns to Chicago. "What does
Chicago mean to me?" he asks, not yet comprehending how he is still
pulled by the memory of his father. Turning from the mourners to the
mourned, the necessity of his labor is made clear. "The living," he reflects,
"paid the retribution, the tribute for the dead. . . . and the tribute he paid
was what? His character! He must finish remoulding his character so that it
would be everything that was different from the character of this man who
had been his father. That was his real, inner struggle."[75]

Bernard's disgust reveals how obsessive his desire is for self-creation.
His wish denies the only human history there is, but can autonomy be
achieved only in terms of historical materialism? This challenge becomes
significant as Bernard realizes that the Marxist interpretation of experi-

ence reduces experience itself. In fact, this is the point the Carr novels themselves make: Farrell argues that Carr cannot be solely portrayed in and by the terms of the political theses he is so attracted to.

In a characteristic flourish, Farrell juxtaposes the individual who feels psychologically incomplete and historically insufficient with an urban institution representing the fullness of man, in this case the University of Chicago. Bernard wonders if the "spirit of truth and free inquiry [could] ever penetrate and conquer the South Side." This is his as well as Danny's plea for the universalizing community, achieved through letters. Speaking of his ambitious literary aims, Bernard hopes to explore the impossibility of realizing an equitable society, given the contradictions of capitalism. He speaks of the "broken promises of American life" and of the "split in ideals and action." The American Dream is the "frame for discussing American culture." He adds: "I want to get at how it is that capitalism, in a very concrete way, stands behind this, how the poets, the novelists have expressed this . . . how [realism] bumps its head against a stone wall of lies."[76]

He must account for his own writing within or outside history. In New York, he can't evade this problem. The city makes him feel the need for a cohesive perspective. He wants to bear witness to what he sees. His writing, he thinks, is "like a call." His laboring day, he finds, flings him "up against humanity even more than in Chicago," and he is moved by the urban spectacle, reflecting how there "was such a sad poetry in all this life."

The two cities are the settings of his life, but they are, finally, inadequate as its metaphors. They are incompleted meanings. His father's death in Chicago and his involvement with the Left in New York are liberating, but the content of his freedom is undecided, as is his politics. He doubts if "anyone in this country know[s] what to say or think."

The last pages of the book weave together the strands of public obligations and private lives. Turning to Elizabeth, Bernard quotes Saint-Just's dictum that happiness is a new idea. Now, the epigraph suggests that his needs cannot be met by the dogmatic community but by the open society. Carr receives a Loewenthal Fellowship and travels to Europe.

However, Farrell did not end Carr's ideological temptations and allegiances. In the late forties Farrell wanted to reexamine Carr's quest for certainty. The need to keep alive the situation of ideation, rather than ideology, characterizes the last of the Carr novels. Revealingly, Farrell prefaced *Yet Other Waters* with Heraclitus's dictum, "Into the same river

you could not step twice for other [and still other] waters are flowing."
Bernard's own struggles are now for an uncommon politics. He wants to
rescue will and deliberation from an iron dialectic while preserving man as
a creature within the processes of nature. As a novelist, he realizes that
histories rather than the apodictics of *a* history are the themes of his life
and vocation. The Party pressures and cajoles him to join and write in its
service but Bernard cannot evade his own judgment of experience.

In this novel, New York is his mentor. For Farrell, historical interpretation had to account for the mundane. Average life, not the critical epochal
situation, tests a theory's adequacy. This, of course, is in keeping with
Farrell's own literary portraiture. The city's placidity makes Bernard pon-
der his loyalty to a Marxism that cannot or does not speak about the
ordinary person, about the inwardness of an individual's life. The movement is at ease treating cataclysms—"new epochs, vast stages of history.
But here were all the little details of life. . . . Where did all this connect
with the broad, historic conceptions of the Movement?"[77] Staring at the
people who give the city its enduring variety, he wants to "penetrate the
mystery behind smiles, behind sad faces. . . ." No small task, this is a
claim that experience is ever fresh, and because of this, subversive of
categories.

His political life is an existence apart, a piece of him on loan to the Party.
Picketing Balch's Department Store, he is attracted to the community of
strikers more than to its politics. He "felt as he had never felt before except
perhaps on the night he had demonstrated for Sacco and Vanzetti across
the street on the square." Even though the Party offers him the safety of its
dogma, Bernard can distinguish between experience and its caricature.
His quandary is that the Party's rendition of events is valuable for its social
consequences, its opposition to the injustices of fascism and capitalism. Yet
he knows that the movement forces a distinction between experience and
inquiry. He cannot accommodate the blind faith of a Don Jones ("I doubted
and I almost lost my faith. . . . I told myself that the leaders of the Soviet
Union couldn't mislead their masses . . .") or accept Eldridge's incantatory profanation of scientific activity ("our policies are based on science,
are scientific policies . . . and we have the science to examine the content
and to test the social purpose of writing").[78]

Sitting in court, the complexity of explanations is forced on him yet
again. Is human nature a concept prior to politics? Can politics resolve or
explain, for example, homosexuality? Or the will to violence? "Dealing
with theories," he muses, "it all appeared easy, but dealing with human

beings in trouble and distress was different." Later he argues that he is no absolutist: "I neither look for nor believe in certainty." The protagonist of his recent novel demands the comfort of a conceptual absolutism, and Bernard points out, "That's why I used the title of one of John Dewey's books on the quotation page—'The Quest for Certainty.'"[79] At the Chicago Art Institute, Bernard remembers how he used to look at its paintings with "untrained" eyes. Farrell reminds us that amidst Bernard's attempts to write about what is characteristically his, this visit is one of the temptations besetting the writer: to train, and narrowly so, a way of seeing so that theory dismisses the complexity of experience.

Turning away from the community of the Party to the city, Bernard understands how much its people will be part of his quest for self. Walking through the Chicago neighborhood of his youth, he discovers that he doesn't need to fight for a subject or to be told how to write about one. The streets of the South Side are *his* landscape. Explaining how his work will deal with *his* Chicago, he asserts "There's continuity in everything, there's an individual continuity of past, present, and future in everybody's life. And I'm going to rediscover and put down if I can, some of my own continuity."[80] His defiant recovery of a life for inquiry becomes his acceptance of a future conferred upon him, paradoxically, by the message of the city and his past.

Toward the end of the novel, he watches a May Day parade, but like the fathers of the American radical imagination he is with his own procession. Wondering if he is right, if he is inside a more spacious, yet indeterminable history, he remembers the night he stood vigil for Sacco and Vanzetti, and he is convinced that "he had made the right decision." He is now a figure given up to the larger community, as he is given up to a freer self-creation. He will not live in or with a bad faith. No longer accepting what the Party claims is history, he is engaged in the novelty of situations that point to freedom.

Reading Farrell's novels, one is always struck by the persistence of their themes. The making of a self within the story of America as he knew it depends, of course, upon the self he wrote about and the *Americas* he knew. Chicago and New York? Perhaps the obsession he had for his subject and theses should remind us of what used to be called the obligations of the novelist. His insistence upon reinterpreting the past from his changing present circumstances (and what he believed were changing national occasions as well) is part of his distinct perspective. Yet Farrell's major works, and even his later ones that are embarrassing palimpsests to an apparently uncapturable past, transcend their minute fidelity to an area and age of the city. They remain anatomies of freedom made possible by the city itself: Farrell's aspiration that a rational, democratic urban life is shared human history and a commitment to face the contingency of experience.

Farrell's allegiances to the naturalism of Mead and Dewey and his exploration of urban ecology could have made his writing more arid and even less contemporaneous. After the Second World War, what novelist acknowledged these thinkers as shaping the literary imagination? In an age in which the concepts of alienation and dread guided American letters, Farrell's intellectual heritage seemed out of place and old-fashioned. Yet he would not turn away from his hope for the democratic community. He did not invert, as did many postwar writers, the liberal, communalizing nature of the city to produce new fables of alienation.

Judging from his critical discussions of Tolstoy, of Dreiser, of Dostoyevsky, and of realism, Farrell would have been at home with a distinctly nineteenth-century audience, one concerned with having the novelist dramatize a new subject or idea. And for him, this subject was, of course, the city as he understood it. His attention to the mundane and seemingly pedestrian is his presentation of how the self grows within the city. His fiction insists that his readers understand this often tedious portraiture as a clue to their own individuality and its *pasts*. In this ethical sense, he is akin to the writers he admired.

He would not accept an idea of the city without testing it in terms of the cities he knew so well. Like Riis and Mumford, he too would have few hesitations in talking about the socially conditioned impoverishment of self or in writing about a city without arguing for the importance of its geography—moral and physical. Like them, he depicted the city in terms of its equitable life. As a result, Farrell's novels remain landmarks in their liberal presentation of the educative power of the modern city. The South Side of Studs and Danny, the New York that Bernard chooses to live in—what are these but reminders of what is possible of communities within larger, more pluralistic communities? And an assessment of what may be tragically foreboding as well?

Paul Goodman would raise these questions anew, insisting that the city be shaped around an original human nature. Like Riis, Mumford, and Farrell, Goodman wrote of *his* experience of the city, arguing that the city can be judged by what kind of civic patriotism it nurtures and by how individuals enact its heritage. And again, like Riis, Mumford, and Farrell,

James T. Farrell

Goodman found that the city was too complex to rely upon abstraction or categorization for analysis or description. His voice and his personality are always present, insisting that there can be no thought without man thinking, and no city without man. People using each other as resources was his epigram for the communal anarchism he found valuable. This brief phrase suggests how he would emphasize the fraternal and humanizing occasions the city called into being.

Chapter 4

Paul Goodman: The City as Self

"**I**T IS false that I write about many subjects," Paul Goodman contended. "I have only one, the human beings I know in their man-made scene."[1] His one literary theme, he wrote, was "Community."[2] Many of his major works are community designs suggesting how human behavior can be radicalized, that is, how a true self can be expressed. He would transform ordinary behavior into civic conduct. He wanted to return the city to its inhabitants by making it libertarian, if not communally anarchistic. Hence, writing about the city was patriotic and Goodman took urban laurels for himself by proclaiming that he was a "regional poet of the Empire City" and by planning, with his brother, Percival, community arrangements for a new generation of Americans. Goodman remains our modern urban Hesiod.

While it would be tempting to make a great deal of his encomia about Nature, in his works it is usually nature. He presents the landscape of the "lordly Hudson" signified by trees and rivers that are inspiriting, sometimes incarnating a mythological deity, and certainly recreative, but these presentations are not as imaginatively suggestive as either his myths about the city or his interpretation of city life. For him, the city was wedded to the richness of human life.

Goodman's urban writing, for all practical purposes, is most of his work. The city was what he knew, and by "city," I mean the totality of its relations, which indicates what human nature authentically is. He insisted upon restoring *the* urban context to seemingly ignored yet momentous occasions. He asked How do we come to recognize ourselves within and as the makers of the city? How do we rediscover what human nature is and the fabricated cities that we have taken for granted?

He summarized his task by speaking about it as a consequence of his urban education: "Born in New York City in 1911, I know the schools of this place and time and the streets of the Empire City and the wild rocks along the Hudson River. I am concerned with naturalizing the family, primary education, and community layouts. I should like to set free the prisoners; to destroy the rationalizations by which we protect ourselves from our primary anxiety, our fear of giving way to joy and creation."[3] His urban thought is most accessible in his meditations given over wholly to community and the city, notably *Communitas* (1947) and his major urban fictions, the Empire City novels (published as one volume in 1959) and *Making Do* (1963). For this reason I want to concern myself with these works.

His inquiry into man and the city is apocalyptic rather than insurrectionary, radical rather than revolutionary. In brief, he disentangles human nature from its historical character. For Goodman, the origin of politics is the self engaging its environment. Freely chosen acts sustain the self. In other words, authentic human nature is self-management, which is the self's appropriation and rejection of what constitutes its surroundings. The self confronts an environment and from it creates a "field" pertinent to its activity. Character is inseparable from this gestalt. Autonomy derives from and is justified by this uncoerced, self-fulfilling contact.

"Growing up," as Goodman calls it, happens when the "ego" protects and guides the instincts of the self. This maturity is expressed, for example, in cooperation, inventiveness, eros, and fraternity. The realization of these acts, however, is contingent upon the kind of society we have. In the best of circumstances, the true self determines its field, in these cases a meaningful vocation; local, democratic control of affairs; useful, necessary production and technologies; a participation in world culture—all within the urban-regional web.

Goodman seems too impatient to be concerned with a systematic approach to the issues he raises. Often he does little more than schematize the historical and political ways an individual becomes ethical. He does not ask how and under what conditions one can know and enact a public will or a general good, even though *Art and Social Nature* (1946), *Gestalt Therapy* (1951), *People or Personnel* (1965), and *New Reformation* (1970) try to bind the authentic self through vocation to community and a vaguely shadowed society. Nonetheless, his fiction and community plans take these links as givens, depending upon what he terms the eros, good sense, and honor of human nature. As a result, his pronouncements about autonomy and coercion, individuality and community are logically as well as temperamentally derived from his assumptions about what a self is. These assumptions control his interpretation of the genesis of politics, accounting for his fable (but not for the social and economic causes) of the rise of the authoritarian State and the decline of the self. These suppositions shape his presentation of the city.

II

Human nature is expressed by its system of contacts, the ways the environment is engaged. Clues about the true self reside in the conditions of its maladjustment to the State and are found in the State's protective rationales such as abnormal psychology, authoritarian politics, and anthropology in the service of social control. Accepting the claims of these disciplines about an empirically known self denies the possibility of any commanding revival of human nature. There is no criterion of adequacy against which "facts" should be read.

Goodman's debate with C. Wright Mills and Patricia Salter (running through issues of *Politics* for July and October 1945) about the claims Marxism and psychology make for a better life deals directly with this. Goodman insists upon an acceptable notion of human nature.[4] "In general," Goodman propounds, "'human nature' refers to a potentiality and as such can only be observed in its acts, which are historical. Human nature is inferred positively from great achievements, from the lively promise of youngsters, etc; it is inferred negatively from the dire effects of obvious outrages."[5] Or, as he states the case two decades later, "I think many social scientists have been making an error in logic. Certainly only society is the carrier of culture (it is not inborn). But it does not follow that socialized and cultured are synonymous. What follows, rather, is that, since culture is so overwhelmingly evident in observing mankind, social properties must be of the essence of original 'human nature,' and indeed that the 'isolated individual' is a product of culture."[6]

These are fuzzy, sometimes ironic, but optimistic theses arguing for the possibility of knowing an original human nature apart from society's contamination. Historical knowledge, as opposed to an understanding of historical situations, is the revelation of human plenitude. "History," Goodman observes "is the actuality of the human powers, and we infer the power from the act. It is Homer and Sophocles that demonstrate that we can be poets. From the peculiar character of an epoch we infer that certain powers, elsewhere actually expressed, were inhibited by the institutions."[7]

Goodman's argument endows individuals with criteria of judgment and

161

Paul Goodman

responsibility for realizing their nature. These tests are the felt nature of healthy, uncoerced contact which is characterized by curiosity, excitement, and anticipation. We can comprehend which acts of ours are "natural." We *can* know the unique way of our being in the world insofar as we understand what we feel. A modern society has been achieved at the expense of memory and contact because we have forgotten what healthy engagement feels like. The crisis of modern life is the disengagement of the individual from everyday existence, not the inevitable nature of repression in civilization. Forgetting how to live independently, we have almost forgotten how to think about autonomy.

Autonomy rests upon the free act, the unique disposition of the individual maturing through a willful appropriation of the environment. In *Art and Social Nature* and *Gestalt Therapy,* Goodman wrote about the biological and psychological norms that define genuinely vital engagement and contrasted them with our culture's notion of the well-adjusted self. For Goodman, there is contact, conflict, and the formation of a figure/field relationship. Our culture's education of the self produces inhibition of appetite, apathy, and indifference.

In "The May Pamphlet" (published in *Art and Social Nature*) Goodman attempted to describe the distinction between the free act and the socially made pathological one. Whatever prevents the realization of a "human power from becoming a living act" is an unnatural convention, an example of coercive politics. Save for those acts that are crimes against and in society in general—coercion of another, for example—the true character of the individual must be maintained. As Goodman put it: "A man must make his own commitments. Any coercion in this sphere is unnatural in that, first, it prevents the ego from realizing its living power of interpreting and defending the most original instinctual demands; second, perhaps more important, it awakens archaic attitudes that then shunt off the power of the ego altogether and reduce the man to a child."[8] Clearly, Goodman was less interested in political theory than in the political context of behavior.

Goodman's notion of coercion is at the heart of his discussion of the self and its relation to the community. He saw the contemporary American legacy as a series of mutually unfinished revolutionary situations, occasions that *seem* to be normal parts of urban life yet hinder "organismic self-regulation." In "The Anthropology of Neurosis" (1950), he traced the divorce of felt satisfactions from the self within modern, industrial society where estrangement is an ironically safe act. In *Gestalt Therapy,* he propounded that the self, in order to satisfy a thwarted need, would try to complete that need by repetition. The "fixed attitude" would fail in a unique situation. "Old-fashioned techniques" and the inability to discharge energy make this compulsion-repetition seem infantile. In *Growing Up Absurd* (1960), culturally significant patterns of experience making for disengagement and repetition (dooming growth by having an individual replicate the failures of the culture) became the physical and cultural environment presented to the young. As he put it, noting the loss of fundamental change for the better in our day, every "profound new proposal, of culture or institution invents and discovers a new property of 'Human Nature.' Henceforth it is going to be in *these* terms that a young fellow will grow up and find his identity and his task. . . . The existing situation of a grown man is to confront an uninvented and undiscovered present. Unfortunately, *at* present, he must also try to perfect his unfinished past: this bad inheritance is part of the existing situation, and must be stoically worked through."9

Growing up ought to be, but is not, the passage from ego dependency (what Goodman had called in "The May Pamphlet" "natural coercion") to autonomy. Instead, our maturity is a regression. To inherit such a cultural situation is to accede to deprivation. In fact, there is no community that provides the trust an adolescent needs to grow up. There is no city as mentor demonstrating what a healthy independence is. The State, mediating experience through its authoritarian institutions and values, makes behavior uniform and productive for the market. Goodman argues that "nothing is more clear, unfortunately, than that certain tensions and blocks cannot be freed unless there is a real environmental change offering new possibilities. If the institutions and mores were altered, many a recalcitrant symptom would vanish very suddenly."10 However, the city and its region can become the "field" for a person's humanization.

Goodman's position was loosely enhanced by some of the writings found in the anarchist *Why? A Bulletin of Free Inquiry* and in the intellectually more capacious, unfortunately short-lived *Politics*. Yet his ideas were uncongenial to, and outside of, the speculations of those who saw the strengthening of the State as the best, albeit imperfect, check on an ambitious and often vicious human nature.11 Unlike such postwar works as Arthur Schlesinger, Jr.'s *The Vital Center*, and Reinhold Niebuhr's *The Irony of American History*, Goodman's writing contended that what was not to be trusted was a *coerced*—a state-coerced—human nature. Opposing historical interpretation of America's progressive spirit such as Richard

163

Paul Goodman

Hofstadter's *The Age of Reform,* Goodman argued that the promise of the early Republic was not to be found in an agrarian myth of the yeoman but in the character of semianarchic society from 1783 to 1815.[12] And finally, in contrast to those who saw the practical difficulties that "free acts" and voluntary, anarchistic associations would encounter in the modern, centralized State, Goodman observed that we suffer from social amnesia. We have lost confidence in our ability to meet the present.[13]

III

What was the city to Goodman? What was at stake in his identification with it as a regional poet and novelist, as a writer of "occasional" urban pieces? Goodman is one of the major writers of our time who *did* want to have a place in the history of the urban region though no doubt he would object to the term "urban" by arguing that it transformed the city into a dehumanized object. He called himself a follower of Patrick Geddes and praised Lewis Mumford as "the dean of us all who work in this field."[14] He found Kropotkin's *Fields, Factories, and Workshops* an eloquent manual of regionalist hopes and he believed Jefferson's democratic writing to be an exemplary statement of the politics of regional life.

For Goodman, city life is the state of affairs within the city (the kinds of behavior, language, shared activities) as well as the urban form itself. The city and its region express an "ecology of the human." The city is a physical and symbolizing environment in process. It is not, as it is for Mumford, a form of the generalized psyche constructed along the axes of nurture and aggression, technics and art. Goodman's grasp of the city, less concerned than Mumford's with this *psychomachia,* is nonetheless anthropological. The city and its region stand for how and what people choose for themselves. It is our self in the making, and by this Goodman means our ability to mature autonomously as well as cooperatively, locally as well as universally.

The city mystifies us. We talk about it as if it obeyed laws of its own. In actuality, we are removed from the human season. "City life," Goodman contends, "is one of the great human conditions, but in Urbanism, no one gives birth, or is gravely ill, or dies. Seasons are only weather, for in the Supermarket there is no sequence of food and flowers. . . . When the sciences are supreme, average people lose their feeling of causality."[15]

Moreover, the modern city privatizes life so that individuals become indifferent to their public roles. The city crowd, for example, should satisfy the need for contact and affability. The crowd (and Goodman distinguishes it from the mob) is now a barricade against the public-making demands of the city. This mass of people provides a defense against self-reflection while protecting the ego from any trial of the self. The individual, Goodman notes, will never be called on.

The crowd expresses the system of urban heteronomy in which uninterested behavior replaces engagement. Certainly public behavior is public: it is made possible by the city's fostering association. The common life, however, is not for the commonweal but is subjection to "*habitual* motivation, plan, timetable" which individuals now assume is normal.[16] "Let us rather take a lesson from the Greeks," Goodman advises,

> who were most often practical in what concerned the chief end, and did not complicate their means beyond what was animating. An Athenian (if free and male) experienced in the public places of the city . . . many of the feelings of ease, intimacy, and personal excitement that we reserve for home-gatherings and private clubs; he lived in the city even more than at home; and these feelings had for their objects the affairs of an empire as well as the passions of private friendship. There was no sharp distinction between private affairs and public affairs.[17]

By nature, we desire the reasonable environment because it satisfies our needs. Having no great environment, no grand community, Goodman exhorts, deprives us of a "human right."[18] Having no adequate environment means living with a permanently impoverishing future.

Democratic regionalism, the large unit of association, partakes of universal affairs. Belonging to a community that is both local and international is a *public* good—the right kind of shared association—and an individual right, for we are given the chance to be at one with others. Community, Goodman insists, is a natural appropriation of what is around us.

Crucial to this thesis is that the political independence of the region speaks to the quality and kinds of relationships that make regional life regional rather than parochial, a point, Goodman argues, ignored by the Southern Agrarians in their reflections on the culture and community of the South, *I'll Take My Stand*. In an unpublished essay written during the forties, "The Working Truth of Jefferson," Goodman pointed out that Jefferson's theory of democracy was a regionalist one. Unhindered dissemination of information creates a public that is given the chance to choose deliberated futures. Attentiveness to what is local, balanced by a receptiveness to what goes on elsewhere, makes everyday life practical, communal, and communalizing. Inventiveness is encouraged; indepen-

165

dence is actual. People live their choices. As a result, patriotism becomes natural behavior.

The diversity that regionalism ensures should remind us of an earlier America:

> In our history, the Americans have thrown away one of our most precious heritages, the Federal system, a system of *political* differences of regions, allowing for far-reaching economic, legal, cultural, and moral experimentation. . . . This was the original idea of our system. When the fathers gave up the leaky Articles of Confederation for the excellent aims of the Preamble, they were not thinking of a land with an identical gas station . . . with culture canned for everybody in Hollywood and on Madison Avenue; and with the wisdom of local law dominated by the FBI.[19]

Historical reconstruction of the American past, therefore, rescues the American spirit for the present. The inevitability of any centralized government is challenged. "The high tide of human freedom," as Goodman called the period in American history from 1783 to 1815, carried the American character. "Inventiveness, adventurousness, classlessness" are an American patrimony.

Yet regionalism had little chance of holding its own in a modernizing world. In a landmark essay of 1944, "The Attempt to Invent an American Style," Goodman wrote of modern technologies as *moral* technics because a preference for doing had displaced "utopian cultural aspirations." International, homogenous technological values eroded a less efficient but more individualized regional culture. As a result, chances for a "humane national style, a style integrated although regional, historical rather than parochial" no longer existed.[20]

Up to a point, this is a cranky primitivism. Surrounded by choices making for efficiency and abundance, Goodman, the urbane writer, prefers the vagaries and limits of local enterprise. Yet he senses a genuine threat to the conditions of self-knowledge. How can we know what our community is if we are prevented from creating it? How can our politics reflect our choices if the way we live is not *our* arrangement for living? How can the writer assert a practical relationship to a community, pointing out what is the "real," if the community does not hold a life in common?

In an engaging short story, Goodman depicted the challenges confronting the American regionalist, an "original" refusing to be cut off from America's common strength and his sense of place. Someone akin to Goodman. Perry Westover, the protagonist of "A Cross-Country Runner at Sixty-Five" (1936), is an athlete whose course is the contemporary civilization his place suffers from. Perry's race takes him through the legacies of his region, across the hunting ground of Indians, through gas stations and the debris of the mechanical age, to the concrete ribbon of Route 4w. As the landscape becomes more crowded with junk, the objects present themselves as signs of false needs. There is no human face to this clutter; he sees a gas pump painted for the third time, an RFD box, and a billboard advertising Castoria. "This age of Iron is the most crowded of all," Goodman writes, having Perry turn our attention to the age of gold, of sensuous awareness and inventiveness.

However, Perry's running is his dialogue with his place and humankind. Perry breaks "forth from the forest like a tired replica of the Race of Man." He runs, as he points out, because it is necessary. He wants to assess what he knows, explaining that

> most often, when asked for a judgment about anything, we have no clear present idea of it, but judge it with the same words we once used, although they have lost their meaning; and this is why we so often contradict ourselves, trying to harmonize past words and present knowledge. But luckily we suffer that vague uneasiness of conscience which tells us (though nobody else knows) when our words are opinion and when they are knowledge. By running across the country . . . I hope to keep my judgments up to date. . . .[21]

This story is a good example of the regionalist as a community writer. Goodman wanted to celebrate those occasions of place and those concerns of man that lead to a preoccupation with Man. He deals with this subject in a number of works, most engagingly in the preface to *Our Visit to Niagara* (1960), and "Notes on a Remark of Seami" (1958).

In *Our Visit*, Goodman tells of his interest in the relationship of place to the surrounding world: an argument for the richness of *his* tradition. "In collecting my stories of the last ten years," he writes,

> I was astonished at how they fell into these two groups [the mythical emerging from the American scene; the realistic suffused with myth]. In the American stories I could not keep Jeremy Owen or the lifeguard or the attendant at Niagara Falls from turning into mythical figures. Yet when I drew from ancient Greece and China, or the Bible, or from Art, I found there my daily business and intimate anxieties—just as I feel that Sophocles, Milton, or Hawthorne are more my personal friends, alas dead, than the literary people I know.[22]

In "Notes on a Remark of Seami," Goodman speaks of the power occasional poetry has for establishing a connection with our history by asserting it as the real, the existent. Poets, by identifying the local with the universal, assert their importance to the community. Goodman's thoughts on this reveal how difficult he thought this role—*his* role—was. "Nevertheless," he writes, it is a great ease and comfort to a poet to be able, just before his climax, to astound us with this particular trump card of factual demonstration, because he can then, at the very moment he is performing his risky and socially dubious deed of giving us the strange, feel the security of a common home from which he cannot be excluded. He has a Public Occasion, as if he were to say, "The occasion for my poem is our one and only world; you cannot deny me the right."[23]

A mentor to the times, a companion of myth-makers—these are no modest claims for either Goodman or any regionalist writer. Yet he insisted upon emphasizing the universal aspirations of this task. Discussing the dilemma of the local writer who sees in his labors no connection to a world culture, Goodman argues that the opposition is false; it leads to an international public, for "abstraction and every other self-conscious method are potentially traditional in several traditions; for they are a passage beyond the stories themselves to the artist in every man universally. . . ."[24]

Goodman's reconciliation of his community with those of all people is found in his devotions to his city, to the "lordly Hudson" and its shore, to those parts of the city that were his informal forums, and to the places that promised sexual dalliance.[25] These places offered him the repose, the fraternity and the teaching the city calls into being. If his writing does reveal the artist in everyone, it does so by its rootedness in Goodman's circumstantial problems: the belief that his city might make much of his citizenship because of what he could wrest from its daily life. The celebration of place, of *his* city, could provide, as the narrator of "A Ceremonial" (1937) proposes, "a unique coupling of love and fastidiousness."

This sentiment animates what Goodman thought of as a new form of writing, the urban pastoral. The data of the city, its machines, its crowds, its schedules, should be seen as humanly fabricated. If this genre succeeds, we can look at our city as "something human again."[26]

IV

Until the publication of *Growing Up Absurd* in 1960, Goodman's audience was small. As Goodman mentions in *Five Years* (1966), he found that he was talking to himself. His sense of his implausible (because marginal) position in American letters must have certainly spurred his construction of a usable eclectic tradition, one in which Judaism, anarchism, gestalt analysis, American pragmatism and regionalism nourished his reading of the city. Yet Goodman also rarely made a secret about how his sexually and emotionally untidy life colored the motives of his writing, calling into question his conduct. "Let me turn it on myself," he writes in *Five Years*, and he ruefully observes how "fucking X., seducing Y., pushing for publicity and money for my books—is all innocent enough as I do it . . . and always it entails fear, illness, being laid low, bill collectors, maybe jail."[27] His search for an adequate situation that would test his solutions to public and private dilemmas and would reward his efforts was all too real. His interpretation of the history of American letters, which emphasized the public's neglect of American genius, validated his position yet revealed an edgy writer aware of how far apart he was from his intellectual contemporaries. In his self-assessment, he was not wrong. By the late 1940s, Irving Howe observed: "Goodman is unique in the contemporary intellectual world. He is quite without roots, quite cut off from any controlling tradition that might yield him richness and perspective. He is the Jewish intellectual alienated to the point of complete reduction, which is one reason why his thought is so eclectic, his prose is so crabbed, and his fiction gives out such a thin trickle of feeling."[28]

Goodman had a reply drawing upon his notion of estrangement and community. "The disease of all real community in America is the most important cause of the specific Jewish community illness," he wrote.[29] His argument, that Creation "justifies itself," that God is immaterial, that the "Messiah will come," and that "all the rest is dubious and unessential" provided a theology for his politics, authenticating engagement, utopian ventures, and speculation. "For 'whatever comes up,'" Goodman wrote, "cannot be but for our good." This faith meets a companionable world— one that can sustain vocation. No less important, what Goodman termed "Jewish community ideas," notably mutual aid, served as his basis for a contemporary politics. The millennial Judaic sensibility nourishes, even in darkness, the fraternal society. One does not justify Creation, he argued, but rather one's own creation.

Yet Goodman's efforts to place himself in an intellectual tradition should not be confused with the categorical behavior that he forced his public to confront. "Jew," "bisexual," and "anarchist" are terms deriving their modernist significance from their potential to overcome an ironic marginality. The alienated writer can share in all traditions and cultures. Goodman seized this thesis; he would speak for the city and for man in general.

Establishing his claim to be a writer of the modern city, he must have enjoyed disputing the polemic that the American novelist had insuperable difficulties in a nation without antiquity and manners. Goodman would vindicate his subject and his heritage. "The social scene," Goodman argued, "is everywhere concrete and various enough to those who dream about it or are excited by it." The "strong artist," a "wild Indian of culture," an American original often becomes the bearer and interpreter of the *common culture*. His position is "exactly nowhere, neither in the government nor in the opposition."[30] This tension is an enduring one; the American creator has to triumph by virtue of character, and character is, Goodman argued in his reading of Louis Sullivan's achievement, "a reflex of society and its mores."[31] Given this, how could Goodman not speak of failure?

It is no surprise, then, that Goodman's engaging studies of American artists who often were victims of obscurity or at worst, ignominy, gave him the chance to propound a tradition that had room enough for him. The major artist, often an unconventional figure, has had, Goodman contended, "a rough go of it": "Hauled up for a breach of manners, taste or morals, he ends by having to teach his crass and ignorant accusers what their own real tradition is (it is also his tradition), so they are ashamed."[32] Rationale or not, this line became a defense of sorts, in his fiction (i.e., *Making Do*) and in his reflections (i.e., *Like A Conquered Province* [1967]). Under the terms of Van Wyck Brooks's argument that failure is the American artist's legacy, Goodman could make himself into something of a native son. However, his defense reveals his determination to be seen in an indispensable—and acknowledged—perspective. His work would outlive its detractors. The importance of his urban themes would be justified.

V

The shape of our environment, Goodman observed, "*is* the functioning community."[33] Coming early to this opinion, probably because of the influence of his brother Percival, an architect, Goodman refused to separate the man-made environment from man making his self. His essays about architecture, city design, and the regional plan are companions to his fiction. They are apposite; works that educate by engagement.

Architecture is the "most social of the arts," presenting to us the spirit of our culture. "A Romantic Architecture" (1931), the unpublished "Our Captious Critics" (1931, written with Percival), "A Rationalistic Architecture" (1932), "A Note on the Materials in Architecture" (1933), and his early essays on building and design announce his neofunctionalist program. They speak of the development of the whole individual within the community as concerns of the city planner and architect. Questions guiding the essays' inquiry are Is the endeavor worthwhile? Is human nature realized?

There is nothing startling about this position. The reader could have found similar concerns in Louis Sullivan's *Kindergarten Chats* and *The Autobiography of an Idea*. Lewis Mumford's *The Brown Decades* and *New Yorker* "Skyline" essays were a tough-minded reading of the social values of architecture. Frank Lloyd Wright's community plans were topical. Yet to a young man who had been a "latchkey kid," who had bicycled across the Washington Heights of his boyhood and the Manhattan of his youth, and who was a gifted and curious writer making the metropolis his home, writing about the city was part of living in the city, and this was open for inspection. One had a right to put questions to it.

Judging by Goodman's lavish attention to the spectacle of the streets, the city had become his house; he was at ease in it. Delmore Schwartz caustically portrayed Goodman and his circle turning every public and private place of the city into a theater of controversy in "The World Is a Wedding." This sketch is nicely balanced by William Barrett's portrait in *The Truants* of Goodman writing on buses and trains.

Yet these early essays are unusual. A point should be made that for an American Jew to take the city as his own, insisting it answer the questions he poses, is a remarkable sign of acculturation. In fact, Goodman in his criticism identifies himself as the rational public. And clearly, his is a small voice measured against a chorus speaking of the city as a concentration of people and capital.

For Goodman, architecture had to be purposive and rational. Architectural criticism separates reason from rationale because the aesthetic of architecture implicates an ethic. The choices of means consonant with ends and of ends meeting the needs of people are designs for living. "A Romantic Architecture," Goodman's querulous scrutiny of Frank Lloyd Wright's "subjectivism," and "A Rationalistic Architecture," Goodman's discussion of the logic of purposive design, ask if architecture can answer what we naturally desire. If it cannot, the essays imply, architecture exists as an ensemble of materials and designs shaped by the market, appearing as an environment we confront rather than engage. Architecture, he insisted in "A Note on the Materials in Architecture," is made "with men, of their lives." It becomes a "choreography" rather than a design for shelter or a pleasing order of materials.

During the early 1940s, Goodman's own wartime difficulties increased, and so did his contribution to the invention of community plans. He asserted his right to be a civic artist opposing the war by discussing the quality of public planning. Percival and Paul Goodman started to explain their regionalist ideas. In "Architecture in Wartime" (1943) they challenged prevailing architectural orthodoxies that guided new opportunities for building. In short order, the essay rebuked the inertia of military architectural policies, defense-housing plans, and temporary buildings that would not outlive their moment.

More important, the piece sketched the problems of a wishful future that was based on a failed past. The American versions of the garden city (Radburn and the plan for Willow Run) were "historically reactionary and morally ruinous." The city and countryside were not functionally integrated: home and personal considerations were separated from industrial production. A truly "regional functional relationship" between farm and factory was thwarted. For example, houses were designed either as escapes from factory life or as carriers of factory style. There was no rethinking the relationship of necessary production to consumption. The personal, domestic, and public sectors of life were accepted as unrelated categories and were planned for as such.

The alternative to the garden city and its commercial relative, the company town, is the integrated community which the Goodmans explain is "interpenetrating in space, correlated in function and meaning, and combining factory and farm." This proposal, the Goodmans note, is ahead of our psychological but not our technological capabilities. "If," they write,

> a more human attitude comes to exist, there may be an architecture of a profounder meaning, smaller in scale, more leisurely in pace, grounded in the classic urbanism of integrated work and life, and in the humanity of integrated city and farm. Such an architecture, to symbolize it, is an architecture of city squares—squares where people stay, not mere junctions of traffic arteries—squares on which homes and public buildings and factories and markets all abut. Such an architecture may even, again, be great.[34]

"Architecture in Wartime" attracted critics. Lewis Mumford argued that the Goodmans misread the achievements of the garden city as conceived by Ebenezer Howard and carried out in Letchworth and Welwyn. The authors, Mumford wrote, were really suggesting a garden city on a regional scale, a settlement with a wider dispersal of facilities and more open form than originally conceived by garden-city planners. The Goodmans replied that their plans to integrate community functions were different from what Mumford thought them to be. A reliance on city squares rather than automobiles to promote community, a real simplicity eliminating all

The City as Self

intermediary facilities neither part of production nor consumption, and a reassessment of what work and culture could become (rather than the closer alliance of labor and a dulling culture) were points ignored by the garden city. The brothers' rejoinder testily misread much of what the garden city idea is, and the controversy continued.[35]

The publication of *Communitas* in 1947 gave the Goodmans a greater opportunity to define their plans and their notion of planning as an ethical project. *Communitas* is nourished by the sensibilities of Victorian forebears such as William Morris and John Ruskin, who argued that an aesthetic education developed a moral disposition. The book is indebted to the work of Geddes and Mumford, the great regionalist thinkers of the twentieth century. *Communitas* draws upon the experiments of American originals such as Ralph Borsodi who lived his community ideas. Finally, the book owes a great deal to Percival's own thoughts about what good modern design was and to his experience with a project for the New York World's Fair in Flushing Meadows.

Just as important, in its first edition and in its 1960 revision, *Communitas* translates the classical questions of political philosophy into urban design. What is the importance of the city? Can it educate us? For what good, and in what ways do people associate? Could the contradictions of civil life between self-interest and public obligation be reconciled?

The book is part of the tradition of utopian planning, refusing to accept conventional social conduct as *the* expression of human nature. The political, economic, and cooperative concerns of humans are categories that fractionate living. The Goodmans argue that urban planning is less an account of urban history than it is an account of human nature. By offering plans to renew life, *Communitas* challenges the tyranny of the conventional city.

Communitas is eutopian. Unlike Mumford's meditations on the city and its fall into urbanism or his pioneering analysis of the historical utopian imagination, *Communitas* is a manual. The Goodmans present as models communities that already exist, such as the kibbutz and the TVA. The book is also sustained by antecedent city invention. The authors summon city thinkers such as Wright, Le Corbusier, and Howard who designed communities based on their views of what the self is and needs. The book analyzes projects such as Broadacres, the Radiant City, and the garden city.

Howard had seen the city, town, and countryside as incomplete communities. The chances for a decent, cooperative life could be realized only

173

partially by each of them. The garden cities would, through cooperation and democratic politics, check the progress of capitalism by subjecting it to public control. However, the center of the garden city is a bazaar. What is produced, what is traded, and what is desired have little to do with a new community idea. The garden city's geometrical layout of circles, green-belts, and avenues reduces adventure to walking about a well-planned place. The emphasis on ultimate community ownership diminishes self-interest, but it also limits the growth of a diverse population. Frank Lloyd Wright's love for the secluded valleys and open stretches of the Midwest led him to oppose the city, calling it a cancer. His community plan is, finally, arid. His uneasiness with a large population and a turbulent plural-ism, and his plan's reliance on technologies make the community a series of arrangements rather than problem-solving inventions. Le Corbusier thought of the city planner as an engineer, even a scientist. His city values authority, concentration, and anonymity.[36] It demonstrates a theory about planning and not a concern for the whole person.

In contrast with these writers, the Goodmans love the city. Its streets, its possibilities for surprise and diversity, its revelation of intellect and energy, its affective qualities make it the place for an enriching, celebra-tory life. Where else, how else could a public and a self be mutually engaging? Or a culture transmitted? Finally, the authors' confidence in the possibility of community and city planning is based upon an affluent economy with surplus goods, and available technologies.

Cities are not independent, autonomous zones. Planning must be com-prehensive in scope. A new urban regionalism could create a democratic public by making accessible what is actually available, the physical and cultural universal community.

Communitas insists that we enact our nature. The authors do not call for enhanced work but for a different method and kind of labor. They are not asking for an ever-mechanizing workplace but for a more lucid strategy for the machine's role in human affairs. They are not arguing for more leisure, a respite from industrial production, but for a reexamination of the means and ends of work.

The new city plan cannot be a scheme satisfying the technological imagination. The metropolis should not be planned as an ensemble of services. Urban design involves the paradox of design. As the Goodmans put it, echoing Mumford's critique of the utopian city: "The best plan . . . is one that recognizes its limitation in itself; *that . . . planning for every-*

thing, includes freedom from the plan as one of the greatest things to plan for."[37]

It is a credit to the Goodmans' good sense that they do not confuse a work of art, shaping and closing experience, with a city plan that does the same. *The latter must be an invitation to improvise.* The contrasts among *Communitas*'s ideograms, Howard's diagrams, Le Corbusier's crisp, arid lines, and Wright's schematics are striking. The Goodmans offer the provisional; the others, a blueprint. (We ought to be reminded of Mumford's use of aerial photographs portraying the city as developing in fixed, spatial patterns regardless of its internal pressures and geography.)

The difference between the first and second editions of *Communitas* is the change in emphasis on the urgency of an "open" plan. The first edition of *Communitas* is, after all, a wartime book (written between 1943 and 1945) looking at an undetermined future. That edition addresses problems dealing with the modern division of labor and the opportunities of technology. "Plasticity" (the choice of means) and "flexibility" (commitment to goals) are chances to be taken. The second edition looks backward to examine lost opportunities. Planners have failed to make more sensible use of what is available in an age of surplus production. In other words, what has become of the postwar promise? Nonetheless, the two editions are a sustained argument, and I shall treat them as such, quoting from the more readily available revision unless noted otherwise.

Intriguingly, the authors rely on ideograms in both editions, insisting that the human figure points to the outsize scale of a technological civilization. However, it is not the ideogram itself but the way we see it that is important. The second edition opens with a gestalt meditation upon "Foreground and Background" that points out how we have become too accustomed to the city as a setting. We are *unused* to, and nonchalant about, our perceptions. The Goodmans will provide the reader with a way of seeing so that the city is no longer a mere background, but instead an environment to be sensuously appropriated. The ideogram is an exercise in engagement. By responding to the provocativeness of the sketch, we realize how modern civil life has transformed the psychologically harmful into the normal.

Communitas discusses a city in which the "whole man" is possible. Therefore, a reading of the city depends on discovering its *humanizing* history. When Paul Goodman elsewhere argues that a grand environment is a human right, he is claiming that the city must realize our natural

175

ambitions. This demand measures our urban literacy. We must learn to interpret the form of the city and the satisfactions it offers in terms of human nature. Urban meditation is, for the Goodmans, demystification: for example, we must discover why our nature is not being fulfilled.

Communitas, a book published after black times, urges its audience to restore choice to its life as much as it proposes optimism. "The future is gloomy," the Goodmans write, "and we offer you a book about the bright face of the future!"[38] On the one hand, the Goodmans were countering the fearful imagination behind modern urban design. Le Corbusier had argued that *his* city, the *Ville Radieuse,* was an appropriate one for the day because it could withstand air raids. Sigfried Giedion, in his now classic *Space, Time and Architecture* (1941), had spoken of the city as the modern target, as Mumford also did in his wartime essays. In the not distant future, Frank Lloyd Wright would design the Guggenheim Museum to withstand an atomic attack on New York.

On the other hand, the Goodmans' designs checked "hard" liberals' notions of a corrupt human nature. The Goodmans claimed that contemporary industrial life damaged the creative spirit of eros. Dispiriting, they argued "is the world-wide anxiety that everywhere produces conformity and brain washed citizens. For it takes a certain basic confidence and hope to be able to be rebellious and hanker after radical innovations."[39]

Privatism impoverishes the city; a thoughtless architecture encourages this withdrawal. Public settings encouraging contact are slighted by the planner. As a result, the city is less and less communalizing. It is also an infrequent environment. The city has become a place in which people transact their affairs. It is no longer *their* affair.

A new city and public had to be created. Asking what a self should be forces a consideration of buried needs. Questioning our wants is a natural, practical activity, the first stage in affective behavior. Returning the city to its inhabitants means planning for human nature that thrives on engagement, on enlargement. The Goodmans' suggestions for city squares, their propositions to return the streets to walkers, their plans for housing that does not isolate dwellers from what is around them are tactics making the urban population confront *felt* but ignored inclinations. In a line that could have easily come from *Gestalt Therapy,* the Goodmans declaim that they want "Style, power and grace. . . . These come only burning, from need and flowing feeling; and that fire brought to focus by viable character and habits."[40] We possess by and with our senses. This possession, dulled by the mechanical routine of the present city, can be enlivened. For instance,

awareness of an unfolding perspective, and of the visible connections
between self and neighborhood and of the past and the present must
become normal.

When the Goodmans talk about returning to the Greeks for salutary city
planning, they appeal to the tradition of the holistic community. There is
no pursuit of the good apart from the erotic, social, and reflective opportunities of the city. In other words, the quest for the good begins with what
completes us, with what we are attracted to. *Communitas* explores, therefore, a city of selves that make our self possible.

The book's analysis of major urban designs is a study of distinctive
cultures, that is, ways of life created by various means of integrating work,
housing, and services. The Goodmans shrewdly look for political initiative,
gregariousness, and cultural flexibility in these plans. The qualities of
conventional neighborhood life point to the value of association. Wouldn't
it be better, the authors ask, "instead of regarding 'non-cooperation' as a
datum, to take the bull by the horns and regard community life as a
continuous group-psychotherapy in our sick society, in which just the
anxieties and tensions of living together become the positive occasions to
change people and release new energy altogether?"[41] This assertion is
faithful to Paul Goodman's principle of voluntary but necessary adjustment
to the only world there is. Psychotherapy, in this case our understanding of
the "field" of human relations, replaces law as an agent of cohesion. We are
offered a contemporary Paulinism: let the community complete us as we
wish to complete it ("people using each other as resources," as one of
Goodman's characters pronounces in *Making Do*).

Yet this is all prelude. *Communitas* is known for its three models:
paradigms, at times parodies, of cities realizing varying degrees of the
whole person. The Goodmans first describe a fevered state: the city as
department store. The antecedents of this city (from Plato's description of
the feverish life, through Aristotle's discussion of a deteriorating political
economy, to Veblen's anatomy of the contemporary situation of workmanship) are obvious. Activity is efficient consumption. Life is the circulation
and use of commodities. Pecuniary emulation is overstimulated. The city is
given its ritual of purgation and a tyrannical mass taste much the way early
utopian writers invented rites of catharsis and enlightenment for their
cities. Public rituals, the grand carnival, for example, eat up reserves of
goods, thereby emptying inventories and preparing the way for another,
hungered round of consuming. Education is the pedagogy of buying.
Character in such a city is truncated or immature. It is dependent upon the

official culture for choices; the official culture, in turn, is indifferent toward purposeful, necessary workmanship.

One of the points *Communitas* is making is that the continuous therapy of community life depends, to a great extent, on having individuals become responsive to their own natures. In this city of consumption, the self is estranged from its nature by a seamless social system: market values are reinforced at every moment. Frustration is rationalized as eccentricity just as a critique of this economic culture is taken as crankiness.

The third city is planned to facilitate the need for vocation, though whether this city could fully make that possible is dubious. The economy (reminiscent of Aristotle's "two tables" as well as the New Deal) is a dual sector exchange. One sector provides subsistence goods and modest jobs. This area is swelled by national conscription. The other sector is the risky capitalist market. This city provides the chance for purposeful work and useful invention. Economic activities are, to a great extent, freely chosen. In addition, the city has social safety nets built into it so that the dangers of the market can be lessened.

The limited sector has its own perils such as estrangement from and bewilderment at the surrounding society. In this area of the economy, freedom and security lead an individual to see those in the capitalist sector as incomplete. His compatriots, the Goodmans note, seem to be creatures in a social zoo. Choosing to live in the subsistence sector means being in a minority and psychologically out of place. It also means being physically apart from the city, living far from the city center, distant from the opportunities of urban life. However, homes at the city periphery are often mobile or exchangeable units. People enjoy, and here the authors quote Homer, a modern odyssey. Their nomadic life lets them learn of the "places and many minds of men." (Yet such folk may well forget that Odysseus yearns for the kingly and domestic rituals of Ithaka.)

The economy of this city has provision for necessary, useful work that is the foundation for civic patriotism. Alienation, as the Goodmans deal with it, is ethical; one chooses one's life and the means toward it. This state is not a mentor but a facilitator.

The second city is the one preferred by the authors. Its political economy can be described as guild anarcho-syndicalism. The daily cycle of metabolism (work, replenishment, rest) replaces the mechanical, unvarying schedule of industrial production. Psychological and moral criteria govern labor so that means and ends logically interpenetrate. Production and consumption are choices. They are based on the region's needs and resources which are assessed by decisions about how deeply to enter the extraregional market. The facts of work reflect the values of the good life. "A way of life," the Goodmans write,

> requires merging the means in the end, and work would have to be thought of as a continuous process of satisfying activity, satisfying in itself, and satisfying in its useful end. Such considerations have led many moralist-economists to want to turn back the clock to conditions of handicraft in a limited society, where the relations of guilds and small markets allow the master craftsman a say and a hand in every phase of production, distribution, and consumption. Can we achieve the same values with modern technology, a national economy, and a democratic society?[42]

This *sehnsucht* for the medieval within the modern, a sensibility shared by some of the Goodmans' contemporary city thinkers such as Lewis Mumford and Murray Bookchin, is based on several things. Certainly among these factors are desires for limits, for fraternity, and for necessary production—criteria that are out of place in the contemporary city as megalopolis. Labor should be, as the Goodmans argue here, a vocation. The attraction of guilds and free cities, in this sense, is that of communities made possible by socially valuable labor. (And here, *Communitas* is close to the aims of one of its contemporaneous American communities, the Catholic Worker movement.) Unlike nineteenth-century English conservatives who resurrected this epoch as a defense against a socially polarizing industrial capitalism, *Communitas* and Paul Goodman's other writings see conflict as necessarily educative (again, the Goodmans' valuation of community as psychotherapy).

Decentralizing technology suggests how efficient this city could be. Energy is already decentralized. Why not production? It is more economical to move material than workers. The labor force can be dispersed and work done according to small-group decisions. Workers would have a say in what they do and how they do it. Moreover, a regionalism based on the union of farm and factory guarantees each unit and area a measure of self-sufficiency and bargaining power in the national economy and politics. The national economy integrates production and exchange, but the Goodmans argue that their plan aims at a different standard of efficiency and a better way of life.

The Goodmans had practical successes at hand. Voluntary agreements, as Kropotkin pointed out, made the European railroad network possible. Ralph Borsodi proved that the small community could develop an interdependent though self-sustaining economy. The kibbutz indicated the long-term future of a cooperative, intentional association. The TVA was American regionalism's triumph. These are not only successful plans but also the achievements of a resourceful, inventive human nature. The community, the city, and the region can reflect as well as serve the whole person. As the authors put it in "Community Buildings" (1954), every "human function— from individual contemplation and creation and domestic life and sexuality to collaboration in industrial production and mass absorption in specta- cle—is by nature a community function. Conversely, the community is nothing but an interrelation of all vital functions. In every activity the sense of community, the integration of all functions, ought to be con- scious—or available to consciousness."[43]

Communities are not nominal entities; their goals are enacted. The task of community (its therapy) is restoring to the individual the authentic environment. Self, community, and region are now linked terms, each invoking the other. Conversely, character is the lived summation of this relationship and the possibilities of reinterpreting this in the future. Again, this is a society of selves, of people engaging each other. As Goodman notes in *Five Years*, "Community might be defined as finding resources in other people, just by their co-presence."[44]

VI

How could literature not be a community idea for Paul Goodman? For all his pronouncements about the meaning of a modern style, about avant- garde art, and about the logic of contemporary fiction, he was more a nineteenth-century writer than not. On the one hand, his novels and short stories are didactic: Goodman tells us, as if he were a modern Tolstoy, how badly we live. On the other hand, his fiction makes psychological conflict the register of the regional society. His protagonists are the community, acting out their character against coercion. And for Goodman, who would inevitably portray coercion as behavior suitable to the State, the tyranny of personal relationships was often depicted as a failure of good will, a lapse of common sense and honor. As a result, his characters are, for all their memorable eccentricities, overbearingly social types. Eliphaz, the Em- pire's financier and Yiddish philosophe, instructs his wards about exchange values in a department store and laments the decline of civilization in a warehouse. Horatio Alger, whom we first meet as a street kid meandering across the city while fleeing the authority of schools, ends as a grown man praying for the success of his citizenship. The "tired man," the narrator of

The City as Self

Making Do, Goodman himself, writes about Goodman the author preaching community and vocation to anyone who listens.

In an argument that weds the development of American nineteenth-century literary aesthetics to gestalt psychology, Goodman insists that art renovate the commonplace. It remains true, as Emerson argued, to the transcendent possibilities paradoxically within the subject, or, in profane terms, true to the *possibilities* we can still entertain for ourselves and the world. In other words, literature asserts faith in engagement. The world and we will "come across." Goodman writes, "An aim, one might almost say the chief aim, of art is to heighten the everyday, to bathe the world in such a light of imagination and criticism that the persons who are living in it without meaning or feeling find that it is meaningful and feelingful to live."[45]

Goodman's fiction had a limited audience. Reading his work is often irritating. Experimental, abrasive, and capricious, his fiction was usually dysynchronous with the literary sensibilities of his time, making it often a tradition of one—Goodman. Influenced, he claimed, by cubism, impressionism, the sonata form, even atonality and a "naturalistic" anarchism, Goodman seemed determined not to let his writing share in the aesthetic and social projects of, for instance, the proletarian fiction of the thirties, the Freudian realism of the forties, or the ahistoricism and later hermeticism of the fifties and sixties.

His work attends to subjects other writers ignored: the need to inherit a city that could enlarge conduct and character. His fiction rarely strays from the city as an agora; the region is the context for life. His works lavishly deal with meetings, lectures, and debates, with colloquys on streets, in apartments, and in classrooms. His descriptions of city doings often turn to the eloquently recreative and ethically critical episodes occurring along the Hudson. The idea of the city and its region is a teaching, could we but know it, and Goodman is the self-appointed visionary proclaiming its messages. With his writing almost wholly given over to what should be termed the rites of the city and how they bring us to maturity, Goodman discovered an entirely new urban scene, though, of course, it was the one he knew as the everyday environment. His oval of vision is his self, and his own sense of freedom became the test of what he felt was problematic in his life.

Goodman's fiction is often thin. His sensibilities are thematic. He has no feel for people who are not exemplars or types. Rarely is he able to create a "full" character defying its creator's theses or reader's expectations. Goodman insisted that his characters behave knowingly: he was their maker and mentor. If there are devils in his work, he claims to know them. His fiction makes *his* solutions sensible if not workable; his prognostications seem sure. No character seriously challenges the legitimacy of the enigmas Goodman finds in the world.

Yet his city novels, *The Empire City* and *Making Do,* illuminate the difficulties of getting on with our lives because of these qualifications. The situations of his fiction and his characters are often audacious, reminding us how Goodman wanted a literature to pierce his audience's sense of normalcy and to make his readers vulnerable to a community beyond themselves. The triumph of Goodman's city fiction rests on this affective claim: the need for a humanizing writing. Early in that chrestomathy of the metropolis, *The Empire City,* a character decides that "a community occasion is under God's providence, but first the occasion must be given."[46] A maxim that might almost have come out of Buber's hasidic parables, this emphasizes Goodman's good sense. There have to be projects that fiction addresses that are also humanly do-able. To his credit, Goodman's fiction has both character and reader confront the conditions of life as they *should* be, given our will. Goodman's protagonists want to be citizens. They are sustained by hope for a community that is both local and universal. In great measure, they invent this community because they identify it with what they believe to be the fully human: individuals in all their powers. Goodman could justify his creation, but Creation would only be justified if providence meets human expectations.

Fabulist, realist, mythographer, Goodman remains almost alone in our time as a celebrant of such an enterprise. His discomfort at being out of place in an age that made it difficult to identify self with city and region, as well as to identify democracy with civic culture ought not to be taken lightly. These are not "postmodernist" concerns as they are defined, but they contest the hegemony of that title. An idea of community remains a concern of modern American letters, in part because of the moment and irritating presence of Goodman's writing.

VII

The Empire City, consisting of *The Grand Piano* (1942), *The State of Nature* (1946), and *The Dead of Spring* (1950) and published in 1959 as a single volume ending with "The Holy Terror" and "Here Begins," is surely one of those overpowering sports in American literature. How does one read it? Its extravagant style trying both to capture and to re-create the meaning of the city and its surroundings, its rendering of public ritual and myth as social amnesia, its Hegelian catalog of facts about the city revealing, gradually, an order of mind—how could these elements not be perplexing? Harold Rosenberg posed, heuristically, *Mardi* as a companion in greatness. [47]

The Empire City describes the journey of "Our Friends," as Goodman affectionately calls its characters, from the late thirties through the early fifties. The novel rejects as protagonists those who find the world absurd and who are devastated by its otherness and intractability. "Our Friends'" growing belief that their common sense and natural powers can sustain them is a modern trial of faith, suggesting what the new city of man portends. These characters experience anxiety but not dread as they summon the resources of their nature. ("Father, guide," Horatio intones.) They create a region of expanding choice and reflection leading to discoveries about autonomy and practical attempts to make a community.

This massive work is epic. Horatio Alger, the work's dominant figure, incarnates the destiny of his circle. His environment, he learns, can be made over to answer to *his* character. The pathos between intention and experience is closed. What he and "Our Friends" come to inhabit is their creation, an honorable community. And an Alger, of course, and his circle are ambitious—ambitious to be of use to their city.

In the first edition of *The Empire City*, Horatio's labor contrasts with that of St. Wayward. The latter, an answer to the age's wish for heroes and the miraculous, perches atop the sculptured horses in Piazza San Marco. In *Five Years*, Goodman writes: "What is most noble in Venice is the *absence* of the centerpiece between the horses of San Marco. . . . When the world again has a center, then we shall put something there. . . . Let me pray: God grant that we—one of our young—will find and place this missing centerpiece between the horses of San Marco."[48] In the revised edition of *The Empire City*, Horatio moves from the backdrop of the city to its forefront as he prays for ground for a next step. The difference in endings suggests Goodman's sense, early and later, of different futures.

Goodman's interpretation of what he saw around him is gnostic. He grappled with what he felt was an intractable culture depriving events of their novelty, and hence, poets of their eloquence. Reality could not be transcribed empirically. It must be constructed as the emergence of the *seemingly* fabulous (though potentially real). Characters who fly in their dreams now fly awake. Those who wish for grace are answered. The book, then, is fond of legends of a golden age in which vocation is possible. Nonetheless, Goodman's writing does not deny the nature of the tragic. His fiction does not forsake his protagonists' agony and society's denial of maturation. Rather, it uses his characters' independence and creativity as a measure of the culture we fabricate.

Characters become reconciled to the only world they have. In doing so, they confront the otherness of the world that they insist yields to their will. However, Goodman's gracing of the ordinary authorizes the richness of what is common. This recognition of the world, as Goodman often reminded his readers, is a paradise of sorts: the only sort given to humans.

The Empire City speaks about those who are initially deprived of power. They are the socially unassimilable—the inventive and creative who try to tend to their own lives yet long for a redeeming city and region. In short, they are urban types dramatizing a social humor.

The city and its region are inseparable from "Our Friends." Goodman is concerned about where and how and for what they work. He dramatizes the moral use of their employment and setting, describing it as either educational or pedestrian. When he describes Manhattan's streets and the Hudson's shoreline, he reminds the reader of early roads to the capital upstate, or to the state of nature itself. When Horatio looks for work in the city or seeks justice in the courts, he sees the city as a pedagogy. For the civil writer's real theme is how one is humanized in a city that is an alma mater.

For an anarchist, how could the city be its coercive institutions? The schools, the courts—these are to be escaped—and they are. Goodman invents no new institutions; he invents, instead, an urban colloquy, a running discourse by free men who want an urban patrimony. This is Goodman's New York. No one, the civic writer argues, willingly forsakes his city. When Eliphaz invites Horatio to gaze out the window at the city and declaims, "I loved as a native son, and now love as a compassionate father, though I am no longer a New Yorker," Goodman writes, reminding us of the preposterousness of this remark, "I am baffled as to the meaning of Eliphaz's statement that he was no longer a New Yorker" (*EC*, 87).

Pacified and distorted, experience under the Empire is experience *of* the Empire. Accepting what the Empire transmits by way of its schools and courts, its language and rationale makes Goodman's characters ill. They find that their speech is as mystifying to themselves as to each other.

As a result, their natures remain mute. "From the very beginning," Lothar, Horatio's older brother (sometimes called Lothair), despairs, "I learned how to warp the language and to aim at ordinary goods by indirection" (*EC*, 205). In a world so narrowed, there is nothing worth looking at and little worth moving toward. Blindness, immobility, and frustration are physical signs of defensive therapy.[49]

With this novel, Goodman wanted to "fashion in our lovely English tongue a somewhat livelier world" and to "impart life to this planet of artifice" (*EC*, 413). The city had to be made over again, by means of a language that could evoke engagement. Self, community, and region had to become realities more concrete and symbolically richer than their conventional, flat connotations. The need to contrast the libertarian with the coerced selves in the Empire accounts for Goodman's rhetorical strategy. The combination of shifting viewpoints, the widening and closing of authorial distance, the use of riddles, graffiti, self-invented myth, and parables define the protagonists within a historical and speculative framework.

Goodman prefaced *The Grand Piano* by recounting the failure of promise that marked his day. The inventiveness of the Paris International style and its political counterparts was spent. The opportunity for artists to speak to their age and community was slender. (Elsewhere, he talked of the "Revolution of the Word," commenting how it heralded an integrated culture "bringing together all times and places as if these things were neighborly here and now.")[50] The book, as he introduces it, is an "Almanac of Alienation" (in its original edition, it was composed of twelve chapters). He called it a "comedy of sociological *humors*" and a "sociological *abstraction*" because motives of character would not be important. (Goodman wanted the book to be practical Dada; he hoped that the novel could be made to explode with firecrackers or sizzlers after it was read.)

The comedy of sociological humors amplifies accidents, the result of overdramatized social causes. In his own interpretation of this genre, Goodman claims that this form of comedy involves us with it because we identify with the *world* of its characters, "which is after all compact of simple childish wants."[51] In *The Grand Piano*, those driving appetites that often seek an innocent fulfillment are deformed by the Empire as a matter of course. Reading the book would be a provisional identification with those subverting society, contingent upon the reader's strength to wrest some comforting meaning from daily life. "I am a regional poet," Goodman announces in the preface, — "of the Empire City—an empire that will *soon* come to be or not." The "or not" heralds either self-creation or State coercion.

Goodman had seen his own development as a writer in terms of stylistic experimentation reflecting his estrangement from his environment. The "Revolution of the Word" had been therapeutic for its readers because it shattered self-rationales: anxiety was released. This, however, occurred in a time when anxiety was tolerable and tolerated. Now, with *The Grand Piano*, Goodman as writer is stymied by Goodman as healer: his art would be out of place. With *The Dead of Spring*, it was. His own passage from naturalism through symbolism to expressionism attempted to close the distance between a culture that made possible the creativity needed to accept the "missing centerpiece" and the intolerable conditions of simple existence.

Describing the first phase of his experimentation, Goodman writes that from 1940 to 1942, the method he developed was an "expressionistic naturalism." He abstracted "the true causes of events" and activated "these in imitation of the likely interplay of causes in the world."[52] There is nothing startling about this statement. It represents an allegiance to the mimetic claims of naturalism in terms of causes not character. Yet its significance is psychological. Expressionistic naturalism became, he writes, "the last stage of the withdrawal that was already apparent in the innocent naturalism. But now the scene was not even admitted to be *my* scene. . . . I was impatient to present anything but its schematism, which I analyzed and abstracted with the more ferocity in order to put it in *its* place, and what had that to do with me?"[53] In fact, the original edition of *The Grand Piano* stopped short of letting *its* characters accept the world of the Empire by ending on "a note lower than normalcy

&

ALSO

FLAT."[54]

Subtitled "Before a War" (in the 1959 edition of *The Empire City*), the book ignores the concrete politics of the thirties and forties. For all of Goodman's explications of how we do in fact live, there is little, if anything, in the book that suggests the nightmare of European politics or even New Deal liberalism. His characters exist in a less specific environment, one that might satisfy his own rationale about the abstraction of cause. Goodman's concern is with what he calls sociolatry: the acceptance of *the* State. The drama of *The Grand Piano* occurs as human nature clashes with its

State-given role. The title of the book was chosen because it speaks to this conflict of nature against convention. What could be a more artificial designation of any polity than a mechanism? "Society," Goodman writes, "is supposed to be a community of the people making the society, and that's not a musical instrument."[55]

In summary, *The Grand Piano* deals with Horatio Alger, who has walked out of a primary school resembling a madhouse. His brother, Lothar, and his sister, Laura, are in, but not of, the State. They make sure their connections are as attenuated as possible. Lothar is unable to register for the draft, and Laura, like her brothers, lives on the dole. The plot turns on the various arguments and means used by society at large, and in large, namely the millionaire Eliphaz, to entrap the Algers within the system. They must be made to feel at one with the aims, if not with the low spirits of the Empire. Naturally, Goodman's Algers resist. Good community anarchists, they believe voluntary association is *the* fundamental American politics, not identification with mass society.

The novel opens upon Maimonides' injunction in the Mishnah Torah against making idols: "Whoever makes an idol for others, although he is punished with stripes, is nevertheless allowed remuneration for his labors. The reason is that an idol does not become forbidden till it is completed, and the last tap of the hammer is worth less than a perutah."[56] A commentary on reification and estrangement, Maimonides' words are also a demand for judging the particular society that we have made. What are the uses of alienation? How can we meet the world in the confidence given us by our nature? And what is the meaning of this assuredness?

The Grand Piano invokes the major theme of the bourgeois novel: who shall inherit the house of rule? Goodman explores this concern's now trivial nature by arguing that society is not worth inheriting. The novel places before us Horatio literally reading the city's doings as the city has come to present itself. "THERE'S PLENTY OF TROUBLE" and "VICE SQUAD ROUND-UP" are the headlines he mouths, teaching himself to read. But as Goodman would ask, reading for what? And what should be looked at? Characters have a hard time seeing what others accept as normal. Mynheer, Laura's would-be lover and Horatio's seductive teacher, has "No eyes in his head." Lothar, unable to give a dignified answer to the draft board, leaves the interview "waving his hands in front of his eyes." Eliphaz has "merry black eyes" though what he wants to gaze upon is the purity of objects deprived of their economic meanings.

At the height of his powers, Horatio is not resigned to "second-best

choices." Cynicism preserves his autonomy. His maxims are a social physics of wariness: "Budge Only for Folding Money," "Never Let On," and
"One Thing Leads to Another." His slogans tell us how often private life
must remain private. In this city, unlike in what Goodman interprets as
Athens, it is hard for someone to be at ease in any place. Morality, as
Henry Adams had feared, has become police. Detectives, social workers,
and truant officers are the instruments of social cohesion.

Yet Horatio preserves his instincts, and his adventures in the city as-
tonish his older friends whose lives are boring. The city is Alger's teacher.
He deciphers the meanings of the city by living in it, by asking questions of
it. He has learned something about construction by watching buildings go
up; grammar, the "spelling and punctuation of the *Herald Tribune* style
book," by reading newspapers; physics, by playing handball.

What Horatio must learn, Mynheer instructs, is the "Habit of Freedom." Horatio will have to know how to sabotage or circumvent the state's
bureaucracy on any needful occasion. Later, Mynheer quickly sketches
the educative city, a project synonymous with much of Goodman's own
writing and reminiscent of Randolph Bourne's *The Gary Schools* and
Dewey's *Schools of Tomorrow*. Using an image of the ego guarding the
instincts, Mynheer envisions gangs of six or so children, guided by shep-
herds who would protect them, "accumulating experiences tempered to
their powers." Children, learning how the city functions, may ask how it
should be made to function. In one of the novel's most poignant scenes,
Goodman describes the high moment of civic conduct, the right kind of
appropriation of the city. "Local Patriotism" celebrates the consequences
of this natural education in community. Of Laura and Mynheer, Goodman
writes that on a

> glittering morning they would be standing on a height overlooking New
> York . . . and she would praise the good features of the city ("my own neighbor-
> hood where I am inscribed on the rolls!"), and not mention the bad features. She
> would praise the dramatic juxtaposition of the heights and the rivers, and the
> concrete-and-steel engineering that bound them together.
> But he would look at her dumb with love because she was praising her native
> neighborhood. (*EC*, 59)

Yet the characters of this novel are exiles. Some are estranged from their
own nature; others, from the city around them. As a result, they cannot act
within the existing world. For practical purposes, they are characters
without selves. Arthur Eliphaz, the millionaire's feckless child, is incapable of dealing with what is concrete. He wishes for pure desire, but cannot

choose or love what exists. "What Arthur wanted," Goodman observes, is "to be able to say, 'I love you—it's nothing personal'" (*EC*, 93). Eliphaz, master and symbol of the imperial exchange, wishes to undo the work of creation, to return from the sixth to the first day. He dreams of converting everything into its pure exchange value (zero) and removing all things from the marketplace. He serves as the daemon of chaos, but points to a time when all things will have the integrity of their being.[57] Mynheer, unable to accept what he sees (and this includes the only world we have), is a metaphysically stateless person. He is a citizen yearning for a situation.

An opera raising the issues of individuals engaged with the community inspirits "Our Friends." The grand piano is artifice; *The Mastersingers* is commentary. Goodman has his characters glimpse a celebration of what could be theirs. With this scene, he becomes a community poet. He is intrusive, asserting his right to be part of the occasion. Insistently, he reminds the reader of stories that affirm human powers.

As the opera begins, Goodman's characters talk about the contests of love and personal fulfillment. Amidst their discussion of the opera's resolution, Goodman urges upon the reader the importance of this and in fact any presentation of fraternity. You can "slip into that world of social peace on its red-letter day," he writes. Hinting at his own recognition that with this novel he would still not have an audience, Goodman has Mynheer wryly point out that art is unable to challenge successfully the Empire's public: "You'd be surprised to study into what a perfect acquiescence the enormities of my friends Jean and Franz and Paul Klee were allowed to fall with a dull thud" (*EC*, 106).

Goodman's concern with his audience counterpoints Eliphaz's ambitions to enslave those who resist being part of the sociolatry. The Algers will be seduced into becoming representative citizens. His attempt to squeeze a grand piano into their apartment and make them people of property is a parody of the opera. It also is a mild refutation of the Marxist claim that the false needs generated by capitalism overwhelm the individual. For Goodman, the Algers are in touch with their natures, resisting Eliphaz's material temptations.

Even though Eliphaz announces that Horatio will have the piano and be his heir—and this means he will own a large part of the city—Horatio insists the piano must be won in contest. However, ownership of society, its "thingness," is Goodman's point. Twisting the theme of actual Horatio Alger novels in which the city can be owned, Goodman asks who could resist this possession? Horatio can. There is nothing to gain by alienation disguised as social harmony. He has wired the piano with explosives. Yet some of "Our Friends" do perform, as Horatio wires and unwires notes. Emily, a social worker, plays Poulenc whose "simple-minded" music is a refuge for the wounded spirit. Lothar, powerless to change what is around him, allows himself a "limited chaos in order to create a world." Shrewd and empathetic, Horatio senses the flatness of the adults. "This is," he realizes, "what it meant to be grown up." The revised edition ends with a completed act. Goodman has Horatio break the conventions of his environment—unlike his peers of a later generation in *Growing Up Absurd*. Horatio plays his animal spirits, ending with a fortissimo silence. Literally playing his nature, he has triumphed in the Empire's battle for him.

Goodman has the crowd laugh, the music deflating their "sadnesses to nothing." Clumsily or craftily, the laughter is Goodman's insistence that there be relief, that instinct be released. As he put it, writing about the comedy of humors: "At the deflation the comic characters are destroyed; they carry off with them the shame and the base imputation. But the point is that what is left is not nothing, but normal persons, we ourselves—nobody has been hurt."[58] Here, of course, there is no unity of character, and no one is destroyed. In fact, the novel ends with the presence of Horatio and his circle; it is the reader who has to leave the scene.

With *The State of Nature*, Goodman committed himself to a more fundamental rhetorical and political strategy. He would turn to the classical point of departure for political philosophy: he would write about the origins of the city and the authentic community. As an anarchist and regionalist, he describes their destruction by the State. Horatio and his elders can undo the society that is given to them, one "organized as a factory and a market"—so Goodman informs the reader at the beginning of the novel. Surviving the war, his characters come out of a wilderness of rubble to found a new community based upon what they value most about their selves and upon what they believe is common to all people. Again, this is Goodman's hope for the libertarian community. This is a fragile, if unrealizable, wish even for the novelist as mythologist. The novel closes with a wedding, interrupted by what Goodman felt was the message of the late forties. Millions will die of the "Asphyxiation"; government will be "one anonymous front"; vocation will be impossible. Community will exist only by determined opposition to the State.

To read this novel, therefore, is to plunge into a social poetics: Goodman acts as a Hesiod explaining why the story of community must be remembered. The title of the novel points to the opportunities Goodman creates for "Our Friends." He liberates them from the social contract, boldly giving them a chance to succeed where, he felt, society had failed. Horatio, called "our heir," must discover what healthy engagement is, and *that* is the state of nature. By acting, to borrow Goodman's phrase, in nature and freedom, the burden of history is thrown off. Self-fabrication is the only theogony. What good was it to talk of a new society if it was a variation of the old? "Reflections on Drawing the Line" contended that "a free society cannot be the substitution of a 'new order' for the old order; it is the extension of spheres of free action until they make up most of the social life."[59]

The section headings of the book move didactically from "The Weakness of the Ego" to "The Strength of the Ego," from the discovery that society has damaged the organization of the psyche to the reassurance that the ego can guide instinct. Goodman wanted our fear to give way to "joy and creation." This confident reading of what the struggles of the past were about and *should have been about* is Goodman at his best.

Yet the major ironies of *The State of Nature* are the absences of a practical community actually living and acting in freedom beyond the initial moments of its creation. "Our Friends" are defeated. At its beginning and at its end, the tragedy of the book is the destruction of natural association. Lothar is prevented from serving society as best he can; Laura, now an architect, disguises buildings from air raids; Horatio has to escape from the city. These are the obvious instances of coercion but they become, in Goodman's book, chances for "Our Friends" to undo the State's repression. In fact, the first edition of *The State of Nature* ends with Mynheer's voicing Goodman's thesis. "By Liberty," Mynheer reminds us, "I mean releasing the forces of original nature; and by Equality, that men exist; and by Fraternity, the fact that by setting excellence against excellence they produce what was not known before."[60]

Here and again is Goodman's argument for a new revolution, human rather than conventionally political. Progressive political thought has been drained of its strength, he contends. It defends and rationalizes sociolatry by appealing to its power rather than undermining its significance. A better politics founded upon the true self is community invention. In fact, Goodman's characters struggle against the Empire's apparatus by defending their nature. Since desirable conduct is State behavior, "Our Friends" have to find out what is authentic about their lives.

A good part of this novel dramatizes, as Horatio points out, a city that is "as grand as a department store." And this is the least compelling part of the book. *Communitas* makes this point though even there it was hardly a revelation. What is unique in this novel, however, is the battle and victory Goodman gives to his protagonists, emancipating their struggle from the context of social realism. *The State of Nature* argues that the politics of autonomy is visionary. A literature of fable about what humans actually are challenges the custodial dogmas of the State and its literature.

In this city akin to the fevered metropolis of *Communitas*, education holds the individual hostage to the State. Wants generated by the marketplace have become confused with needs, original nature with convention. In contrast, the nameless war Goodman describes forces us to know what we *will*. Fear, at least, is a feeling; combat is, at least, commitment. Arthur, later killed in the war, rewrites the opening of Genesis: commitment is creation. "That God created the world at a blow—and made the grass spring on the hillside!" he explains: "He committed Himself. Such a blow, out of all the possibilities of being or not-being, is a commitment! And soon it is storming at every heart!" (*EC*, 175). This is also Goodman's commentary on Maimonides' epigraph appended to *The Grand Piano*. Creation is not idolatry; it binds the maker to his nature.

"Our Friends" escape the authoritarianism of the Empire by insurrection and, later, through its devastation. Goodman describes their acts expressionistically. For instance, in images representing the relation of ego and instinct, Goodman depicts Lothar freeing animals from the zoo; Mynheer becomes their protector. That Goodman saw this rhetoric as necessary suggests the impasse confronting him. By rejecting the sensibilities of realism, *The State of Nature* found it easy to invert realism's ironic and major theme, that of social maturation. Traditionally, the young man from the provinces who makes his way in society by duplicity sees civic life as worthwhile struggling *within* if only to have an object for his energy. For "Our Friends," however, faith in the restorative power of their natures supplants the politics of the conventional realistic novel. Horatio is the young man from the city wanting to return to the condition of existence in which all social relations have to be reinvented.

Fleeing the Empire City's soldiers patrolling the city's boundaries, Horatio runs along the Hudson shore. In a short, quickening passage, Goodman speaks of the barriers placed in the way of renewal. The fences and railroad lines around the Hudson are literal and conceptual walls barring citizens from their regional estates and instinctual natures. Horatio, fighting to keep his freedom as he walks waist deep in the lordly river, hears Goodman's voice: "It's around the next bend that you must change from convention to nature." Making his way to Harry Tyler, a patriot by disposition, Horatio passes from a society besieging itself (the classical image of the tyrannical psyche) to a natural existence. Horatio enters America's past of salutary anarchism.

"Our Friends" refuse to build a postwar society. They choose, instead, to create an intentional community. Goodman's neofunctionalist criteria guide arrangements for living. Peter Ringland explains the relation of his machines to the human body and praises industrial designs that are easily comprehended. Laura plans a town square that will encourage friendship. Lothar, trying to relearn a language that he has forgotten, affirms its power to express what humankind is. The first words he utters are "Yes, men and women, people." However, the novel ends with a literal fall. Hearing the prophecy of Eliphaz—"You are going to live in the Sociolatry"—Laura faints.

The Dead of Spring offers the reader a countermovement: rising, levitation, and flying are the book's metaphors for transcendence and happiness. This work is Goodman's "mourning labor": it deals with Horatio's problem "of how, these days, to be in love," amidst the suicide (of Laura), cancer (of Emilia), deformation (of Droyt and Lefty), and blindness (his own) of "Our Friends."[61] *Gestalt Therapy* points to the limits of creative adjustments the self can make in a hostile world. *The Dead of Spring* depicts this boundary situation. People suffer from civil society. Goodman's fable of a golden age could not sustain this novel. Now, the novelist's imagination surrenders to the authoritarianism and comprehensiveness of the imperial city. *The Dead of Spring* ironically begins with a community meeting that has come to a dead standstill. "We have exhausted the strength of fraternity," Goodman observes. The book raises Emerson's questions in "The American Scholar." What if no synthetic, heroic act occurs to integrate the explosive American penchant for doing and evaluating? In what ways would a culture of the new further separate itself from, and ultimately war against, human nature?

In *The Dead of Spring*, Emerson's foreboding is a problem to be confronted with the understanding that the only tradition accessible and helpful is the one to be discovered. Goodman as healer demands that people invent a therapy that undermines conventional normalcy, making them able to engage their environment. Radical anthropology demands that individuals originate their own behavior. Goodman, speaking of Horatio in terms applicable to his friends, proposes that he must learn again to express his feelings without panic. "When we try to do a natural act or come to a natural learning we are stricken with anxiety. And these joint causes, not knowing the real words and guilty paralysis" of expression have crippled the community (*EC*, 334). Emily and Lothar cannot copulate even though they long for a child. Their friends have to be instructed in how to eat (a gestaltist example of assimilating the environment). Horatio, blind because there is nothing of importance to look at, has to be taught to see.

Mynheer's observation, that no matter how inconsolable they are, simple acts of nature are practical and communalizing, is Goodman's theme. Set against much of the arid prose of the novel, "An Urban Pastoral" gracefully portrays the wedding of self and city. In this case, the city is "Our Friends'" mentor. Goodman portrays the city as a Futurist would. He praises the speed and roar of the subway; the patterns made by city lights; the efficiency of city marketing. Yet Horatio and Rosalind do not know how to bind their love for the authentic city to their love for each other. Affection has to be learned; figuratively they must move up and down Plato's ladder, stepping from the love for a beautiful self to the love for one's city, surrendering themselves to the compulsion to apprehend the good.

Bufano, composer and avatar of opera bouffe, pushes them together. Bufano instructs them, urging that they look at what they usually ignore— city streets:

> Your friends say these people are dead, but you see there's nothing but life, stories, imagination, form, color, rhythm and harmony.
> It's the outpouring of fruitless longing, that must be stayed with some feeling or other. By fruitless longing I do not mean what is not satisfied, but what does not want to be satisfied. . . . Without the excitement of these arts everybody would lie down and stifle. (*EC*, 372–73)

Bufano's ballet, with Rosalind as its star, is a recovery of graceful human movement. Within the Empire, people can be reminded of a desirable way of life. In *The Grand Piano*, the revelation of community was frozen in opera. In *The Dead of Spring*, art makes the audience become aware of its own life.

Tried for persistent treason (he has never registered with the State), Horatio announces he is in love. His outburst is a proclamation of man for himself. For Horatio is aflame with what he has seen in the city, and "his body spoke what he did not know he knew" (*EC*, 319). At a given point, being itself draws the line. Nature heals. "What is needed from us," Horatio teaches his detractors, "is to stand out of the way, to allow a little freedom for the regenerative forces (no forces of ours), and in heaven's name, an abeyance of the pathological pressure" (*EC*, 388). So Goodman's anarchist-gestalt politics refutes the "Dilemma." If one conforms, one is sick; if one does not conform, one is demented because there is no other society.

"Lothair's Couvade," the last chapter, dramatizes the practical way out of "fruitless longing." What is this but self-constriction? In this city, boredom is the only feeling Lothar can cling to, expecting yet ignoring what is really happening. Stung by this revelation, he looses his grip upon himself. Restoration of community will begin with self-healing.

"The Holy Terror" (subtitled "Modern Times") continues Goodman's quarrel with society. The vocation of man is a fitting theme for this section of *The Empire City*. What is socially desirable and what is human have to be distinguished. The whole man must oppose the socially acceptable one. Somehow, the grand civic patriotism that nurtures character must inspire a protagonist to redeem the city.

Collapsed possibilities mark our day; our slogans are a truth "fit for pigs." *The Grand Piano* is an "Almanac of Alienation." "I now am concluding with a kind of Register of Reconciliation, a Domesday Book," Goodman writes, pointing out that "commonplace matter is my theme" (*EC*, 427). The commonplace is providential: knowing how we must comport ourselves, we find that we can. This, of course, is Goodman's guiding faith. As he explains it, drawing upon the traditions of American pragmatism and existential theology: "In its trials and conflicts the self is coming to be in a way that did not exist before. In contactful experience the 'I' alienating its safe structures, risks this leap and identifies with the growing self, gives it its services and knowledge, and at the moment of achievement stands out of the way."[62] At the end of the novel, Horatio makes his own leap of faith and confidence. He prays for ground "for a next step."

Vocation is more than a reconciliation of individual to world. It is a reparation of the world. It insistently calls for the fraternity of man to be realized. Acting for one's self is acting on behalf of others as well. This paradoxical situation makes the future discontinuous with the past, giving it an "otherness" that summons our faith. "Our Friends" fight not only for themselves but now, ethically, for the impoverished character of others. Their yearning to be civic patriots is a recognition of how mutely others suffer as well, for citizenship completes the unfinished revolutions that make for anxiety in our day.

Chapters entitled "Conversing," "Dancing," "Eating," and "Relaxing," form the section "Neolithic Rites" describing the outward movement of the protagonists. Learning about themselves, they can minister to those around them. Community occasions can be willed. Horatio and Rosalind complete their friendship by marriage. Antonicelli and Minetta develop a therapy for their patients that pushes them into both the city and a struggle for a decent public life.

The search for the "real" situation liberating natural powers is shared by Horatio and his friends. He wakes one morning realizing that he is voting for the "General." He discovers himself reading the *Herald Tribune* and accepting the apathy of the Empire. His argument, "It's more important to have common sense, honor and eros" restores him to sanity (*EC*, 544). Wayward, exemplifying Freud's dictum that no man is truly free until his father is dead, murders Lothar. Mynheer describes his adventure to a corner of the universe (in effect, a fable about curiosity in this world), comprehending that his affections have to be lavished upon the community of "Our Friends."

What happiness can be gotten from our "only world" is the theme of Droyt's account of his brother, Lefty. The tale is simple. It affirms the power of man as creator, as progenitor. Horatio sums up Droyt's report with this commentary: "you have come to us with a marvelous story. We find it hard to believe our ears. You speak of a free artist who has an immediate audience; of lovers who wish each other well; of a man who gets paid for a useful job that fits him; of the confidence that there will be some use for another human being in the world. . . . It means that all along the time a certain number of people are not committing an avoidable error" (*EC*, 578).

This achievement deserves Goodman's accolades, but after all, it is Goodman's invocation of the fabulous: a recognition of the therapy the community writer offers. Lefty's triumph out of socially absurd conditions encourages the other characters to resolve their own exasperating situations. A community meeting ("like the olden times," Goodman notes) is called to discuss the general impasse. *"The irresistible force has met the immovable obstacle: what to do?"* (*EC*, 587).

Community wisdom, in this case a combination of gestalt therapy and common sense, points to the community of "Our Friends." They will to form it. Their maxims—"Go about your business" (know what is given to you by your nature); "Have another ounce of strength" (persist in disheartening times); "Get a handyman" (find a mentor who can teach you what the field of action actually is)—are means shot through with ends. Unlike the theses of contemporary letters arguing for the irrelevancy of meaning in the engagement of self and world, *The Empire City* proposes that there is no other project. Its ending emphasizes this. The community meeting is the background for Horatio's resolve: he will battle a society that degrades the self by making its nature inauthentic. Horatio prays for ground for a "next step."

Throughout the course of the Empire City novels, Horatio and his friends turn their love for the city into a solidarity with all that they believe is human. The city that confronts them as a place in which to wander gives way to their need to appropriate its civil culture, and finally, is seen in the light of their commitments to make it over into a new city of and for all. Community *is* their labor and in a Pauline way, it is a beloved and loving community committing itself to what is significant in life: the empowerment of the true self.

Yet this strenuously made proposition had no then contemporary analogues in American fiction. *The Empire City* remains an interim fiction, an urgent task undertaken in the absence of interested writers. At present, the book has almost vanished. Like much of Goodman's writings, it is out of print, still without its audience.

VIII

The only novel Goodman wrote after *The Empire City* is *Making Do*. It has earned the reputation of being his least attractive novel. Its plot seems as mechanical as its characters seem unendurable. "Our Friends" of *The Empire City* find that their irascible persistence makes a difference in the life of the city.

Making Do is deprived of the richness of Goodman's rhetorical experimentation, as well as the allure (or crankiness) of his fables. The novel describes an incurious landscape. There is little in the city and in the New Jersey community called Vanderzee (in reality, Hoboken) that sustains the will to civility. The city and community are depicted as coercive and debasing. The police courts, the ineffective university symposia, the tedious life of the narrator, the cynical politicians and salesmen make the environment barren. The inspirited meetings of *The Empire City* are replaced by almost furtive and private colloquys as characters discover that they simply cannot find a way to sustain a community. Looming over all their doings is the threat of the Cold War: nuclear testing has resumed.

Yet characters who would be marginal in other novels insofar as they resist civil society are, in this novel, representatives of those caught in the social contract. The misguided teenagers, the Puerto Rican child hustlers, the stoned would-be poets, and the sexually dysfunctional serve Goodman's teachings well. They point out that being absorbed into an urban economy cannot protect them from the State's coercion. The scars that mark these individuals—an inability to speak, an ethical incapacity to imagine a world of others, impotency—are failures of humans to define themselves and create their environment. Goodman asks, How can "normal" politics or "usual" work resolve the difficulties besetting a self unable to know and express its needs?

Making Do is ambitious in other ways. It is an American testament weaving together hope for and identification with one's city and region. Classic and modern aspirations for a redeeming city of humanity drive Goodman as writer and narrator to assess the culture of the Cold War and the possibilities for a life of significance. Diotima's instruction of Socrates, John Robinson's exhortation to the Pilgrims founding a kingdom of the faithful, and Professor Davidson's loving praise of the traditions of scholarly commitment become civic instructions to those populating *Making Do*. We have an opportunity, Goodman insists, for America to become again experimental, to test its principles by reviving the congregationalist anarchism and regionalism of the early Colonial period. The book's characters *will* to belong to their city, whereas their failures, so Goodman intimates, point to the retrograde situation of American life. They have never fully matured. We are presented with a collection of well-intentioned individuals who cannot make their private interests cohesive enough to form the voluntary, ethical associations—the anarchist communities— that Goodman praises in his reading of the autonomous, associative spirit. Yet before we dismiss these inhabitants too quickly because of their derelictions and abnormalities, we should remember that Goodman saw the struggles of so-called outcasts in American history as signs of the meanness and poverty of an official culture.

The plot of *Making Do* is contrived and symmetrical so that the repetition of an action and the restatement of a crisis augment common failure and disappointment. Goodman as the "tired man" recounts his involvement with a group of younger people who have migrated from New York to Vanderzee. On the one hand, he tries to protect Meg and her baby from her demented husband, Amos, who is believed to be stalking her. On the other hand, he is the mentor of an anguished college dropout, Terry, who moves from Columbus, Ohio, to Vanderzee and discovers what a true community is. Out of desperation, he invents it. The narrator's care embraces Jason, a college instructor who cannot finish his dissertation and temporizes about marrying his pregnant girlfriend, Connie, who, in turn, worries if she should have Jason's baby, and Harold, an electronics worker whose need for love is accompanied by humiliation and danger from the adolescent hustlers he keeps. By the novel's end, Terry is committed to an institution; Harold and Meg are betrayed to the police by Harold's child consort; the "tired man" can't effectively intervene in the chaos around him.

The book opens upon and elaborates throughout the character of the unfinished act, specifically its signification of the thwarted, punitively stifled satisfaction of the self. Jason's scopophilia, Meg's sexual passivity, Harold's reluctance to accept his nature, and Terry's inability to stop his self-destruction illustrate these characters' inability to have their natures guided by the strengths of their ego. They are unable to commit themselves to an act that redefines themselves and their surroundings. *Making Do*, then, is an apt title for this book. The first chapter is entitled "hammering out a rule of thumb," taking us back to Maimonides' epigraph in *The Grand Piano*. The State is, and should remain, here, a human creation.

Meg, never far from her infant, is afraid that Amos will return and shoot her. The "tired man" and Harold stand guard. The wearying lookout for someone who can end their suspense prefigures a series of urban encounters (students looking for mentors, lovers seeking each other, even police closing in) that tests the first criterion of freedom—the hope of autonomy must be sustained. The demanding habit of anarchy must be kept. "We couldn't call the police," the narrator recollects, "because we were anarchists and pacifists and didn't believe in policemen, we did not want them messing in our lives which were innocent but in many ways illegal."[63]

The narrator's weariness becomes a loving allegiance to the nature of his city. A Socratic, urban walker whose *paideia* is the city, the narrator hopes that he will be consecrated by a vision of the good itself. Even though he remains caught on a rung of Plato's ladder, as he puts it, he recounts Diotima's instruction of Socrates. Goodman reminds us that "man's eros turns to the institutions and customs of the city" (*MD*, 274).

This is an unusual account of a self in the modern city. But the city of *Making Do* is where the search for the good does occur. The city is, ultimately, a recognition of the humanly attainable good itself. To apprehend urban life at its best is to be purified of those derelictions that detract from community. Free association, a civic culture that nurtures a public, and cooperation call into being the city which in turn is a mentor for community. This is Goodman at his best even though at its suggestive level the book does little to represent the more practical notions of urban planning found in *Communitas* and his fugitive essays on architecture.

Whereas *Making Do* may be, next to *The Empire City*, our time's most intense novel about a voluntary urban community, it can hardly pose—even in its rhapsodies—as an adequate strategy for making the city a conceptual whole for the reader. This central irony was not lost on Goodman. The narrator has problems seeing, and the quest for community is also a kind of a blindness, albeit a necessary blindness. It is not surprising that Amos is first given credit for trying to form a community, although he needs a "building sacrifice"—his wife. Rescuing Amos's rage for the sake of its attenuated reason, the narrator contends that Amos "could not tolerate that people should continue as they were: he generously had to offer them what they did not know enough to want" (*MD*, 8). His desire for a ritual that makes fraternity sacred is an evocation of a persistent human longing. Even crazy, he knows that someone has to remedy the fragmentation of human nature. He urges a return, like his namesake, to a life in which the plowman shall overtake the reaper. He is not stalking his wife, however, but is in a new promised land, Israel, committed there to an insane asylum.

Pointing out what people need but cannot articulate is Goodman's novelistic strength. He can elaborate upon their infirmities. Harold "*made* himself stupid, the way he kept the parts of himself out of touch with one another" (*MD*, 5); Meg loves the narrator because he "drew her out of her speechlessness" (6); Terry has denied his own brightness for he has "never studied a subject, never lost himself in a stroke of art or discovery, never acted like a citizen" (75). The failure of these characters to recognize what they long for ends in pathos. By virtue of their incompleteness, they refuse to sustain their community.

Their moral incompleteness reveals their slender psychic resources; it also signifies a culture that makes growing up a disinheritance of nature. Elsewhere, Goodman remained unconvinced that ignorance and violence were revolutionary acts. The withdrawal and asociality preached by then contemporary leaders of youth movements had no commanding value.[64] In *Making Do*, the prospects for vocation abound and the chance for meaningful work energizes the narrator.

Making Do might well have been provisional therapy for Goodman; for the narrator it is *actual* therapy. He contends: "I had too much real work to do in America to be exhausted by the inevitable fuck-ups of my young friends and these hang-ups of my older friends who should have known better than to marry crazy persons. Yet I could not stay away . . . because any vitality that there was in my work came from my contact with my friends, such as they were" (*MD*, 3).

The hazards of urban life and mental health (one of the conferences the narrator speaks at is called "Urban Environment and Mental Health") exemplify a vulgar civility. The police harass Vanderzee's bohemians; academics shy away from controversy; public, genteel conversation at symposia stymies urgent, exciting discussion; politicians disregard the common good. As a result, Goodman's protagonists come to accept frustration and duplicity as the normal state of affairs.

There is a justice to this reading of city doings though Goodman often overdetermines a situation, making it silly or worse. The difference between the extreme and the probable is lost. Turning from his generous, earlier use of myth in *The Empire City* that transformed a shrewd political observation into an illumination about the nature of culture, Goodman's theses now seem to commit him to describing occasions that can only justify his distaste for the State. "The police," the narrator tells us, " . . . were torturing the screaming children of the poor" (*MD*, 8). And the police "of Vanderzee . . . Madrid, Warsaw, Moscow were the instrument of the worldwide system of states in which man was hounded from one baroque jurisdiction to another . . ." (9). These rhetorical tactics in which distinctions collapse and people are seen either as prisoners or as refugees are foolish, yet they are also tropes of a moral imagination aggressively opposing the idea of coercion.

Goodman has some self-obvious complaints: the values of the city are not maintaining human nature at all. The "tired man" recounts that "suburban flight and urban housing, narcotics and narcotics laws (as usual the laws were more of a problem than the delinquencies), lifeless jobs and a phony standard of living, traffic congestion and bad schools and segregation and the lapse of citizenly initiative—all these were only properties of the kind of community that we had" (*MD*, 41). Goodman as therapist wishes for the promised city and restores to the reader the aspirations of its thinkers. Whereas the impossibility of love is the impasse of modern times (as "Our Friends" have discovered), the "tired man" is guided by and incarnates the spirit of Eros. A genuine civic life, Goodman claims, wars against the soporific charms of the commercial city. Paraphrasing Diotima's words to Socrates, the narrator, who "did not love" is recalled to *his* being:

201

My crowded days were this love affair with my city, a thorny adventure, but often I was so busy at it that I didn't know whether I was unhappy or happy, and that meant, I suppose, that I was sometimes happy.

But at last, said Plato, a man begins to have intimations of God in whom the city exists, and he comes to love Him. And presumably God comes across. (*MD*, 274)

"Presumably" is the catchword. Anticipation and expectation are significant characteristics of the religious experience. In *The Empire City*, Horatio calls upon the Creator Spirit for ground for a "next step"; the characters of *Making Do* take that step. Goodman's rational anarchist, like Kierkegaard's knight of faith, lives a public vocation. He is the model for a differing life. The narrator's self-assumed task also is the making of a new public—the like-minded, here—and he begins a therapy for his Vanderzee friends making their selves and world desirable.

Communitas described community arrangements and designs that maintained the independence of the ego. *The Empire City* portrayed Horatio's repugnance at second-best choices. *Making Do*, with little significant difference, argues that vocation is possible only insofar as a true human nature is realized. This is presented by fiat: Goodman insists that somehow this does happen. *Natura sanat* is his gestaltist metaphysics. The narrator tells the reader: "I did not trust to let the nature of things be, although it certainly worked out according to its nature, in spite of all my efforts" (*MD*, 274).

In *The Empire City* self-creation let Goodman create a rhetoric of the fabulous so that character and mythology reinforce the appearance of the whole man. He is as real as he is timeless. In *Making Do*, this new man is impossible. Modern civil society smothers the appetites and contacts of the self so that instinct and ego are estranged. Goodman's protagonists can't answer their needs; they have been trained to be wary of them, to suffer them.

The transforming powers of the Socratic eros are damaged. Language and sexuality reveal a character's helplessness. Terry does not know how to ask for help; his girlfriend, Joanna, becomes "depersonalized" when Terry admits he loves the narrator; Dr. Blumberg, an educator who makes the rounds of conferences and symposia, cannot directly answer the questions he is asked. Dr. Davidson, a Nobel laureate physicist and Terry's professor, is at a loss to find the right words to deal with Terry. The numerous panels the narrator is invited to can't reach an audience beyond the room. Conclusions seem impractical and will not be tried. Eloquence and pertinence are irrelevant.

The City as Self

The impotence of language to re-create experience is part of the sexual agonies of the narrator's friends. Jason is indifferent about the birth of his child; Harold is victimized by those he loves; Meg is sexually exploited. Rabbinic and radical here as elsewhere, Goodman argues that language and sexuality are the agents of self- and community-creation. The sexual and linguistic trials of the characters in *Making Do* mark their temporizing about living within the legacy of the community.

Making *his* own vocation important for and in the novel, Goodman has Terry quote Goodman the social thinker: a community is people using each other as resources. The work confronting the "tired man" is making the people of the novel recognize their own salutary nature. Advising, teaching, making love, using a diction that is a witness to one's being—these, the novelist points out, should be redeeming. The claims the characters make upon each other are those of *menschlichkeit*. Whereas the narrator easily despairs over his unseemly lover, it is Terry, careless in most things, who emancipates his older mentor from an importunate life. "I need his health," the narrator confesses. Similarly, Meg reminds Harold that he can commit himself to his feelings, rather than be shamed by his acts. Professor Davidson argues that nature indeed is ordered: it comes across. Terry, in turn, makes Professor Davidson aware that scientific activity must be governed by moral criteria; Davidson joins the demonstration against the bomb.

In *Making Do*, fraternity is an affective idea; fraternity itself is only temporary. *"You said we had to be careful, for the community"*: Terry's own preaching provides the cautionary note for the book. The novel's characters jeopardize the trust and friendship of one another because they are not practical minded enough, not cunning enough to hide their aspirations. For example, consulting with Meg's lawyer in order to win her battle for custody of her child, they tediously debate whether the court is true to American ideals, whether they, as anarchists, can testify in a court, and so on. Some simply cannot be "good" character witnesses because they are good people, following their sexual and social inclinations. They are not naifs whose affection and innocence condemn pretense. Instead, they are always perplexed that integrity counts for naught. In fact, their associations do not collapse; they are betrayed. Involvement with drugs, petty theft, and juvenile delinquency invites the police, the lawyers, and the authority of the city.

In *The Empire City*, the Algers reject Elpihaz's offer of bourgeois life, the grand piano. They turn the piano to their own ends by sleeping under

203

and on it, and, later, by wiring it with dynamite. In contrast, *Making Do* contends that people no longer have enough imagination to preserve their integrity. The Vanderzee group is all too responsive to society.

Predictably, the narrator grows bored at having to aid this helpless circle at the expense of his energy. As the need for and talk about community increase, its opportunities diminish. The fraternity and inventiveness that Goodman argued were found in free associations are here neither communalizing nor actual. The narrator and his friends are isolated from the public they wish to teach and from each other. The peace demonstrations "exerted no influence: they meant that people were powerless and at a loss . . ." (*MD*, 269).

The hopelessness of vocation underlines its significance: "We did our work," the narrator reflects," did it because it was worthwhile and because it was the work we chose." He adds, "we were futile because . . . our countrymen—suddenly seemed too base" (*MD*, 204). Lamenting Terry's breakdown, the "tired man" tells a friend "I taught him useless secrets that are the art of life among men, but not here" (269).

Against the collapse of the Vanderzee community and the daily humiliations he endures (his plans for decent schooling are ignored; he can't help Terry; his home life is trying), the narrator finds he must do more than save appearances by recounting them. He must vindicate their significance. His discovery is that his wayward affairs in and with the city are a pedagogy. Plato's observations are true, Goodman adding that "I used to think it was only literature." Recounting Plato's odyssey of reason, Goodman writes, "And then, he said, surprisingly, a man's eros turns to the institutions and the customs of the city, that educate character and nurture physical beauty; and now his lively concern is with these. I should never have believed it when I was younger! But as I grew up, I found that it was true" (*MD*, 274).

The narrator remains "frozen on the ladder," unable to climb higher. Goodman the writer closes the novel with a look at the true self. Our own nature sums up our engagements with the world. We are driven to will and to do. Nature does heal. Amos makes his timely discovery. He returns to America and lives by "making his own choices." He accepts the sense of *his* being. Attributing lines to Amos that Goodman wrote about himself, Goodman observes that Amos "had spent nearly forty years glaring at those he loved! until he stopped loving his world his only one. But now he and she had commenced to live on civil speaking terms, since he didn't care for that so much anymore" (*MD*, 276).

The City as Self

Making Do ends upon the discordancy of America's early promise as a refuge for the intentional community and its modern coercive nature. Refusing to close the novel with Amos's resignation, Goodman invokes the loving exhortation of the Puritan divine John Robinson. God does come across if we make the occasion. His spirit rests on those who seek a saving habitation of man. "No," Goodman declaims, taking us from Amos's thoughts to Robinson's words: " 'The Lord has yet more light and truth to break forth,' as John Robinson said to the Pilgrims embarking toward America" (*MD*, 276).

Whether read as yet another invocation to the Creator Spirit or seen as Goodman's restoring anticipation to experience under the Empire or as his own preaching to the reader about early America, this brief, concluding section refuses to pacify the rhythm of the plot through a rounding of the aesthetic experience itself. There would be no pronouncement of an end. The issues of the book would extend *into* the reading audience.

I X

What are we to make, finally, of Goodman's urban thought? It would be easy to point out that the anarchist community, the libertarian program, the medieval city, and the regionalist idea are attractive because they address an easily recognized conceptual whole, whether it is the individual acting autonomously and cooperatively or the small community. Most important, his theses sustain our belief in individuality and fraternity. His city and his community are entities open for individual action and humane control. Arguments that condemn their impracticality or their possible failure because of an open, pluralistic capitalism seem mean-spirited and contemptuous of the frustrations most people feel about their associations, their way of work, and their prospects for a valuable life.

Similarly, Goodman's invocation of human nature seems talismanic: rhetorically and poetically, it often serves as a way out of the challenges posed by political emergencies. As a novelist, Goodman could set his version of human nature against the Empire and remain insightful, but as a social critic he would eristically dodge Meno's claim that people may knowingly and happily seek things other than the good, and, tragically, their good. It is unsettling that as *Gestalt Therapy* and *Art and Social Nature* unfold, it becomes obvious how deeply inventive and assuming Goodman was. Though he rarely talks about the roots of the American radical spirit in Emerson and Thoreau, it is tempting to see Goodman's praise of natural energies as similar to the notions of graceful will that the transcendentalists inferred, which became distorted and nonsensical. In exasperation, one can call naive Goodman's depiction of the repressions of American society: his novels are unusually disengaged from the opportunities of American life.

Yet in his rendition of the potency of human nature, Goodman's city meditation is, of course, a call for what classical poets identified as patriotism: a love for the knowledge—and often, ironically, for the boundaries—the city makes possible. To identify with one's city and region was, finally, to affirm a knowledge of the values that made one confident of one's self and one's patrimony within the world. In Goodman's terms, it means a better faith in what we might become. Clearly, he had few contemporaries who could have made his task smoother and more acceptable.

Goodman's urban landscape is a therapeutic invention: his city designs and fiction are a topography of an all-too human gregariousness demanding that a solution for an impoverished human nature be found in new arrangements for self- and community creation. An authentic self, an authentic community are the goals his writing envisions. How and in what ways does the city answer to this true self? Can it maintain a culture of autonomy? These questions are Goodman's hazarding Plato's ladder. One begins with the need for a human satisfaction—for love, for fraternity, for useful work—and ends with a common vocation: citizenship. The urban associations that Goodman attentively describes in his nonfictional prose and his novels present themselves as stewards of a full, "original" human nature making the city an agora in which our independence and cooperation are discovered anew.

As Paul and Percival Goodman write in their conclusion to *Communitas:* "In this difficult art, the people are not philosophical, they do not know the concrete and central facts. Yet only the people *can* know them."[65] The commanding civic culture that Goodman's works make us catch sight of is the mentor of freedom, as he saw it: a grand regionalism that he aspired to call into being, as if his works were incantations summoning and inspiriting the emergence of humankind. This is not a utopian enterprise. It is, to paraphrase Goodman, a community idea.

Epilogue

I**N SUMMARY**, how the city *is known* and how it is *made known* are questions at the core of the urban writing I have examined. Riis, Mumford, Farrell, and Goodman "de-categorize" urban meditation by arguing that, above all, it is *engagement* with the city, *engagement* that is subjective. There is a danger in abstracting values from concrete situations. Once the city is represented as a quantifiable object, the city as an expression of humanly created relations and meanings is either lost to inquiry or becomes secondary. These writers point out that the lesson of the city is found in urban conduct, an individual's enactment of civic culture. A preference for the qualitative nature of experience, a refusal to deny the paradoxes that cities generate and individuals live by and with are writers' loyalties to the figure of man, to life *in situ*.

The city is not simply its location, describable in quantifiable terms. Rather, its cultural as well as its physical legacies must be accounted for. The city not only preserves but also generates those intangible values giving it a context as well as a direction. Seeing the city this way is an allegiance to the dreams as well as the accomplishments of reason. As a result, the writers I have discussed diminish the most powerful claim of a modern social science: what is empirically verifiable constitutes legitimate experience.

In their assessments of the city, these four writers remained true to what they believed was the idea of an authentic self and community. Human nature is fraternal and creative; the metropolis is not a city; its teaching estranges individuals from their powers. In this sense, the informing nature of the writer's past and place seemed to them self-justifying and indubitable. Even if they were creatively self-deceiving, never far from their writing is the portrait of the city as a maelstrom, a necropolis, a habitualizing environment, and an agent of authoritarianism. They understood all too well the danger of their own optimism. By giving weight to their own aspirations and fears they emphasized what the economy of

207

theory pushes aside yet what every significant writer submits to: the ambiguous, rich, and not fully accountable nature of experience itself.

The human figure is these writers' point of reference and point of accession. As a result, what these four men take as human incompleteness is their reading of a potential that must be realized. They passionately argue that urban planning and city writing without human beings and their needs at the center are, at very best, exercises in abstraction and meaningless. After all, individuals build the city to satisfy themselves; how can it not be accountable to them? Moreover, writing without the felt presence of the writer diminishes the hope for a public colloquy. How could writing about the city not involve making the liberalizing society?

The city transmits the generative symbols and historical-making consciousness of man. As the grand humanizing agent, the city must be democratic. A shared city liberates people from an isolating existence, delivering them to the legacies of the human community and its creativity. How could one be fully human living apart from such a city? Opportunities for sharing the urban heritage must be accessible to everyone. Logically, these range from education to housing, from work to recreation. Moreover, the city is part of a regional ecology; criteria for urban technology and development have to preserve the balance of nature and account for necessity of use, distribution of goods, and amenities.

These points are prologue. What is the practical importance of these writers' work is a question that must be asked. For all their inclinations to raise problems that are within the realm of classical political thought, these city thinkers are interim urban philosophers, or better, interim men of letters. That is to say, their work is culturally portentous because there are so few philosophers in and of the city, so few individuals willing to write about the task of letters for the American city. If the individuals I have written about did not address the logical and technical implications of their questions, if they have not provided the city with a systematic philosophy out of which a detailed politics flows, they nonetheless kept alive questions that are often shoved aside by those responsible for city planning and by those who write about it.

We can look back upon these four and talk about their inadequate knowledge of the city, or their too grand aspirations. Obviously, we are no longer tied to the physical conditions of the city which they took as a given. American cities are not based on brown coal economies; they are not invariably situated in the river valley; they are not physical products of hundreds of years of continuous settlement; they are not small villages writ

Epilogue

large; they are not without laws regulating housing density and sanitation; decentralization is a fact of our existence. For all these qualifications, these four thinkers restore the city for us. In one way, they revive Socratic quarrels, in this case asking who really writes *for* the city? What discipline, what specialty is able to know and to write most tellingly about the idea and actuality of the city? The claim of these writers, of course, is that any specialty impoverishes the intelligibility of human affairs.

In another way, looking upon a city unable to meet human needs, these writers speak of what human nature and civics are. Their claims about how we should live and our actual arrangements for living demand that urban planning keep alive the terms of civility and the future it pushes us toward. Yet writing such as theirs about the chances for an authentic city culture and its realized human nature is infrequent. Without more such labor, we will confront our cities as something we are unprepared for, as habitations unknown to and unexperienced by previous generations and unamenable to our own.

Notes

Introduction

1. It is worth asking if Riis, Mumford, Farrell, and Goodman knew each other. There are tangible connections among three of them, but these are not *central* to my reading of them or the literature they helped create. Their public exchanges were infrequent, and focusing on them would diminish the common questions their works present—though such questions often animate these writers' critiques of one another. Goodman and his brother Percival, an architect, met Farrell in the early 1940s. Paul Goodman clearly impressed and perhaps dazzled the older Farrell, who entered in his diary brief remarks about Goodman's wit, his poverty, and his sketchy observations on community planning. Mumford and Farrell quarreled in 1930 over the meaning of Dewey's naturalism, and Farrell seemed to have nurtured a grudge against Mumford, or so Farrell's letters indicate. Later, Farrell awkwardly attacked Mumford over the significance of regionalist theory. In his turn, Mumford cautioned Van Wyck Brooks not to pay attention to Farrell's criticism. In their turn, the Goodmans wrangled with Mumford about the achievements of the garden city, though Paul later honored Mumford by calling him the "dean" of American urban thinkers. For these three living in New York, Riis may have been a name to them, but it would have been a name with a presence. The city they inhabited was physically transformed by him. The city they wrote about depended, in large measure, upon *his* pioneering conception of it.

2. Historically convenient origins, excluding the scientism of a Henry Adams, a Walter Bagehot, and a Herbert Spencer, are August Meitzen, *History, Theory, and Technique of Statistics*, translated by Roland Parker and published in English by the American Academy of Political and Social Science in 1891; Marcus Reynolds, *The Housing of the Poor in American Cities* (1893), the prize piece of the American Economic Association; and Adna F. Weber's brilliant study, *The Growth of Cities in the Nineteenth Century: A Study in Statistics* (1899).

1. Jacob A. Riis: The City as Christian Fraternity

Unless otherwise noted, newspaper material and letters come from the Riis Collection at the Library of Congress. This newspaper file of articles by and about Riis constitutes the largest holding of such material. In a scrapbook, apparently put together with material gathered by a press-clipping service, Riis saved accounts of his doings. Often, the citation of dates appears to be in his hand. Because of the incomplete nature of archival newspaper files dating back some one hundred years, I have relied upon Riis's "sign-posting." He did not record page numbers.

1. "A Police Reporter's Camera," (New York) *News,* January 27, 1888; "The Society of Amateur Photographers of New York," *The Photographic Times and American Photographer,* February 3, 1888; "Pictures of Police Life," *New York Tribune,* January 26, 1888; "Flashes from the Slums," (New York) *Sun,* February 12, 1888 (Alexander Alland, Sr., in his invaluable *Jacob A. Riis: Photographer and Citizen* [Millerton, N.Y.: Aperture, 1974], suggests that Riis wrote "Flashes" [p. 26]. Since Riis was usually scrupulous about identifying his own work in his scrapbooks, I suspect someone else wrote this account).

2. A. F. Schauffler, letter of March 3, 1888; W. T. Elsing, letter of March 12, 1888; Lyman Abbott to Jacob Riis, May 10, 1888.

3. "Help Save the People," *Thrift,* October 16, 1889; Mrs. Amelia B. Sears to Jacob Riis, December 7, 1888.

4. Robert W. De Forest and Lawrence Veiller, eds., *The Tenement House Problem,* 2 vols. (New York: Macmillan, 1903), 1:105.

5. Ernest Poole, *The Bridge: My Own Story* (New York: Macmillan, 1940), p. 60. Crane heard Riis's illustrated lecture in Asbury Park, N.J., and the young writer's account was published as "On the Jersey Coast," in the *New York Tribune* of July 24, 1892. Crane's urban fiction is set in the slums of lower New York. Lincoln Steffens, *The Autobiography of Lincoln Steffens* (New York: Harcourt, Brace and Co., 1931), see pp. 203–7.

6. James Russell Lowell, quoted in "Jacob A. Riis, Roosevelt's Ideal Citizen," *American Review of Reviews* 50 (July 1914): 97–98.

7. "Visible Darkness," *New York Morning Journal,* February 12, 1888.

8. Dr. Roger Tracy, undated document.

9. Steffens, *Autobiography,* p. 204.

10. Jacob A. Riis, *The Making of an American* (New York: Macmillan, 1902), p. 370.

11. Steffens, *Autobiography,* p. 223.

12. Riis, *Making of an American,* pp. 198–99.

13. Marcus T. Reynolds, *The Housing of the Poor in American Cities* (1893; reprint, College Park, Md.: McGrath, 1969), p. 29. See Lawrence Veiller, *Housing Reform: A Hand-Book for Practical Use in American Cities* (New York: New York Charities Publication Committee, 1910), for the professionalism of a new generation of urban reformers; Adna F. Weber, *The Growth of Cities in the Nineteenth Century* (1899; reprint, Ithaca: Cornell University Press, 1967), pp. 3–4; Riis to Lincoln Steffens, August 8, 1906, Lincoln Steffens Papers, Rare Book and Manuscript Library, Columbia University.

14. See Theodore Roosevelt, "Jacob Riis," *Outlook,* June 6, 1914, p. 284; Lincoln Steffens, "Jacob A. Riis: Reporter, Reformer, Useful Citizen," *McClure's* 21 (August 1903): 419–25; Jane E. Robbins, "A Maker of Americans," *Survey,* June 6, 1914, pp. 285–86.

15. Riis, *Making of an American,* p. 3. Subsequent citations of this work will be given parenthetically in the text as *MA.*

Notes to Jacob A. Riis

16. Riis quoted in "Children of the Tenements," *New York Mail and Express*, March 29, 1895.

17. Jacob A. Riis, *The Old Town* (New York: Macmillan, 1909), pp. 32–33.

18. Ibid., p. 128.

19. See, for example, Riis's recollections of his youth in *Making of an American*, p. 399.

20. Jacob A. Riis, Commencement address to Barre, Massachusetts, High School, no date.

21. "A Great Hearted American," *Outlook*, June 6, 1914, p. 267; "Casual Comment," *Dial*, June 16, 1914, pp. 487–88.

22. See, for example, the summary of reviews of *The Making of an American* in Lewis Fried and John Fierst, *Jacob A. Riis: A Reference Guide* (Boston: G. K. Hall, 1977).

23. "Jacob A. Riis: Friend of the American People," *Craftsman* 26 (July 1914): 459–61; "A Great Hearted American," p. 267.

24. Carolina Riis to Jacob A. Riis, March 26, 1873; Niels Riis to Jacob A. Riis, March 28, 1873.

25. Jacob A. Riis to Emma Riis, January 1, 1895.

26. Jacob A. Riis, letter, no addressee (possibly written January 20, 1907).

27. James Macgregor, *Reports of the Superintendent of Buildings for the Years 1870 and 1871* (New York, 1872), quoted in I. N. Phelps Stokes, *The Iconography of Manhattan Island, 1498–1909*, 6 vols. (1915–1928; reprint, New York: Arno Press, 1967), 5: 1948.

28. See William Dean Howells, "An East Side Ramble," in *Impressions and Experiences* (New York: Harper and Brothers, 1896). It is worth looking at Henry James's genteel disgust: "It was as if we had been thus, in the crowded, hustled roadway, where multiplication, multiplication of everything, was the dominant note, at the bottom of some vast sallow aquarium in which innumerable fish, of over-developed proboscis, were to bump together, for ever, amid heaped spoils of the sea" (*The American Scene* [Bloomington: Indiana University Press, 1968], p. 131).

29. James S. Redfield, *Redfield's Traveler's Guide to the City of New York* (New York: Redfield, 1871), p. 72; R. G. White, "Old New York and Its Houses," *Century Magazine* n.s. 4 (October 1883): 845; Moses King, *King's Handbook of New York City 1893* (1893; reprint, New York: Benjamin Blom, 1972), p. 158.

30. *New York State Laws*, sess., 1867, chap. 908, sec. 17. The definition of a tenement is found in the more accessible work, Roy Lubove, *The Progressives and the Slums* (Pittsburgh: University of Pittsburgh Press, 1962), p. 26. *Report of the Tenement House Committee, as Authorized by Chapter 479 of the Laws of 1894* (Albany: James B. Lyon, 1895), p. 14.

31. *Report of the Tenement House Committee*, p. 32.

32. Rev. Peter Stryker, "A Discourse," in *The Lower Depths of the Great American Metropolis* (New York: Schermerhorn and Bancroft, 1866), pp. 1–2. The New York City Mission Society Papers held by the New York Historical Society should also be looked at.

Notes to Jacob A. Riis

33. Charles Loring Brace, *The Dangerous Classes of New York* (1872; reprint, Montclair, N.J.: Patterson Smith, 1967), p. 29; "A Volunteer Special," *The Volcano Under the City* (New York: Fords, Howard, and Hulbert, 1887), p. 333. The fascination with a city redeemed or scourged by fire can also be found, for example, in titles such as *Civilization's Inferno* by B. O. Flower (1893) and *New York's Inferno Explored* by Commissioner and Mrs. Ballington Booth (1891). In addition to Jewish apocalyptic and prophetic literature which uses such imagery, it is worth exploring the connection between the nineteenth-century imagination connecting cataclysmic evolution and the turbulent metropolis: for example, see the works of Ignatius Donnelly.

34. Stokes, *Iconography of Manhattan Island*, vol. 5, with its almost daily catalog of New York events is an indispensable work for chronicling the city's riots. For treatment of the scare articles, see, for example, J. B. Manheim and M. Wallace's extremely useful *Political Violence in the United States. 1875–1974: A Bibliography* (New York: Garland, 1975). For Josiah Strong, see *Our Country*, ed. J. Herbst (1891; reprint: Cambridge: Harvard University Press, Belknap Press, 1963), p. 151.

35. See Rev. J. M. King et al., *The Religious Condition of New York City* (New York: Baker and Taylor, 1888).

36. G. G. Foster, *New York by Gas-Light* (New York: DeWitt and Davenport, 1850), p. 50.

37. Ibid., p. 47.

38. Junius Henri Browne, *The Great Metropolis: A Mirror of New York* (Hartford, Conn.: American, 1869), p. 429; "Editor's Easy Chair," *Harper's* 45 (October 1872): 779.

39. Charles Loring Brace, "The Little Laborers of New York City," *Harper's* 47 (August 1873): 330.

40. Jacob A. Riis, "Across the Ocean: Leaves from the Journal of a Traveler," *South Brooklyn News*, March 4, 1876. The *South Brooklyn News* has disappeared.

41. Jacob A. Riis, "Are We So Soon Forgot," (New York) *World*, October 2, 1883.

42. Ibid.

43. Jacob A. Riis, "People Who Disappear," (New York) *World*, June 4, 1883; Jacob A. Riis, "The River's Unknown Dead," *Cincinnati Enquirer*, August 30, 1885 (datelined "Correspondence of the *Enquirer*, New York, August 25, 1885").

44. Jacob A. Riis, "Pestilence Nurseries," (New York) *World*, June 11, 1883.

45. Jacob A. Riis, "The Era of Suicides," *Mail and Express*, October 9, 1884; see Riis's "Secrets of the River," (New York) *World*, May 25, 1883; "The Foundling Boom," *Morning Journal*, April 15, 1883; "Pestilence Nurseries"; "The Tramps Marching," (New York) *World*, June 25, 1883.

46. Jacob A. Riis, "The Oldest 'Finest,'" *Morning Journal*, April 29, 1883; Jacob A. Riis, "The Police Telegraph," (New York) *World*, August 17, 1883; Jacob A. Riis, "Accomplished Beggars," (New York) *World*, July 6, 1883; Jacob A. Riis, "Tramps Back in Town," *Mail and Express*, December 26, 1885.

47. Jacob A. Riis, "Keeping an Empty Chair," (New York) *Tribune*, March 21, 1886; Jacob A. Riis, "He Never Returned," *Mercury*, June 14, 1885; Jacob A. Riis, "Missionaries By Night," (New York) *World*, July 23, 1883.

Notes to Jacob A. Riis

48. Jacob A. Riis, "Gotham Doings," (Green Bay) *Advance,* no date given other than 1884.

49. Ibid., February 14, 1884, and February 27, 1884.

50. It is interesting to see Riis's attempt to resolve the personally and socially warring oppositions he faced as symptomatic of a larger struggle of "progressive" Americans to do the same. See, for example, Kermit Vanderbilt's "Howells among the Brahmins," *New England Quarterly* 35 (September 1962): 291–317; and Christopher Lasch's discussion of Jane Addams in *The New Radicalism in America. 1889–1963* (New York: Vintage, 1965).

51. Jacob A. Riis, "The Tenement-House Question, II:—The Remedy," *Christian Union,* May 1889, p. 624; and "The Tenement-House Question, I:—The Question Stated," ibid., April 1889, p. 590.

52. Jacob A. Riis, "How the Other Half Lives," *Scribner's Magazine* 6 (December 1889): 643, 660.

53. "New York Tenements," (London) *Saturday Review,* December 12, 1891; "Literary Brevities," *Chicago Times,* December 20, 1890; "Charles Scribner's Sons New Books," *Dial* 11 (April 1891): 364.

54. Jacob A. Riis, undated letter, no addressee given, Riis Papers, Cohen Library, City University of New York.

55. See Fried and Fierst, *Riis: A Reference Guide,* for abstracts of critical responses to the book.

56. Franklin H. Giddings, "The Province of Sociology," *Annals of the American Academy of Political and Social Science* 1 (July 1890): 77.

57. Jacob A. Riis to John Riis, October 9, 1905.

58. Jacob A. Riis, *How the Other Half Lives,* with an introduction by D. Bigelow, (1890; reprint, New York: Sagamore Press, 1957), p. 7. Subsequent citations of this edition will be given parenthetically in the text as *HOHL.*

59. Jacob A. Riis, "Shadows of a Great City," *Jamestown Journal,* July 27, 1891; Jacob A. Riis, "The Man Who Is an Immigrant," *Survey,* February 18, 1911, p. 868.

60. See Jane Addams, *Twenty Years at Hull-House* (New York: Macmillan, 1910); Frederic C. Howe, *The Confessions of a Reformer* (New York: Charles Scribner's Sons, 1925); and Leo Hershkowitz's reinterpretation of New York's politics in *Tweed's New York* (New York: Anchor, 1978).

61. "International Convention of the Brotherhood of St. Andrew," *Churchman* October 23, 1897, p. 501; "Want Sunlight in Slums," *Chicago Tribune,* November 12, 1899.

62. See Paul T. Ringenbach, *Tramps and Reformers, 1873–1916* (Westport, Conn.: Greenwood, 1973), and Kenneth Allsop, *Hard Travellin'* (New York: New American Library, 1967). Well worth looking at are Josiah Flynt's *Travelling with Tramps* (1899) and *My Life* (1908). Flynt is a pseudonym for Willard. See also Jack London, *The Road* (1907).

63. Jacob A. Riis to John Riis, March 4, 1904.

64. Jacob A. Riis, *The Children of the Poor,* with an introduction by F. Cordasco (1892; reprint, New York: Garrett Press, 1970), pp. 1–2. Subsequent citations of this edition will be given parenthetically in the text as *CP.*

Notes to Jacob A. Riis

65. Jacob A. Riis, *The Battle with the Slum* (New York: Macmillan, 1902), p. 431.

66. Ibid., pp. 402–3.

67. Jacob A. Riis, *The Peril and Preservation of the Home* (Philadelphia: George W. Jacobs, 1903), p. 188.

68. Ibid., pp. 108, 24.

69. Ibid., pp. 95–96.

70. Riis, *Battle with the Slum*, p. 229.

71. Jacob A. Riis, "On Jews," undated speech.

72. Ibid.

73. Jacob A. Riis, Chautauqua, Summer 1908, untitled lecture.

74. Jacob A. Riis to John Riis, 1913.

75. Riis, Commencement address to Barre High School, no date.

76. See James Lane, "Bridge to the Other Half: The Life and Urban Reform Work of Jacob A. Riis" (Ph.D. diss., University of Maryland, 1970), for an important discussion of Riis's accomplishments as a reformer. This dissertation served as the basis for Lane's valuable *Jacob A. Riis and the American City* (Port Washington, N.Y.: Kennikat Press, 1974).

77. Jacob A. Riis to Mary Riis, November 15, 1913.

78. Jacob A. Riis, "Statement," February 2, 1895.

79. Jacob A. Riis to Emma Riis, March 5, 1913 (the attribution to Emma is probable but not certain).

2. Lewis Mumford: The City as Man

1. Lewis Mumford, *Sketches from Life,* (Beacon Press: Boston, 1982), p. 3. Subsequent citations of this edition will be given parenthetically in the text as *SL*.

2. Lewis Mumford, "Architecture as a Home for Man," in *Architecture as a Home for Man: Essays for "Architectural Record,"* ed. Jeanne Davern (New York: Architectural Record Books, 1975), p. 149.

3. Ibid. In his later writing, especially *The Brown Decades*, Mumford often returns to the bridge: its form resolves the use of modern materials and enduring grace. The bridge weds art and technics.

4. Lewis Mumford to author, 1984.

5. Lewis Mumford, "The Modern City," in *Forms and Functions of Twentieth Century Architecture,* ed. T. Hamlin, 4 vols. (New York: Columbia University Press, 1952), 4:778.

6. Lewis Mumford, "A Brief History of Urban Frustration," in *The Urban Prospect* (New York: Harcourt, Brace and World, 1968), p. 209.

7. Lewis Mumford, "Architecture and History," *Journal of the American Institute of Architects* 12 (April 1924): 192. This publication has changed its name several times. Hereafter it will be referred to as *AIA. Journal.*

8. Lewis Mumford, "Apology to Henry Adams," *Virginia Quarterly Review* 38 (Spring 1962): 197, 215.

9. Walter Moody, "The 'New' Profession—City-Planning," *AIA. Journal.* 4 (March 1916): 119.

Notes to Lewis Mumford

10. Lewis Mumford, "The Garden City Idea and Modern Planning," in Ebenezer Howard, *Garden Cities of To-morrow*, ed. F. J. Osborn (Cambridge: MIT Press, 1972), p. 40. (Mumford's essay is an introduction to Howard's book.)

11. For some of the debates about the garden city, see Lloyd Rodwin, "Garden Cities and the Metropolis," *Journal of Land & Public Utility Economics* 21 (August 1945): 268–81. Catherine Bauer and Lewis Mumford reply to this scrutiny of Howard's ideas in "Garden Cities and the Metropolis: A Reply," ibid. 22 (February 1946): 66–69, and Rodwin responds with "Garden Cities and the Metropolis: A Rejoinder," ibid., 69–77.

12. Excluding Howard's book itself, the garden city idea came to America most fully by way of report, especially in the *AIA. Journal*, edited by C. H. Whitaker. Under Whitaker's guidance, the magazine from 1913 to 1920 (years in which Mumford would have known about the garden city only through reading) ran a number of pieces exploring experiments in workers' housing, the housing and planning movements in Europe, and, in the aftermath of the war, studies of urban reconstruction. The range of ideas was large and the garden city was variously interpreted, from its placing human welfare at the center of housing, to its part in emptying cities of intelligent leadership. (See George Hooker, "Garden Cities," *AIA. Journal* 2 [February 1914]: 80–91; and Carol Aronovici, "The Garden City Idea in Urban Development," ibid. 3 [August 1914]: 399–401.) Certainly worth looking at is Mumford's essay "Garden Civilizations: Preparing for a New Epoch," written in 1917 but first published in *Town and Country Planning* 23 (March 1955): 138–42. The fact that the garden city offered a variety of meanings to those familiar with it or its literature suggests the unsettled nature of interpretation it carried, as well as the hopes of those who championed it. This diversity of interpretation, growing wider as time progressed, led Mumford to argue that the garden city and Howard's book had been misconstrued:

> *Garden Cities of To-morrow* has done more than any other single book to guide the modern town planning movement and to alter its objectives. But it has met the traditional misfortune of the classic: it is denounced by those who have plainly never read it and it is sometimes accepted by those who have not fully understood it. Nothing could be a more timely contribution to building a life-centered civilization than the republication of Sir Ebenezer Howard's famous book. (*Garden Cities of To-morrow*, p. 29)

13. The difference, for instance, between the American Progressives' idea of a survey and that of Geddes lies in a view of what the city encompasses. For the Progressives, the city was both unknown and seductive. It was an unregulated system of power that deprived its population of a voice. To be managed, it had to be known and brought within scientific control; this usually meant a census of some kind. American Progressives advocated civic surveys that charted neighborhood minorities, housing densities, family sizes, and the like. The regional survey, however, is stupefying in its demands for a catalog of the elements and opportunities within an entire region; for example, power sources, mineral deposits, agricultural production, road surveys, population tallies. The contrast is crucial: the Progressives, at best, believed the city to be defined by the style of its power: the regionalists saw the city itself as the summation of human civilization. For a

dramatic illustration of this difference, see, for example, Patrick Geddes, *City Development* (1904), and Jane Addams, *Hull-House Maps and Papers* (1895).

14. Patrick Geddes, *City Development* (1904; reprint, New Brunswick, N.J.: Rutgers University Press, 1973), p. 218.

15. Patrick Geddes, "Talks from the Outlook Tower," p. 357, and "Cities in Evolution," pp. 125, 124, in *Patrick Geddes: Spokesman for Man and the Environment*, ed. Marshall Stalley (New Brunswick, N.J.: Rutgers University Press, 1972).

16. It is worthwhile looking at Mumford's various pieces on Geddes to see Mumford's changing evaluations of his mentor. Of special interest are "Neighbors," *Survey Graphic* 50 (April 1923): 44; "Patrick Geddes, Insurgent," *New Republic*, October 30, 1929, pp. 295–96; "Patrick Geddes," in *International Encyclopedia of the Social Sciences*, 17 vols. (New York: Macmillan, 1968), 6: 81–83.

17. Lewis Mumford to Van Wyck Brooks, August 5, 1942 in *The Van Wyck Brooks—Lewis Mumford Letters*, ed. Robert Spiller (New York: E. P. Dutton, 1970), p. 217.

18. Van Wyck Brooks, "On Creating a Usable Past," *Dial*, April 11, 1918, p. 341.

19. Van Wyck Brooks, "A Reviewer's Notebook," *Freeman*, May 5, 1920, p. 191.

20. Lewis Mumford, "Regional Planning," in *Planning the Fourth Migration*, ed. Carl Sussman (Cambridge: MIT Press, 1976), pp. 201, 203. For others, most notably Louis Wirth, regionalism and the concept of the region were problematic. On the one hand, regionalism was often a "one-factor theory" (Wirth's term) that distorted the complex relationship between society and environment. The idea of the region simplified or ignored other influences—ranging from politics to communications—that demanded a redefinition of what an area and its institutions are. See Louis Wirth, *On Cities and Social Life*, ed. Albert Reiss, Jr. (Chicago: University of Chicago Press, 1964). Especially useful is "The Limitations of Regionalism," pp. 207–20.

21. Lewis Mumford, "Abandoned Roads," *Freeman*, April 12, 1922, pp. 101–2; "A Very Royal Academy," ibid., June 16, 1920, pp. 327–28; "The Adolescence of Reform," ibid., December 1, 1920, pp. 272–73 (quotation from p. 273).

22. See Mumford, "Garden Civilizations" (Mumford's evaluation of Salt and others); "England's American Summer," *Freeman*, June 7, 1922, p. 296 (on Geddes vis-à-vis other thinkers); "Miscellany," *Freeman*, August 3, 1921, pp. 495–96 (on Cobbett and the transformation of the medieval town).

23. Lewis Mumford, "The Heritage of the Cities Movement in America," *AIA. Journal* 7 (August 1919): 354, 349.

24. Lewis Mumford, "Nationalism or Culturism? A Search for the True Community" *Menorah Journal* 8 (June 1922): 137.

25. Lewis Mumford, "Herzl's Utopia," *Menorah Journal* 9 (August 1923): 168.

26. At the center of the RPAA were Clarence Stein (who served in 1919 as secretary of the New York Housing Committee and who would be fittingly termed a "designer of communities" by the *AIA. Journal*), Stein's long-term partner, Henry Wright (who had worked on housing problems for the U.S. Shipping Board in 1918), and Benton MacKaye (of the Forest Service and the major proponent of the Appalachian Trail and townless highways). The group also included, among others, C. H. Whitaker, an economist and the creative editor of the *AIA. Journal;*

the architect F. L. Ackerman; housing planner Stuart Chase; and the future-housing expert Catherine Bauer.

Mumford had been introduced in 1922 to Stein by Whitaker and became the executive secretary of what was then called the Regional Planning Association. By 1925 he assumed an important editorial role in the May issue of *Survey;* his paper delivered at the symposium at the University of Virginia in 1931 remains one of the best presentations of regionalist aims. The group's theoretical statements—plans for a regional future—are found most notably in Stein's *Report of the Commission of Housing and Regional Planning to Governor Alfred E. Smith* (1926), the May 1925 issue of the *Survey,* and the 1931 symposium at the University of Virginia.

For studies about the RPAA, see Daniel Schaffer, *Garden Cities for America* (Philadelphia: Temple University Press, 1982); Roy Lubove, *Community Planning in the 1920's* (Pittsburgh: University of Pittsburgh Press, 1963); Carl Sussman, ed., *Planning the Fourth Migration* (Cambridge: MIT Press, 1976); and, of course, Clarence Stein, *Toward New Towns for America,* intro. Lewis Mumford (Cambridge: MIT Press, 1966).

27. "Notes," *AIA. Journal* 11 (July 1923): 292.

28. See Lewis Mumford, "Ex Libris," *Freeman,* May 2, 1923, pp. 190–91; "When Spring Comes," *AIA. Journal* 11 (April 1923): 174–76; "Architectural Piety," ibid. (August 1923): 304; "Architecture and History," ibid. 12 (April 1924): 191–92; "The Autobiography of an Idea," *New Republic,* June 25, 1924, pp. 132–33.

29. See Mumford "Neighbors," p. 44; "Seaboard Architecture," *AIA. Journal* 11 (November 1923): 420–21; "Architecture and History," ibid. 12 (April 1924): 191–92.

30. Lewis Mumford to Dorothy Loch, December 8, 1925, in Mumford, *Findings and Keepings* (New York: Harcourt Brace Jovanovich, 1975), p. 98.

31. Lewis Mumford, Preface to *The Story of Utopias* (New York: Compass Books, 1962), p. 2.

32. Lewis Mumford to Patrick Geddes, March 29, 1922, *Findings and Keepings,* pp. 74–75.

33. Ibid., p. 75.

34. Mumford, *The Story of Utopias,* pp. 306–7.

35. Ibid., pp. 301, 278. This argument, reminiscent of parts of Dewey's *Reconstruction in Philosophy,* should also remind us of Comte's lack of interest with a continually theorizing and counter-testing agenda.

36. Lewis Mumford, *Sticks and Stones* (1924; reprint, New York: Dover, 1955), p. 234.

37. Ibid., pp. 17, 16.

38. Mumford's essays dealing with this subject and written during this period are well worth looking at. See, for example, "Regional Planning Schemes, *AIA. Journal* 11 (October 1923): 404–5; "Community Planning and Housing," ibid. (December 1923): 492; "City Planning and the American Precedent," *New Republic,* June 11, 1924, pp. 79–80. See also "Architecture and the Machine," *American Mercury* 3 (September 1924): 77–80.

39. Lewis Mumford, "The Fourth Migration," *Survey*, May 1, 1925, p. 130.

40. Ibid.

41. Lewis Mumford, "Regions—To Live In," *Survey*, May 1, 1925, p. 151.

42. Nonetheless, this issue of the *Survey* is vastly superior as a regionalist meditation to the overpraised, skeletal *Report of the Commission of Housing and Regional Planning* of 1926. Compared by regionalists to the Russel Sage Foundation's *Regional Plan of New York and Its Environs* (to the disadvantage of the latter), the *Report of the Commission* charted the future of New York State's development on the regional basis. One part of the plan is a historical study of state development pointing out that areas of settlement were not fortuitously located but rather shaped by topography and resources. The second part of the plan, based on an earlier discussion of the web formed by city and country, energy and production, suggests strategies, such as new methods of transportation, to make decentralization and decongestion a reality. For Mumford's review of the Sage Plan see his "Plan of New York," *New Republic*, June 15, 1932, pp. 121–26; and June 22, 1932, pp. 146–51.

43. Lewis Mumford, "Architecture and Broad Planning: Realities vs. Dreams," *AIA. Journal* 13 (June 1925): 199.

44. Lewis Mumford, "Regionalism," in "After Dullness—What? A Miscellany of Brief Answers by People in Their Thirties," *Survey Graphic*, November 1, 1926, p. 182.

45. Lewis Mumford, "The Sacred City," *New Republic*, January 27, 1926, pp. 270, 271.

46. Lewis Mumford, *The Golden Day* (New York: Boni and Liveright, 1926), p. 73.

47. Ibid., p. 87.

48. Ibid., p. 204.

49. Ibid., p. 283.

50. Lewis Mumford, *The Brown Decades* (1931; reprint, New York: Dover, 1955), p. 55.

51. See Lewis Mumford, "The Buried Renaissance," *New Freeman*, March 15, 1930, pp. 12–13.

52. *Brown Decades*, p. 34.

53. Ibid., pp. 162, 204.

54. Lewis Mumford to Van Wyck Brooks, June 21, 1933, *Brooks–Mumford Letters*, p. 94.

55. Lewis Mumford, "A Philosopher of History," *New Republic*, March 20, 1929, p. 140. For Mumford's earlier view of Spengler, whose writing at that time had appeared only in a first volume, see ibid., May 12, 1926, pp. 367–69.

56. Lewis Mumford, "A Modern Synthesis," *Saturday Review of Literature*, April 12, 1930, p. 920; May 10, 1930, pp. 1028–29. Here and in "The Pragmatic Acquiescence," *New Republic*, January 19, 1927, and in "What I Believe," *Forum* 84 (November 1930), Mumford felt that he was countering the "New Mechanists" (Dewey among them) who had underestimated the role of human interest in a discussion of experience. Whereas Mumford's reading is partial and, at times,

inaccurate, his argument suggests that *The Golden Day* and *The Brown Decades* would redefine the interests of an American philosophy.

57. Mumford, "What I Believe," pp. 265, 268.

58. A claim for this distinction occurs in his 1939 review of *The Decline of the West*. Reassessing Spengler in "Books That Have Changed Our Minds," Mumford faulted his imagination for its inhospitality to willful change. For Spengler, "civilization meant . . . the deliberate abdication of the organic and vital elements, and the reign of the mechanical. . . . The region was shriveling to a point: the world city, megalopolis." To face Spengler's civilization of despair, the "engineer, the businessman, the soldier" alone have the requisite hardness. For Mumford, however, the organic implied the vital interdependent order of nature and culture, not the hierarchical. See Mumford, "Books That Have Changed Our Minds," *New Republic,* January 11, 1939, p. 276.

59. Lewis Mumford, *Technics and Civilization* (1934; reprint, New York: Harcourt Brace and Co., 1963), pp. 370, 371.

60. Lewis Mumford, *The Culture of Cities* (1938; reprint, New York: Harcourt, Brace and World, 1966), p. 9. Subsequent citations of this edition will be given parenthetically in the text as *CC*.

61. For example, writing of the contemporary city, Mumford contends that its compelling paradox is "the existence of a rational collective organization of the physical means of life without the necessary organs of collective association and responsible social control" (*CC,* 239).

62. For Mumford, this pattern reflects successful organic behavior. In *The Culture of Cities,* as in his later books *The Condition of Man* (1944) and *The Conduct of Life* (1951), the ecological matrix of human life is an ever-expanding one—and this includes symbolic manipulation and change. By containing what might be called the items of the anthropological encyclopedia, the city can be read as the text of people placing themselves within nature and their own creations; it "represents the maximum possibility of humanizing the natural environment, and of naturalizing the human heritage" (*CC,* 6).

63. Meyer Schapiro, "Looking Forward to Looking Backward," *Partisan Review* 5 (July 1938): 18; James T. Farrell, "The Faith of Lewis Mumford," *Southern Review* 6 (Winter 1941): 417–38.

64. See, for example, Rodwin's "Garden Cities and the Metropolis" and Mumford's "Garden Cities and the Metropolis"; and Mumford, "Cities Fit to Live In," *Nation* 166 (May 1948): 530–33; "The Goals of Planning," *Planning 1948* (Proceedings of the National Planning Conference of the American Society of Planning Officials, New York City, October 11–13, 1948), pp. 1–7; "The Modern City"; "Utopia, The City and the Machine," *Daedalus* 94 (Spring 1965): 271–92; "City: Forms and Functions," in *International Encyclopedia of the Social Sciences,* 17 vols. (New York: Macmillan, 1968), 2: 447–55.

65. The "Renewal of Life" series opposes the necessity of the modern state. *The Condition of Man* (1944) contends that we live in an age surfeited with historical interpretation that paradoxically impoverishes, for there is little discussion of our history as a species. Darwin and Marx, as Mumford interprets them, make possible modern explication joining the meaning of culture with nature.

Notes to Lewis Mumford

Mumford's differences, again, with the theses of the Left are easily apparent. Witness his transformation of the character of labor into something close to Spinoza's *conatus*. "If work," he writes, "is the chief end of man's self-maintaining activities, every act he performs has the same underlying purpose: to effect within the organism a dynamic equilibrium and to enable it to continue the processes of growth and to postpone those that make for death" (*The Condition of Man* [1944; reprint, New York: Harcourt Brace Jovanovich, 1973], p. 5). Instead, "communication, communion, [and] co-operation" are the agents and results of human self-creation.

66. Lewis Mumford, "The Nature of Our Age," *Sociological Review* 39, no. 1 (1947): 84.

67. See Emerson's "Divinity School Address" for perhaps the best-known American source of this idea. Elsewhere, Mumford describes the renewal of society by invoking the calendar as a rhetorically organizing device. Relying on an intricate, almost byzantine and unclarifying metaphor of organic unity that binds the harmony of culture (the orchestra) with society (the organism) and these with nature (ecological balance), Mumford writes:

> The transformation of a culture is unlike either a change in the seasons or a breakdown in the body's organs and functions. But there are parallels to both processes. As with the seasons, a certain orderly succession of changes can be observed and even predicted. As with the body, the institutions of society cease to maintain a dynamic equilibrium: morbid conditions undermine normal reactions; and the whole culture no longer forms a unified whole, into which the individual part blends like the theme of an instrument in an orchestra. Once the over all pattern of meaning dissolves, the breakdown becomes inevitable. But precisely because the parts of the culture are no longer united, separate activities, no longer restrained and moderated by their union, may exhibit a bounding vitality. Hence this paradox: the downfall of the culture as a whole may lead to rapid advances in this or that part of it. This social fact is fairly close to what follows when an ecological balance in nature is upset. (*The Condition of Man*, pp. 152–53)

What these terms concretely mean and the significance of their ancestry are compelling questions that point to the hypnosis that the organic metaphor can exert. In Mumford's use, the early analogical function is lost; the metaphor now expresses a general law that is composed of images. Ironically, the distaste for human sciences is now a scientism. The distrust of social planning offers instead the good will. Nonetheless, the appeal to the organic is an argument that makes social reconstruction a matter of deliberation, a sign of autonomy for the organic is the justification of the social structure. Mumford's argument insists that post- and prewar meditations about the immanence of evil in human nature may be expressed by social wholes, but are not reducible to them. We are justified, however, in asking if Mumford's notion of renewal remains more rhetorically inventive than historically useful.

68. See respectively Mumford's essays in *Introduction to the History of Sociology*, ed. Harry Barnes (Chicago: University of Chicago Press, 1948), pp. 677–95; in *Planning 1948*, pp. 1–7; in "The Model City," in Hamlin, *Forms and Functions*, 4:775–819.

Notes to James T. Farrell

69. Lewis Mumford, *City Development: Studies in Disintegration and Renewal* (New York: Harcourt Brace and Co., 1945), p. 157.

70. Ibid., p. 181.

71. Ibid., pp. 193–94.

72. Lewis Mumford, *The City in History.* (New York: Harcourt, Brace and World, 1961), p. 3. (Subsequent citations will be given parenthetically in text as *CH*.) It should be noted that Mumford does not deal with Oriental, African, Middle Eastern, and Soviet cities. Although this is a shortcoming, Mumford forthrightly admits that he writes about those cities he knows.

73. Mumford writes: "it is along a quite different evolutionary line, represented by the social insects, that one finds the closest approach to both 'civilized life' and the city. The social functions of the beehive, the termitary, and the ant-hill—structures often imposing in size, skillfully wrought—have indeed so many resemblances to those of the city that I shall put off further observations till the city comes into view" (*CH*, p. 6).

74. "Once the city came into existence," Mumford observes, "with its collective increase in power in every department, this whole situation underwent a change. Instead of raids and sallies for single victims, mass exterminations and mass destruction came to prevail. What had once been a magic sacrifice to ensure fertility and abundant crops, an irrational act to promote a rational purpose was turned into the exhibition of the power of one community, under its wrathful god and priest-king, to control, subdue, or totally wipe out another community" (*CH*, 42).

75. Lewis Mumford, *The Myth of the Machine: The Pentagon of Power* (New York: Harcourt Brace Jovanovich, 1970), p. 395.

76. Lewis Mumford, *The Urban Prospect* (New York: Harcourt Brace and World, 1968), p. 165.

3. James T. Farrell: The City as Society

Unless otherwise noted, all letters and manuscripts are found in the Farrell Archives at the University of Pennsylvania. Dates are given when available.

1. James T. Farrell, "Dreiser and Chicago," pp. 4–6, Box 294.

2. James T. Farrell, "Chicago Reflections and Memories," pp. 4–5. Box 499.

3. Farrell to Richard Wright, April 23, 1942. This letter, written from New York, was never sent.

4. James T. Farrell to Stanley Pargellis, July 25, 1949. See also Farrell's discussion of Bernard Duffey's *Chicago Renaissance:* James T. Farrell to Stanley Pargellis, July 10, 1949.

5. James T. Farrell, "Literature in Chicago," p. 2, Box 348.

6. See "A Visit to Chicago," Box 303. Not surprisingly, Farrell believed that the emotions and thoughts of people in Chicago were more accessible, clearer to the writer than those of people in New York. See "A Few Observations on the Problem of Chicago and American Culture," Box 366. This may be the first page of "Chicago and American Culture" (see n. 8), which is missing page 1.

Notes to James T. Farrell

7. James T. Farrell to Saul Alinsky, January 19, 1942.

8. James T. Farrell, "Chicago and American Culture," p. 4, Box 382.

9. James T. Farrell to Hortense Farrell, April 14, 1936.

10. I am indebted to Edgar M. Branch, *James T. Farrell* (New York: Twayne, 1971), for the details about Farrell's grandparents.

11. James T. Farrell to Kenneth McCormick, May 13, 1968.

12. See "True" MS., 1964, Box 460; Farrell to McCormick, May 13, 1968; "Chicago During the Twenties," Box 212.

13. James T. Farrell to Saul Alinsky, January 24, 1942.

14. James T. Farrell, "The Writer and His World," November 19, 1957, Evening Lecture to the University of Chicago.

15. James T. Farrell to Saul Alinsky, January 24, 1942.

16. James T. Farrell, "Studs," in *The Short Stories of James T. Farrell* (New York: Vanguard Press, 1962), pp. 304, 298.

17. James T. Farrell, "Some Correspondence with Theodore Dreiser," and "Joyce and Ibsen," in *Reflections at Fifty* (New York: Vanguard Press, 1954), pp. 127–28, 67.

18. James T. Farrell to John Switalski, August 12, 1942.

19. James T. Farrell, "Theodore Dreiser: In Memoriam," in *Literature and Morality* (New York: Vanguard Press, 1947), p. 32.

20. James T. Farrell to Mary [Farrell], probably written soon after July 11, 1939.

21. James T. Farrell to Felix Kolodziej, June 14, 1937.

22. James T. Farrell, *Slum Street, USA* [originally published as *Boarding House Blues*] (New York: Paperback Library, 1967), pp. 210–11.

23. "James Farrell on James Farrell," *New Republic*, October 28, 1940, pp. 595–96.

24. James T. Farrell, "Ingredients of the Personality," *Chicago Evening Post*, May 31, 1929, p. 7.

25. James T. Farrell to Theodore, September 15, 1931.

26. Farrell, "The Story of Studs Lonigan," p. 5, Box 12.

27. "The dominant theme of the sequel will be the decay of the neighborhood," Farrell writes to Frederic Thrasher, March 15, 1932. Also see James T. Farrell to E. W. Burgess, January 9, 1937.

28. This schematic, as Burgess put it, "brings out clearly the main fact of expansion, namely, the tendency of each inner zone to extend its area by the invasion of the next outer zone. This aspect of expansion may be called *succession*, a process which has been studied in detail in plant ecology" ("The Growth of the City," in Robert Park, E. W. Burgess, and Roderick McKenzie, *The City*, intro. Morris Janowitz [Chicago: University of Chicago Press, 1967], p. 50).

29. Robert Park nicely sums this up: "The growth of new regions, the multiplication of professions and occupations, the incidental increase in land values which urban expansion brings—all are involved in the processes of city growth, and can be measured in terms of changes of position of individuals with reference to other individuals, and to the community as a whole" (Robert Park, "A Spacial Pattern and a Moral Order," in *The Urban Community*, ed. E. W. Burgess [Chicago: University of Chicago Press, 1925], p. 6).

Notes to James T. Farrell

30. James T. Farrell to Clifton Fadiman, July 10, 1929.

31. James T. Farrell, "The Influence of John Dewey on My Writing," 1961, p. 6, Box 293.

32. Farrell cites Mead's "The Scientific Method in Creative Thinking," in his letter of September 15, 1931, to Theodore. Also see James T. Farrell, "La filosofia del presente, di G. H. Mead," *Il Mare, Supplemente Letterario,* November 12, 1932, p. 3; and Farrell's letter of November 25, 1939, to Ferdinand Lundberg.

33. Edgar M. Branch, "Freedom and Determinism in James T. Farrell's Fiction," in *Essays on Determinism in American Literature,* ed. Sydney J. Krause (Kent, Ohio: Kent State University Press, 1964), p. 95.

34. "An In-Depth Interview with James T. Farrell," *Writer's Forum* 1 (May 1965): 55.

35. James T. Farrell, Introduction, *Studs Lonigan* (New York: Random House, 1938), p. xiv.

36. John Dewey writes: "Freedom is found in that kind of interaction which maintains an environment in which human desire and choice count for something. There are in truth forces in man as well as without him" (Dewey, *Human Nature and Conduct,* [New York: Modern Library, 1957], p. 10).

37. Ibid., p. 170.

38. Dewey contends: "Good consists in the meaning that is experienced to belong to an activity when conflict and entanglement of various incompatible impulses and habits terminate in a unified orderly release in action. This human good [is] . . . a fulfillment conditioned upon thought" (Ibid., p. 210).

39. Ibid., pp. 216–17.

40. "We traverse a spiral," Dewey writes, "in which social customs generate some consciousness of interdependencies, and this consciousness is embodied in acts which in improving the environment generate new perceptions of social ties, and so on forever. The relationships, the interactions are forever there as fact, but they acquire meaning only in the desires, judgments and purposes they awaken" (Ibid., pp. 328–29).

41. See James T. Farrell's "Reflections on John Dewey," Box 296.

42. James T. Farrell to Ferdinand Lundberg, November 23, 1939.

43. George Herbert Mead, "The Genesis of Self and Social Control," in his *The Philosophy of the Present* (Chicago: University of Chicago Press, 1932), p. 180.

44. Pointing out the necessity of this tension between institutions (the attitude of the public) and the individual which characterizes the democratic society, Mead writes:

> without social institutions of some sort, without the organized social attitudes and activities by which social institutions are constituted, there could be no fully mature individual selves or personalities at all; for the individuals involved in the general social-life processes of which social institutions are organized manifestations can develop and possess fully mature selves or personalities only in so far as each one of them reflects or prehends in his individual experience these organized social attitudes and activities which social institutions embody or represent. (*Mind, Self, and Society,* ed. and intro. Charles W. Morris [Chicago: University of Chicago Press, 1962], p. 262)

45. Mead, "Genesis of Self and Social Control," p. 194.

46. See, for example, James T. Farrell to Sidney Hook, October 28, 1939.

47. James T. Farrell to Ferdinand Lundberg, January 13, 1939.

48. James T. Farrell, "The Social Obligations of the Novelist: I," *Humanist* 7 (Autumn 1947): 58.

49. Randolph Bourne, "Trans-National America," in *The Radical Will: Randolph Bourne: Selected Writings, 1911–1918*, ed. Olaf Hansen (New York: Urizen Books, 1977), p. 254.

50. Farrell, Introduction, to *Studs Lonigan*, pp. xiv–xv.

51. Ibid., p. xi.

52. See "Collection of Reviews of Books by James T. Farrell, 1928–1946." This scrapbook, apparently drawn from the files of a press-clipping service, was donated by Farrell to the New York Public Library.

53. Farrell, *Young Lonigan*, in *Studs Lonigan*, p. 19.

54. Ibid., pp. 135–36.

55. Dewey, *Human Nature and Conduct*, p. 211.

56. Farrell, *The Young Manhood of Studs Lonigan*, in *Studs Lonigan*, p. 4.

57. Ibid., pp. 312–13.

58. Ibid., pp. 371 and 372.

59. Ibid., p. 412. In "Farrell Revisits Studs Lonigan's Neighborhood," Farrell commented that "it is years since we moved away from Fifty-eighth Street. The same year we left, 1928, a Negro boy moved into South Park Ave. He went to the same parochial schools I attended and he grew up to be a poet. . . . His remarks and stories told me how the old patterns had been repeated. The Negro boy, Stephen Lewis, in *The Young Manhood of Studs Lonigan* predicated a continuation of the pattern. A legacy of change, suspicion, prejudice hung over this neighborhood and new families . . . have [inherited] this legacy" (*New York Times*, June 20, 1954, p. 4).

60. James T. Farrell, *Judgment Day*, in *Studs Lonigan*, pp. 42, 45, 46.

61. Ibid., p. 335.

62. See Gunther Barth, *City People* (New York: Oxford University Press, 1980), for the most sustained reading of this claim.

63. James T. Farrell, to Henry Allen Moe of the Guggenheim Foundation, January 23, 1938.

64. James T. Farrell, *Father and Son* (Cleveland: World Publishing Company, 1947), pp. 12, 16.

65. Ibid., p. 602.

66. James T. Farrell, *My Days of Anger* (New York: Vanguard Press, 1943), p. 401.

67. Ibid., p. 303.

68. James T. Farrell to Meyer Schapiro, June 27, 1943.

69. The trilogy consists of *Bernard Clare*, 1946; *The Road Between*, 1949, and *Yet Other Waters*, 1952. The eponymous protagonist's name was changed, because of a law suit, from Clare to Carr.

70. James T. Farrell to Jim [Switalski], May 29, 1943. The reader should also look at Farrell's *Sam Holman* (Buffalo: Prometheus, 1983).

71. James T. Farrell, *Bernard Clare* (New York: Vanguard Press, 1946), p. 83.

72. Ibid., pp. 160, 159–60.

73. Ibid., pp. 316, 367.

74. James T. Farrell, *The Road Between* (New York: Vanguard Press, 1949), p. 54.

75. Ibid., p. 372.

76. Ibid., p. 106.

77. James T. Farrell, *Yet Other Waters* (New York: Vanguard Press, 1952), p. 111.

78. Ibid., pp. 24, 48, 104.

79. Ibid., pp. 56, 88.

80. Ibid., p. 79.

4. Paul Goodman: The City as Self

1. Paul Goodman, "Preface," *Utopian Essays and Practical Proposals* (New York: Vintage, 1964), p. xiii.

2. Paul Goodman, *Five Years* (New York: Brussel and Brussel, 1966), p. 13.

3. I am quoting Paul Goodman's note on the dust jacket of *The State of Nature* (New York: Vanguard Press, 1946).

4. See Paul Goodman, "The Political Meaning of Some Recent Revisions of Freud," *Politics* 2, no. 7 (July 1945): 197–203; C. Wright Mills and Patricia Salter, "The Barricade and the Bedroom," and Goodman, "Reply," ibid., no. 10 (October 1945): 313–15; and 315–16. See also the more accessible volume of Goodman's psychological meditations, *Nature Heals*, ed. Taylor Stoehr (New York: Free Life Editions, 1977).

5. Goodman, "Reply," in *Nature Heals*, p. 68.

6. Paul Goodman, *Growing Up Absurd* (New York: Vintage, 1960), p. 9.

7. Paul Goodman, "Unanimity," in his *Drawing the Line*, ed. Taylor Stoehr (New York: Free Life Editions, 1977), p. 45. The essay was first published in Goodman's *Art and Social Nature* (New York: Vinco, 1946).

8. Paul Goodman, "Reflections on Drawing the Line," in *Drawing the Line*, p. 8.

9. Goodman, *Growing Up Absurd*, pp. 230–31.

10. Fritz Perls, Paul Goodman, and Ralph Hefferline, *Gestalt Therapy* (1951; reprint, New York: Bantam, 1977), p. 276.

11. See Robert Booth Fowler, *Believing Skeptics: American Political Intellectuals, 1945–1964* (Westport, Conn.: Greenwood Press, 1978); Mary Sperling McAuliffe, *Crisis on the Left: Cold War Politics and American Liberals, 1947–1954* (Amherst: University of Massachusetts Press, 1978), and Richard Pells, *The Liberal Mind in a Conservative Age: American Intellectuals in the 1940s & 1950s* (New York: Harper and Row, 1985).

12. Paul Goodman, "A Conjecture in American History, 1783–1815," *Politics* 6 (Winter 1949): 11–13.

13. It is worthwhile recalling Judith Shklar's summary of the "romanticism of defeat": "The outer world is crushing the unique individual. Society is depriving us of our selfhood. The entire social universe today is totalitarian, not just some

political movements and some states. Technology and the masses are the conditions of life everywhere today, and these, forming the very essence of totalitarianism, are the epitome of all the forces in society that have always threatened the individual personality" (*After Utopia: The Decline of Political Faith* [Princeton: Princeton University Press, 1957], p. 18).

14. Goodman, *Utopian Essays and Practical Proposals*, p. 34; Goodman, "The Pragmatism of His Boyhood," *Hudson Review* 14 (Autumn 1961): 444–47. This last is a review of Mumford's *The City in History*.

15. Goodman, *Growing Up Absurd*, p. 144.

16. See Paul Goodman, "City Crowds," *Politics* 3 (December 1946): 390–91.

17. Paul Goodman, "Notes on Neo-Functionalism," *Politics* 1 (December 1944): 64, 336.

18. Goodman, *Growing Up Absurd*, p. 97.

19. Paul Goodman and Percival Goodman, *Communitas* (1947; reprint, New York: Vintage, 1960), p. 111. This revised edition is more accessible.

20. Paul Goodman, "The Attempt to Invent an American Style," *Politics* 1 (February 1944): 17.

21. Paul Goodman, "A Cross-Country Runner at Sixty-Five," in *A Ceremonial, Stories 1936–1940,* ed. Taylor Stoehr (Santa Barbara: Black Sparrow Press, 1978), p. 22.

22. Paul Goodman, Preface to *Our Visit to Niagara,* reprinted in *Creator Spirit Come! The Literary Essays of Paul Goodman,* ed. Taylor Stoehr (New York: Free Life Editions, 1977), pp. 251–52.

23. Paul Goodman, "Notes on a Remark of Seami," in *Creator Spirit Come!* p. 70. Also see "Occasional Poetry," ibid., pp. 76–78.

24. Paul Goodman, "Western Tradition and World Concern," in *Creator Spirit Come!* p. 9.

25. See Paul Goodman, "Literary Method and Author-Attitude," in *Art and Social Nature,* and "Advance-Guard Writing in America: 1900–1950," in *Kenyon Review* 13 (1951); reprinted in *Utopian Essays and Practical Proposals.* Both essays are reprinted in *Creator Spirit Come!.*

26. Paul Goodman, "Towards Urban Pastoral," *Commentary* 8 (July 1949): 92–93. This is a review of Ethel Rosenberg's *Go Fight City Hall,* and it is, for Goodman, an uncharacteristically generous appraisal.

27. Goodman, *Five Years,* p. 255.

28. Irving Howe, "The Discovery of Sex," *Commentary* 3 (February 1947): 196.

29. Paul Goodman, "The Judaism of a Man of Letters," *Commentary* 6 (September 1948): 241.

30. Paul Goodman, "The American Writer and His Americanism," *Kenyon Review,* 21 (Summer 1959): 478, 479.

31. See Paul Goodman, "Louis Sullivan—Artist in America," *Commentary* 30 (October 1960): 335–39. This is a review of Willard Connely's *Louis Sullivan As He Lived.*

32. Goodman, "The American Writer and His Americanism," p. 478.

33. Goodman, *Growing Up Absurd,* p. 110.

Notes to Paul Goodman

34. Paul Goodman and Percival Goodman, "Architecture in Wartime," *New Republic*, December 20, 1943, pp. 881, 882.

35. See *Politics* 1 (January 1944): 55 for letters by Mumford and the Goodmans. *Politics* 1 (February 1944): 283 has a further response by Mumford and a rejoinder by the Goodmans.

36. See Robert Fishman, *Urban Utopias in the Twentieth Century* (New York: Basic Books, 1977), for an insightful discussion of Howard, Wright, and Le Corbusier.

37. Goodman and Goodman, *Communitas* (1947 ed.), p. 131.

38. Ibid. (1960 ed.) p. 16.

39. Ibid., pp. 15–16.

40. Ibid., p. 20.

41. Ibid., p. 105.

42. Ibid., pp. 153–54.

43. Paul Goodman and Percival Goodman, "Community Buildings," in *Forms and Functions of Twentieth Century Architecture*, ed. T. Hamlin, 4 vols. (New York: Columbia University Press, 1952), 4: 653.

44. Goodman, *Five Years*, p. 245.

45. Paul Goodman, "Advance-Guard Writing in America: 1900–1950," in *Creator Spirit Come!* p. 161.

46. Paul Goodman, *The Empire City* (New York: Vintage, 1977), pp. 102–3. Subsequent citations will be given parenthetically in the text as *EC*.

47. Harold Rosenberg, Preface, ibid., p. xi.

48. Goodman, *Five Years*, pp. 110–11.

49. See Paul Goodman, "The Unalienated Intellectual," *Politics* 1 (November 1941): 318–19; "Better Judgment and 'Public Conscience'—A Communication," *Partisan Review* 9 (July–August 1942): 348–51.

50. Paul Goodman, "Western Tradition and World Concern," in *Creator Spirit Come!* p. 7. This essay was originally published in *Art and Social Nature*.

51. Paul Goodman, *The Structure of Literature* (Chicago: University of Chicago Press, 1962), p. 93.

52. Paul Goodman, "Literary Method and Author-Attitude," in *Creator Spirit Come!* p. 24. This piece was first published in *Art and Social Nature*.

53. Ibid., p. 25.

54. Paul Goodman, *The Grand Piano* (San Francisco: Colt Press, 1942), p. 218. I am quoting the first edition; Goodman revised it when it appeared in *The Empire City*.

55. Paul Goodman, "An Interview on *The Empire City*," in *Creator Spirit Come!* p. 263. This essay was first published in *Kulchur*, Summer 1965.

56. Goodman, *The Grand Piano*, epigraph.

57. See Goodman's jeu d'esprit, "The Moral Idea of Money," in *Journal of Philosophy* 32 (February 1935): 126–31.

58. Goodman, *The Structure of Literature*, p. 93.

59. Paul Goodman, "Reflections on Drawing the Line," in *Drawing the Line*, p. 2. This essay was first published in *Art and Social Nature*.

60. Goodman, *The State of Nature*, p. 227.

61. See Paul Goodman, "A Decade of Writing Projects," in *Creator Spirit Come!* p. 235. This is Goodman's Guggenheim Fellowship Application (1952).

62. Goodman, *Gestalt Therapy*, p. 544.

63. Paul Goodman, *Making Do* (New York: Macmillan, 1963), p. 3. Subsequent citations will be given parenthetically in text as *MD*.

64. See Goodman, *Drawing the Line*, as well as his *New Reformation* (New York: Random House, 1970), and *The Community of Scholars* (New York: Random House, 1962).

65. Goodman and Goodman, *Communitas*, p. 224.

Bibliographical Notes

Jacob A. Riis

Anyone interested in Riis as a reformer should find James Lane, *Jacob A. Riis and the American City* (Port Washington, N.Y.: Kennikat Press, 1974), an invaluable work that succeeds Louise Ware's pioneering but adulatory, *Jacob A. Riis: Police Reporter, Reformer, Useful Citizen* (New York: Appleton-Century, 1938). At this writing, the most recent consideration of Riis as a photographer is Sally Stein, "Making Connections with the Camera," *Afterimage*, May 1983, pp. 9–16. Alexander Alland, *Jacob A. Riis: Photographer & Citizen* (Millerton, N.Y.: Aperture, 1974), is a necessary companion to any work by or about Riis. It is also *the* accessible and invaluable presentation of Riis's photography. Rune Hassner, *Jacob A. Riis: Reporter med kamera i New Yorks slum* (Stockholm: Norstedt and Soners, 1970), is a valuable study with a selective bibliography. An intriguing reading of Riis as a photographer is J. Riis Owre, "Jacob A. Riis: Photographer in Spite of Himself," *American Scandinavian Review* 55 (March 1967): 48–55. No reader should ignore I. N. Phelps Stokes six-volumed *The Iconography of Manhattan Island. 1498*1909* (1915–1928; reprint, New York: Arno Press, 1967). For a photographic essay of Manhattan's history, see Charles Lockwood, *Manhattan Moves Uptown* (Boston: Houghton Mifflin, 1976). The reader should also refer to John A. Kouwenhoven, *The Columbia Historical Portrait of New York* (New York: Doubleday, 1953). Although Riis appended population statistics to *How the Other Half Lives,* the reader should also look at John Billing, *Vital Statistics of New York City and Brooklyn Covering a Period of Six Years and Ending May 31, 1890* (Washington, D.C.: Government Printing Office, 1891). For discussions of urban resources, James Reynolds, *Civic Bibliography of Greater New York* (New York: Charities Publication Committee, 1911), and W. H. Tolman and W. Hull, *Handbook of Sociological Information with Especial Reference to New York City* (New York: City Vigilance League, 1894), are richly rewarding. The problematic nature of Riis's concerns about ethnicity and Jewishness has been examined by a number of writers; central to my interests are Jeffrey Gurock, "Jacob A. Riis: Christian Friend or Missionary Foe? Two Jewish Views," *American Jewish History* 71 (September 1981): 29–47, and Richard Tuerk, "Jacob Riis and the Jews," *New York Historical Society Quarterly* 63 (July 1979): 179–99. I found immensely useful Sam Bass Warner's Editor's Introduction to *How the Other Half Lives* (Cambridge: Harvard University Press, 1970), and Donald Bigelow's Introduction to the Sagamore Press edition of *How the Other Half Lives*, and Francesco Cordasco's Introduction to *Jacob Riis Revisited: Poverty and the Slum in Another Era* (Garden City,

Bibliographical Notes

N.Y.: Doubleday, 1968). I profited greatly from William Boelhower, *Immigrant Autobiography in the United States* (Verona: Essedue edizione, 1982); Paul Boyer, *Urban Masses and Moral Order in America, 1820–1920* (Cambridge: Harvard University Press, 1978); Thomas Bender, *Community and Social Change in America* (New Brunswick, N.J.: Rutgers University Press, 1978); Robert H. Bremner's capacious *From the Depths: The Discovery of Poverty in the United States* (New York: New York University Press, 1956); David Fine, *The City, The Immigrant, and American Fiction, 1880–1920* (Metuchen, N.J.: Scarecrow Press, 1977); Park Dixon Goist, *From Main Street to State Street* (Port Washington, N.Y.: Kennikat Press, 1977); Thomas Haskell, *The Emergence of Professional Social Science* (Urbana: University of Illinois Press, 1977); Leo Hershkowitz, *Tweed's New York: Another Look* (New York: Anchor, 1978); Jean Quandt, *From the Small Town to the Great Community* (New Brunswick, N.J.: Rutgers University Press, 1970); Werner Sollors, *Beyond Ethnicity* (New York: Oxford University Press, 1986); R. Jackson Wilson, *In Quest of Community* (New York: Oxford University Press, 1968); Roy Lubove, *The Progressives and the Slums* (Pittsburgh: University of Pittsburgh Press, 1968), and *The Professional Altruist* (Cambridge: Harvard University Press, 1965); and Roy Wiebe's now classic *The Search for Order, 1877–1920* (New York: Hill and Wang, 1967).

Two works that do not deal with Riis but that are valuable in understanding the historical nature of his labors are James Machor, *Pastoral Cities: Urban Ideals and the Symbolic Landscape of America* (Madison: University of Wisconsin Press, 1987), and Patricia Melvin, *The Organic City: Urban Definition and Neighborhood Organization, 1880–1920* (Lexington: University Press of Kentucky, 1987).

Lewis Mumford

Elmer S. Newman's invaluable *Lewis Mumford: A Bibliography, 1914–1970* (New York: Harcourt Brace Jovanovich, 1971) lists Mumford's publications and archival holdings. I found useful the Van Wyck Brooks and Waldo Frank Collection at the University of Pennsylvania and the Mumford Collection at the New York Public Library. I am grateful for Lewis Mumford's gracious replies to my own questions, especially about Jacob Riis.

Important critical assessments of Mumford are found in the special Mumford issue of *Salmagundi:* "Prophecy Reconsidered," no. 49 (Summer 1980). I have found the following very useful: Eddy Dow, "Lewis Mumford's Passage to India," *South Atlantic Quarterly* 76 (Winter 1977): 31–43; and "Van Wyck Brooks and Lewis Mumford: A Confluence in the 'Twenties," *American Literature* 45 (November 1973): 407–22; Maria Laura Franciosi, "Lewis Mumford," in *I Contemparanei Letterature Americana* (Rome: Lucarini, 1982), vol. 1; Park Dixon Goist's chapters on Mumford in *From Main Street to State Street* (New York: Kennikat Press, 1970), and in *The American Planner: Biographies and Recollections*, ed. Donald Krueckeberg (New York and London: Methuen, 1983); and Peter Shaw, "Mumford in Retrospect," *Commentary* 56 (September 1973): 71–73.

In addition, Patrick Boardman, *Esquisse de l'Oeuvre educatrice de Patrick*

Bibliographical Notes

Geddes suivie de Trois Listes Bibliographiques (Montpelier, France: Imprimerie de la Charite [Pierre-Rouge], 1936); Paul Edwards, Jr. "Lewis Mumford's Search for Values" (Diss. American University, 1970); Roy Lubove, *Community Planning in the 1920's: The Contribution of the Regional Planning Association of America* (Pittsburgh: University of Pittsburgh Press, 1963); F. J. Osborn, *Green-Belt Cities* (New York: Schocken, 1971), and *New Towns: Their Origins, Achievements and Progress* (London: Leonard Hill, 1977); Daniel Schaffer, *Garden Cities for America: The Radburn Experience* (Philadelphia: Temple University Press, 1982); Marshall Stalley's collection of Geddes's writing in *Patrick Geddes: Spokesman for Man and the Environment: A Selection* (New Brunswick, N.J.: Rutgers University Press, 1972). Clarence Stein, *Toward New Towns for America* (Cambridge: MIT Press, 1977), should certainly be read.

Paul Goodman and Percival Goodman, *Communitas* (Chicago: University of Chicago Press, 1947), and Jane Jacobs, *The Death and Life of Great American Cities* (New York: Random House, 1961) are significant readings, opposing Mumford's, of the garden city.

James T. Farrell

The major bibliography of Farrell's writings is Edgar M. Branch, *A Bibliography of James T. Farrell's Writings, 1921–1957* (Philadelphia: University of Pennsylvania Press, 1959), updated by Branch in bibliographies published in *American Book Collector* 11 (June 1961); 17 (May 1967); 21 (March–April 1971). The best surveys of Farrell's life and work are Edgar M. Branch's *James T. Farrell* (New York: Twayne, 1971) and "James T. Farrell," in Charles Child Walcutt, *Seven Novelists in the American Naturalist Tradition* (Minneapolis: University of Minnesota Press, 1974), pp. 245–89. Farrell's work at the University of Chicago also has been studied by Branch in "American Writer in the Twenties: James T. Farrell and the University of Chicago," *American Book Collector* 11 (June 1961): 25–32. The pioneering reading of Farrell's naturalism is, also by Branch, in his "Freedom and Determinism in James T. Farrell's Fiction" in *Essays on Determinism in American Literature*, ed. S. J. Krause (Kent, Ohio: Kent State University Press, 1964), pp. 79–96. Another important discussion is that of David H. Owen in "A Pattern of Pseudo-Naturalism: Lynd, Mead, and Farrell" (Ph.D. diss., University of Iowa, 1950).

Donald Pizer insightfully reads Farrell's work during a turbulent decade in "James T. Farrell and the 1930s" in Ralph Bogardus and Fred Hobson, *Literature at the Barricades: The American Writer in the 1930s* (University: University of Alabama Press, 1982), pp. 69–81. Though I disagree with him about the Farrell-Conroy feud, Alan Wald has written an important study of Farrell and the Left in *James T. Farrell: The Revolutionary Socialist Years* (New York: Gotham Library Press of New York University, 1978). A noteworthy collection of essays on Farrell is Jack Salzman's edition of *Twentieth-Century Literature* 22 (February 1976).

Among numerous commentaries about *Studs Lonigan* that I found influential are: Edgar Branch, "James T. Farrell's *Studs Lonigan*" in *American Book Collector* 11 (June 1961): 9–19; Branch, "Destiny, Culture and Technique: *Studs Lonigan*,"

Bibliographical Notes

University of Kansas City Review, 29 (December 1962): 103–13; and Ann Douglas, "Studs Lonigan and the Failure of History in Mass Society: A Study in Claustrophobia," American Quarterly 29 (Winter 1977): 487–505. Also important is Henry Hopper Dyer, "James T. Farrell's Studs Lonigan and Danny O'Neill Novels" (Ph.D. diss., University of Pennsylvania, 1965), and Richard Mitchell, "Studs Lonigan: Research in Morality," Centennial Review 6 (Spring 1962): 202–14.

Isaac Rosenfeld's comments in the 1940s on Farrell are characteristically perceptive: see "The Anger of James T. Farrell" and "Farrell's Work in Regress" in Preserving the Hunger: An Isaac Rosenfeld Reader, ed. Mark Shechner (Detroit: Wayne State University Press, 1988). Blanche Housman Gelfant's interpretation of Farrell's urban imagination in her now classic American City Novel (Norman: University of Oklahoma Press, 1954) remains central to any reading of Farrell.

Among histories of the literary imagination in and of Chicago, I found most useful Bernard Duffey's pioneering The Chicago Renaissance in American Letters (East Lansing: Michigan State University Press, 1954) and Kenny J. Williams's In The City of Man: Another Story of Chicago (Nashville, Tenn.: Townsend Press, 1974). Carl W. Condit, Chicago, 1910–1929 (Chicago: University of Chicago Press, 1973); Harold M. Mayer and Richard C. Wade, Chicago: Growth of A Metropolis (Chicago: University of Chicago Press, 1969), and Thomas Lee Philpott, The Slum and the Ghetto: Neighborhood Deterioration and Middle-Class Reform, Chicago, 1880–1930 (New York: Oxford University Press, 1978), are crucial studies of Chicago's form and making. Dominic A. Pacyga and Ellen Skerrett, Chicago, City of Neighborhoods (Chicago: Loyola University Press, 1986), is a photographic and diagrammatic guide to Chicago that has a section—"Old South Side"—invaluable for Farrell's readers.

Robert Faris, Chicago Sociology, 1920–1932 (Chicago: University of Chicago, 1967), and Fred H. Matthew, Quest for an American Sociology: Robert E. Park and the Chicago School (Montreal: McGill-Queens University Press, 1977), are landmark analyses of the Chicago School of sociology. Also see Lester Kurtz's important bibliographical guide, Evaluating Chicago Sociology (Chicago: University of Chicago Press, 1984). Lucid summaries and commentary are to be found in Dennis Poplin, Communities: A Survey of Theories and Methods of Research (New York: Macmillan, 1972), and Linda Stoneall, Country Life, City Life (New York: Praeger, 1983). John J. McDermott's important reading of the city and his discussion of Dewey are immensely rich and compelling: see his Streams of Experience: Reflections on the History and Philosophy of American Culture (Amherst: University of Massachusetts Press, 1986).

Paul Goodman

I am indebted to Sally Goodman for information about her husband, her willingness to reminisce, and her suggestions about what should be looked at; to Percival Goodman for recollections about the writing of Communitas; to Taylor Stoehr for invaluable advice about parts of this essay. In addition, Taylor Stoehr was helpful in

Bibliographical Notes

allowing me to look at several of Goodman's unpublished essays. Sally Goodman gave me permission to examine the galleys of *The Empire City*.

Tom Nicely, *Adam and His Work: A Bibliography of Sources by and about Paul Goodman (1911–1972)* (Metuchen, N.J. and London: Scarecrow Press, 1979), is the major reference source for Goodman bibliography. It is added to in Nicely's "Adam and His Work: A Bibliographical Update" in Peter Parisi, *Artist of the Actual: Essays on Paul Goodman* (Metuchen, N.J. and London: Scarecrow Press, 1986).

A great deal of Goodman's writing has been reissued recently, though much of it is still out of print. Taylor Stoehr has edited and provided indispensable introductions to four volumes of Paul Goodman's short stories written from 1932 to 1960 (Santa Barbara: Black Sparrow Press, 1978–80), and to three volumes of Goodman's essays: *Drawing the Line, Nature Heals,* and *Creator Spirit Come!* (New York: Free Life Editions, 1977), and to Goodman, *Don Juan or, The Continuum of the Libido* (Santa Barbara: Black Sparrow Press, 1979). Stoehr has also edited and written an afterword to Goodman, *Parents' Day* (Santa Barbara: Black Sparrow Press, 1985).

The Winter/Spring 1976 edition ("The Writings of Paul Goodman") of *New Letters,* edited by David Ray and Taylor Stoehr, is a landmark volume that contains a number of short stories by Goodman and critical essays about him.

Bernard Vincent, *Paul Goodman et la reconquete du present* (Paris: Le Seuil, 1976), and *Pour un bon usage du monde* (Paris: Desclee, 1979), are crucial readings of Goodman's thought.

There is a wealth of literature about Goodman. I found the following influential: Morris Dickstein, *Gates of Eden: American Culture in the Sixties* (New York: Basic Books, 1977); Richard King, *The Party of Eros: Radical Social Thought and the Realm of Freedom* (Chapel Hill: University of North Carolina Press, 1972); Sherman Paul, "Paul Goodman's Mourning Labor: *The Empire City,*" *Southern Review* 4 (October 1968): 894–926; Leo Raditsa, "On Paul Goodman—and Goodmanism," *Iowa Review* 5 (Summer 1974): 62–79; Theodore Roszak, *The Making of a Counter Culture* (New York: Doubleday, 1969).

There are a number of dissertations on Goodman. Among them, I have found very useful Elliot Glassheim, "The Movement Towards Freedom in Paul Goodman's *The Empire City* (University of New Mexico, 1973); Michael Kelley, "Paul Goodman: The 'Rhetoric' of a Neolithic Conservative" (University of Pittsburgh, 1976); Mark Penta, "Education As a Function of Community: Paul Goodman's Concept of the Educative City" (Michigan State University, 1972); and Nadine S. Schwartz, "Beyond John Dewey: Paul Goodman's Theory of Human Nature" (Rutgers University, 1970).

Epilogue

For assessments of how one knows and writes about the city, see Hadley Arkes, *The Philosopher in the City* (Princeton: Princeton University Press, 1981); Murray

235

Bibliographical Notes

Bookchin, *The Limits of the City* (New York: Harper and Row, 1974); M. Christine Boyer, *Dreaming the Rational City* (Cambridge: MIT Press, 1983); Percival Goodman, *The Double E* (Garden City, N.Y.: Anchor, 1977); Jane Jacobs, *The Death and Life of Great American Cities* (New York: Vintage, 1961); Andrew Lees, *Cities Perceived* (New York: Columbia University Press, 1985); Oscar Handlin and John Burchard, eds. *The Historian and the City* (Cambridge: MIT Press, 1966); Michael Jaye and Ann Watts, *Literature and the Urban Experience* (New Brunswick, N.J.: Rutgers University Press, 1981); Burton Pike, *The Image of the City in Modern Literature* (Princeton: Princeton University Press, 1981); Edward Relph, *The Modern Urban Landscape* (Baltimore: Johns Hopkins University Press, 1987); Mel Scott, *American City Planning Since 1890* (Berkeley: University of California Press, 1969); Peter J. Steinberger, *Ideology and the Urban Crisis* (Albany: State University of New York Press, 1985); Eugenio Trias, *The Artist and the City* (New York: Columbia University Press, 1982); Christopher Tunnard, *The Modern American City* (Princeton: D. Van Nostrand Co., 1968); David Weimer, *The City as Metaphor* (New York: Random House, 1966); Hayden White, *Tropics of Discourse* (Baltimore: Johns Hopkins University Press, 1978); Morton White and Lucia White, *The Intellectual Versus the City* (Cambridge: MIT Press, 1962).

Index

237

Index

Christian Conference of 1888 (Chickering Hall), 33
Christian Union, 11, 42
Cité Antique, La (de Coulanges), 75
Cities in Evolution (Geddes), 74, 77
"City: Forms and Functions" (Mumford), 115
City, The (Max Weber), 81
City and Suburban Home Company, 58
City Beautiful (movement), 86
City Development (Geddes), 77
City Development (Mumford), 108–9
City in History, The (Mumford), 72, 109–15, 116
Cobbett, William, 85
Collins, Ellen, 44, 61
"Commencement Address, Barre High School" (Riis), 60
Communitas (Paul and Percival Goodman), 102, 109, 160, 172–80, 200, 202, 206
"Community Buildings" (Paul and Percival Goodman), 180
Condition of Man, The (Mumford), 107
Crane, Stephen, 12, 14, 15, 83. Works: *Maggie,* 14
Criminal, The (Ellis), 43
"Cross-Country Runner at Sixty-Five, A" (Paul Goodman), 166
Culture of Cities, The (Mumford), 72, 102–6, 109, 110, 112, 113, 115, 145

Daly, Ella, 123
Daly, John, 122
Daly, Julia, 122
Daly, Tom, 123
Dangerous Classes of New York, The (Brace), 31
Daniel (biblical book), 46
Dead of Spring, The (Paul Goodman), 182, 186, 193–95
Decline of the West, The (Spengler), 100–101
de Coulanges, Numa Denis Fustel, 75, 84. Works: *Cité Antique, La,* 75
De Forest, Robert W., 12, 63. Works: *Tenement House Problem, The* (with Veiller), 63
de Hirsch Fund, Baron, 22
Dewey, John, 119, 121, 125, 126, 128, 129, 131–33, 135, 136, 140, 188. Works: *Experience and Nature,* 132; *Human Nature and Conduct,* 131, 132–33, 138; *Individualism Old and New,* 132; *Public and Its Problems, The,* 132; *Quest for Certainty, The,* 132; *Reconstruction in Philosophy,*

132; *School and Society, The,* 132; *Schools of Tomorrow,* 188
Dial, The, 43, 82
Diotima, 198, 199, 201
Doblin, Alfred, 136
Dostoyevsky, Feodor, 157
Dreiser, Theodore, 126, 157

Elsing, W. T., 11
Emerson, Ralph Waldo, 23, 71, 85, 97, 98, 181, 193, 205. Works: "American Scholar, The," 71, 193
Emigration and Immigration (Mayo), 43
Empire City, The (Paul Goodman), 182–97, 200, 201, 202, 203
Evolution (Geddes and Thomson), 74
Experience and Nature (Dewey), 132

Face of Time (Farrell), 146
Farrell, James (grandfather), 122
Farrell, James T., 3, 4, 5, 6, 7, 8, 106, 118, 119–58, 206–9; Burgess, influence of, 129–30; Chicago "school" of sociology, impact of, 119, 128–31, 135–36, 142; death of "Studs" Cunningham, 125; Dewey, influence of, 119, 128, 131, 132–33, 135, 138, 140, 157; family, 122–24; literary traditions, 126–27; Mead, influence of, 119, 131, 133–35, 140, 157; Thrasher, influence of, 129, 130–31, 139; views of, on Chicago, 120–22, 137; views of, on city, 127–28, 135–36, 137; views of, on Mumford, 106; writing, themes of, 119–20, 121, 123, 124, 125–26, 128, 133, 136, 150, 156–57; writing program, 122. Works: Bernard Carr [Clare] series, 150–51; *Bernard Clare,* 151–53; Danny O'Neill series, 146–47; *Face of Time, The,* 146; *Father and Son,* 146, 148–49; *Judgment Day,* 136, 143–46; *My Days of Anger,* 146, 149–50; *No Star Is Lost,* 146; *Road Between, The,* 153–54; "Story of Studs Lonigan, The," 129; "Studs," 125, 131; *Studs Lonigan,* 125, 130, 132, 136–37, 145, 147; *World I Never Made, A,* 129, 146, 147–48; *Yet Other Waters,* 154–56; *Young Lonigan,* 129, 130, 136, 137–40; *Young Manhood of Studs Lonigan, The,* 136, 141–43
Father and Son (Farrell), 146, 148–49
Ferriss, Hugh, 96
Fields, Factories, and Workshops (Kropotkin), 74, 77, 164
Five Years (Paul Goodman), 168, 169, 180, 183

238

Index

Index

Index

Index

242

Index

243

Index